PROTECTING THE PEOPLE

PROTECTING

DAVID WELCH

THE PEOPLE

THE **CENTRAL OFFICE OF INFORMATION** AND THE
RESHAPING OF POST-WAR BRITAIN, 1946-2011

First published in 2019 by

The British Library
96 Euston Road
London NW1 2DB
www.bl.uk

Text © David Welch 2019

All images © British Library Board unless otherwise stated

The right of David Welch to be identified as the author of this work has been asserted by him in accordance with the Copyright, Design and Patents Act 1988

Cataloguing in Publication Data

A catalogue record for this publication is available from the British Library

ISBN: 978 0 7123 5325 0

Edited by Christopher Westhorp
Designed by Steve Russell
Picture Research by Sally Nicholls

Printed and bound in Spain by Grafo

CONTENTS

PREFACE

WHAT IS IN THE ARCHIVE?

The Central Office of Information (COI) Archive at the British Library consists of a unique collection of over 15,000 free information and guidance leaflets, posters, booklets and other promotional materials dating from the 1940s to 1997. The materials were designed and produced for a range of UK government departments and agencies by the Central Office of Information, which deposited its master set of file copies with the British Library in 2000. The leaflets, posters, book and pamphlets in the collection were intended to:

⊙ **Inform the public about their rights and entitlements,
  for example to social security benefits**

⊙ **Provide straightforward guidance to employers, their workers, professionals
  and the public about government initiatives, programmes and current regulations,
  for example discipline in schools or education at work**

⊙ **Influence behaviour, such as the anti-drink-driving or anti-smoking
  campaigns**

⊙ **Inform citizens about current government policies and their implementation,
  for example nationalisation, privatisation, the national curriculum or race
  relations legislation**

⊙ **Provide information about careers opportunities in the public sector,
  such as teaching, nursing, the Civil Service and the armed forces**

⊙ **Inform people overseas about the United Kingdom (UK)**

The collection covers the whole spectrum of contemporary life, including:

- ⊙ **Education, schools and the curriculum**

- ⊙ **Social security benefits and pensions**

- ⊙ **Public health issues, for example HIV and AIDS**

- ⊙ **Food safety and hygiene**

- ⊙ **Environmental issues and nature conservation**

- ⊙ **Overseas trade and exports**

- ⊙ **Housing issues, for example 'How to Protect Your Home from Fire Risks'.**

This unique collection reveals what the government wanted its citizens to think or know about topical issues at the time of publication and the image of Britain that it wanted to project to the outside world. As such it is of enduring interest to social historians. Because the collection also reveals what regulatory guidance was being given to citizens at a certain date, it could also be used for the resolution of disputes about benefits and entitlements. The justification (or otherwise) of greater governmental intervention in the lives of ordinary people goes to the heart of the historic ideological division between Conservatives and Labour about the appropriate size and role of the state. One of the questions I have addressed is whether or not the Central Office of Information contributed to the emergence of a 'nanny' state by excessive state interference, at the expense of greater individuality and personal responsibility. It closed on 30 December 2011 when it fell victim to the coalition government's austerity programme.

While the British Library's Central Office of Information (COI) archive is huge, it is not easily navigable for the researcher; partly because it has yet to be fully catalogued, and because it also contains substantial deposits on the Ministry of Information – the organisation that the COI replaced in 1946.[1] It is not unusual therefore to discover boxes that contain both MOI and COI material, which can be somewhat disconcerting. Nevertheless, once you can separate the two organisations and identify specifically COI material, the archive remains an extraordinarily rich historical source to mine. Some boxes contain multiple copies, including the same publication reprinted and translated in many languages. This could be a pamphlet intended for an overseas audience to supplement a British trade fair in Spain, or it might be a benefit entitlement aimed at specific ethnic groups who have settled in the UK, or even the Green Cross Code explained in Welsh. Frustratingly, many of the official publications were not dated by the COI. I have provided publication dates wherever possible, or approximate dates based on the historical context and the content of the publication. I have also encountered problems with some of the COI's public information films, which were often produced quickly and cheaply, and as a result are of poor quality. When discussing such iconic films I have endeavoured, wherever possible, to provide links to YouTube or to special collections which may be purchased from BFI on DVD. Sadly, however, a few of the films analysed are not of sufficient resolution to reproduce in this volume.

My aim in writing this book is to provide an insight into the nature and scope of the work carried out by the COI since the end of World War II. The COI and its political masters – successive British governments – would classify the work undertaken as providing 'public information'. I have used this term interchangeably with propaganda, which is my preferred terminology. I have spent my academic life writing about propaganda and arguing that historically the act of propagandising is ethically and morally neutral – it may be put to good or bad use.[2] Too often *effective* propaganda is associated with the control of the flow of information and with duplicity and falsehood. But propaganda has the potential to serve a constructive purpose. Writing in 1928, Edward Bernays (the father of modern advertising) argued that: 'Propaganda will never die out. Intelligent men must realise that propaganda is the modern instrument by which they can fight for productive ends and help bring order out of chaos.'[3]

The loosely chronological structure of this book represents a significant departure from most of my previous works, for which I have adopted a thematic approach. Although I *have* included the major themes and campaigns disseminated by the COI, I decided that it made more sense to place them in a historical context because the period being covered is one that lasts sixty-five years. Nevertheless, I wanted the chronological structure to be as flexible as possible to allow me to trace the roots and antecedents of specific themes and campaigns. For example, I have positioned the theme of Civil Defence (a major concern for the COI since its inception) in the 1980s because this was when the final *Protect and Survive* publications and films were produced. By adopting such a chronologically flexible approach, I avoid being encased in a strict historical straitjacket; rather, I can go back and trace the origins of Civil Defence from the early post-war years, illustrate the shifting concerns in the 1960s and 1970s, and bring it up to the 1980s when it virtually ceased as an issue with the ending of the Cold War.

This approach does, I feel, provide for greater historical continuity and helps to highlight some of the major shifts in technology and mass communications that have developed since the late 1940s. Such technological advances massively influenced how the COI communicated to its audiences both at home and abroad. The press, radio and film remained prominent in the 1940s and 1950s, but by the 1960s television was dominant, and more recently we have seen the rise of the Internet and social media. These changes represented huge challenges to which the COI was forced to respond. To this end, although most of the visual representation in the book is largely of printed material such as posters, pamphlets and leaflets, I have, wherever possible, also included analyses of film and video propaganda that were either produced or sponsored by the COI but which are not in the British Library's collection.

The campaigns and artefacts that I have selected provide a revealing insight into how the British state attempted to inform, guide and alter the behaviour of its citizens, and what the government wanted its citizens to think or know about topical issues at the time of publication. It also offers us a fascinating insight into the changing concerns of central government in the post–1945 world (the shifting nature of the anti-smoking campaigns is an excellent example of this). As such the COI material is of enduring interest to social historians and political scientists.

Does such activity on the part of the state constitute a form of social engineering? Moreover, does it suggest an increasing tendency towards a 'nanny state' following the sacrifices made by citizens in the immediate aftermath of 'total war'? Or does it instead reveal a more-enlightened form of social contract on the part of a modern democratic state intent on utilising the media and the message to encourage rather than coerce its citizens to adopt certain behaviour and attitudes and show greater social responsibility? The history of the Central Office of Information raises questions about how different political administrations with their own priorities engage with the dilemma of how a government communicates with its citizens to sustain a credible democracy. After all, democracies should not be afraid of selling democracy. ♔

CHAPTER ONE

THE CENTRAL OFFICE OF INFORMATION

The Central Office of Information (COI) was established by the Clement Attlee Labour government on April Fools' Day 1946. It replaced the wartime Ministry of Information (MOI), which was considered inappropriate for a post-war democracy. The COI continued to be responsible for conducting government public relations campaigns until it was disbanded in 2011. However, very little is known about the roots and antecedents of the COI or indeed the campaigns that it launched. This is surprising given that much of its work formed the backdrop to the lives of the British people throughout the period of the Cold War and beyond. How did the COI differ from the MOI, who was in charge of it, how was it financed and what were its responsibilities? Did it conduct propaganda in the same way as the MOI, and if not, how did it differ? To answer such questions it is first necessary to trace the events that led to the COI's establishment.

DISMANTLING THE MINISTRY OF INFORMATION

During World War II, the Ministry of Information (MOI) disseminated an extraordinarily wide-ranging collection of propaganda material (although it would vehemently deny that it was engaged in propaganda), which eventually – after initial failures – helped to foster a sense of a common purpose and maintain the morale of the British people during the bleakest of times. By engaging in a largely frank and open partnership with the people, the work of the MOI helped to shift the relationship between governors and governed.[1]

Nevertheless, at the end of World War II the MOI's task was done. It would have no place in the post-war world. In August 1943, Winston Churchill had created a committee of permanent officials and government ministers to consider the official machinery of government in post-war Britain.[2] In November 1943, Brendon Bracken, Churchill's trusted Minister of Information, had expressed the view that he did not want the wartime propaganda machinery automatically converted for post-war use.[3] It was an open secret, according to the *Evening Standard* in June 1944, that Bracken 'would not tolerate the continuation of his Ministry at any price'.[4] Civil Service officials, on the other hand, argued for some form of permanent peacetime machinery. Their view was expressed by Sir Alan Barlow of the Official Committee on the Machinery of Government (which Churchill had established):

> *The Haldane Committee laid much stress on the importance of well-informed Government: it is at least as important to the proper operation of democratic institutions that there should be a well-informed public. Therefore, though admittedly the dividing line between presenting facts and inviting particular inferences from them is sometimes thin, it can never be a misuse of the Government's resources to provide machinery by which knowledge relevant to a proper discharge of citizenship is presented accurately and attractively to as wide a public as possible.*[5]

It should also be remembered that many British citizens had now lived through two world wars and the Great Depression, which had tested their allegiance to liberal democracy rather than being seduced by the alternative communist or fascist ideologies. The Official Committee on the Machinery of Government's final recommendations clearly took this into consideration and recognised that continued participation in the democratic process would only be enhanced through greater information; continuity of information policy was therefore essential. This applied equally to British publicity (or propaganda) overseas. To this end, the committee's final report argued:

> *Whatever limitations may be placed on publicity at home by political and other factors, quite different considerations will apply to British publicity overseas and that, in the face of the efforts made by other countries, a*

positive British policy will command universal approval at home and pay handsome dividends abroad. In this as in other fields laissez faire *is no longer regarded as good enough.*[6]

The conclusion reached by the committee was that there would be a continuing need in peacetime, although on a reduced scale, both for government information and publicity services at home and for British information services overseas – 'their functions, if properly conceived, are useful and indeed essential in modern government'.[7] Britain was at last taking seriously the business of peacetime propaganda on the domestic front and at the same time recognising that the representation of Britain overseas transcended party politics and was of national (rather than merely sectional) importance.

When the Labour government took office in the summer of 1945, it largely accepted the detailed proposals for peacetime information services. On 6 December 1945 the Cabinet formally agreed not to retain the Ministry of Information but to charge Herbert Morrison, Lord President of the Council, with the task of setting up a new organisation along the lines recommended by the Official Committee on the Machinery of Government.[8] In a parliamentary statement on 17 December 1945, the Prime Minister, Clement Attlee, informed the House that the Ministry of Information (now shorn of censorship power and of executive authority) would be brought to an end in March 1946. However, according to Attlee, official information services both at home and abroad had 'an important and permanent part in the machinery of government under modern conditions':

It is essential to good administration under a democratic system that the public shall be adequately informed about the many matters in which Government action directly impinges on their daily lives and it is, in particular, important that a true and adequate picture of British institutions and the British way of life shall be presented overseas.[9]

Herbert Morrison brought his considerable weight to bear in support of an independent Central Office of Information (COI) responsible for co-ordinating the information services. Questions remained over how the COI would be controlled and financed. It was under Morrison's direction that details of the new organisation were agreed. A central agency was created to establish the departments that would be required for defined common services and which itself would respond to requests from and under the policy direction of ministers in specific areas of responsibility.[10]

THE BIRTH OF THE CENTRAL OFFICE OF INFORMATION

The title of the new organisation was announced on 7 March 1946 by the Prime Minister in a statement to the House. In the course of his statement, Attlee referred to 'the Office' and also outlined its functions and status:

The Office will take over most of the common service duties now carried out by the Ministry of Information and in the first instance it will be mainly staffed from existing officers of the Ministry. Provision will be made for the interchange of staff between the Office and the departmental information branches, both at home and abroad.... The Office will have a separate Vote, for which the Treasury Ministers will be responsible to Parliament.... Treasury Ministers will also deal in Parliament with matters affecting the staffing, efficiency and methods of the Office.[11]

The Central Office of Information (COI) formally came into existence on 1 April 1946. At the time of its inception, it was not considered to be a continuation of the MOI into the Cold War era. Politicians of all political persuasions had been affected by the unifying experience of the 'People's War' and the new post-war national information agency would ensure more-equal access to the public at home and a more-coherent policy of centralised publicity abroad. The COI's role was restricted to that of a central national publicity agency serving the needs of Whitehall. This formula was intended (mistakenly as it turned out) to defuse any potential political opposition at home while enabling the Foreign Office to conduct the projection of Britain abroad.

The first Director-General was Sir Eric Bramford, formerly of the MOI, who was soon replaced by Robert Fraser, a journalist on the *Daily Herald*, then edited by Francis Williams who became Attlee's public relations adviser in 1945. Fraser had worked with Morrison in the Labour Party's London County Council campaign in 1937 and he continued to work closely with Morrison while working for the Ministry of Information during the war.

The COI began life with a staff of 1,500 and a crisis of morale. Robert Fraser outlined the initial problems facing the COI in a report on the first six months of its existence:

It (the COI) had lost almost all of its wartime leaders... These losses, plus the exodus of many key technicians at lower levels, had sapped its powers. Its internal self-confidence was shaken by the prolonged anxiety about its future... Happily, a number of officers of talent had taken the decision that they would accept the personal risk of remaining on a ship with its decks awash. They had formed a genuine liking for public information work and a belief in its value to the democratic process; and they had a sense of group loyalty which was moving. The policy was followed of bold promotion from among them, and others like them working elsewhere in the information services. The policy is beginning to bring its expected results...[12]

It would take many years before an acceptable staffing policy was established. In the meantime there remained considerable doubts whether, under the existing conditions of service, the COI would be able to attract and retain first-class recruits.

In the immediate post-war years there was a major reconstruction of the Civil Service and out of the Crombie Committee, which had been set up in 1946, came the recommendation in the following year that a new Information Class be established and that the work of the COI should be regarded as coming under this category.[13] The new class would not, however, come into effect until August 1949, when it was finally agreed by the Treasury and the Institution of Professional Civil Servants.

One of the earliest recruitment problems was that when the Treasury Circular was introduced, the information officer was not regarded as anything more than a press officer and there was no hint of the enormous range of disciplines contained in the Information Service. Unlike the more-traditional departments, the COI was acutely affected by the changing whims of successive governments. As a result, staff recruitment fluctuated wildly. In 1952–53, as part of a general retrenchment, substantial cuts were introduced at home and overseas, which led to a reduction from 1,518 in March 1952 to 862 in April 1953. Two years later, total staff employed by the COI amounted to 745, the lowest in the department's history.[14] In 1975 there were 1,250 information officers, but only 18 per cent were engaged in press work. The dramatically changing figures illustrated the need for a high degree of flexibility in the staffing of the department. The problems facing it were formidable.

The situation was not made any easier by the fact that the COI was constantly forced to justify its existence and, more specifically, its expenditure. The Conservatives witnessed the announcement of the COI with considerable apprehension, having assumed that there would be no further need for a government-controlled propaganda service in post-war Britain. Brendan Bracken, now a Conservative backbencher, remained a relentless critic of the COI. In a bad-tempered parliamentary exchange with Morrison in May 1949, the former Minister of Information challenged the Labour view that the COI was merely 'disseminating facts': 'The late Dr. Goebbels' most effective propaganda did not consist in spreading frigid and calculated lies. He arranged his facts to suit his argument.' Bracken went on to question the need for a 'Government bureau' ... 'the best way of describing the COI':

> Having read its report with the greatest care and having tried to follow its operations, I cannot see any justification for maintaining this enormously over-staffed office. In addition to this staff, the Government maintain an army of public relations officers and publicity men at home and abroad. Here I am not taking into account the immense number of public relations officers in the new nationalised industries. I maintain that there is no justification for all the money and the manpower thus expended. ...I must tell the Lord President [Morrison] that even if the Angel Gabriel were in charge of a Government information service, most of the editors would suspect it of propaganda.[15]

Some politicians, like Bracken, viewed the work of the COI as unnecessarily expensive, while others continued to regard overseas information services with suspicion. As a result the COI suffered annual cuts to its budget on 'a more or less arbitrary basis' throughout the 1940s and 1950s.[16] The gross Vote for the COI (which at this time was divided almost equally between home and overseas) fell from almost £4.5 million in 1947–48 to just over £1.6 million in 1955–56. This financial retrenchment happened at a time of growing international tension (increased Soviet oppression in Eastern Europe, and the Suez Crisis, for example), when paradoxically there was a greater need for propaganda activity. In spite of the MOI's success during World War II – or precisely because of its success – many people unfamiliar with the nature of the new global propaganda conflict, and the struggle for hearts and minds it entailed, continued to regard propaganda activity (and even public information work) as something to be ashamed of and which, moreover, failed to produce transparent benefits that would justify the expenditure. Because the COI was never the responsibility of a specific minister, it continued throughout its existence to have to defend its activities.[17]

In 1949, for example, the COI commissioned the Crown Film Unit to make a tongue-in-cheek short film about post-war austerity entitled *What a Life* starring Richard Massingham, who featured regularly in propaganda films for the MOI during World War II. Displaying Massingham's fondness for black humour, the film addressed the challenges Britain faced in the post-war era. The film caused some controversy in Parliament when on 15 February 1949 the Conservative MP for Twickenham, Edward Keeling, asked the Lord President of the Council (Herbert Morrison) how much the film had cost, what revenue has been obtained from it, and whether he had any evidence that its declared purpose of persuading people that things were not as bad as they seemed had succeeded? Morrison explained that it had cost £6,260, plus £2,512 for distribution, and was one of 12 films a year supplied and shown free under a long-standing agreement with the Cinematograph Exhibitors' Association, so the question of revenue did not arise, adding, 'This is a light little film about two men who, in the end, take a cheerful view of life's troubles, and there is no reason for thinking it unsuccessful'. Keeling pressed on regardless, and mischievously replied:

> Has the Lord President seen this film? Does he know that it shows two men so depressed by the conditions of life in England today that they try to drown themselves, but make a mess of it? Does he really think that this is the sort of film on which £9,000 of the taxpayers' money should be spent without any possibility of a return?

Wearily, Morrison retorted that the Hon. Member had given a very short and incomplete critical review of the film 'because he forgot to add that, having

---

1. *Crime: Together We'll Crack It* (1988). Two sections taken from the COI's advertising campaign brochure setting out a detailed six-month strategy that involved television, posters, national press, local press and response material (such as handbooks). Note the comment on the sixty-second television commercial: '…nine out of ten people will see the commercial at least six times.' (BL, HOME/1/22/88A)

We open close in on a young boy's face. He is at the age of innocence with beautiful skin. A good looking lad of, say, 10. After he has said the opening words we dissolve every few seconds to see other children, just head and shoulders, speaking directly to the camera, looking you straight in the eye. Other children will be the same age but mostly white boys and girls.

Boy's Voice throughout:
I WANT TO GROW UP IN A PLACE WHERE PEOPLE DON'T MUG OTHER PEOPLE.
I WANT TO GROW UP WHERE KIDS DON'T SNIFF GLUE.
I WANT TO GROW UP IN A STREET WHERE MY GRAN CAN OPEN THE FRONT DOOR WITHOUT BEING FRIGHTENED.

Voice Over
WE'RE ALREADY WORKING TOGETHER TO CRACK CRIME. WHY NOT JOIN US?
('Practical Ways To Crack Crime' is placed in screen so we can see how thick it is)
START HERE.

AND NO ONE BREAKS IN OUR HOUSE AND STEALS OUR THINGS.
I WANT TO GROW UP WHERE THE BIG KIDS DON'T GO ROUND SMASHING THINGS UP.
AND WHERE MY SISTER CAN WALK HOME SAFELY WITHOUT BEING WORRIED BY HORRIBLE MEN.
(Fade under but we still see the kids faces and their lips moving.)

(Hands turn the pages and point to three interesting and surprising headings which are easily readable)
THIS BOOK IS FULL OF IDEAS, TO HELP YOU, THE POLICE, ALL OF US
PROTECT OUR FAMILY. (We see page relating to children/teenagers)
OUR PROPERTY. (We see page relating to care)
OUR COMMUNITY. (We see page relating to The Community Programme)
(The hands continue to turn pages as the phone number is supered over)

Voice Over
IS THIS TOO MUCH TO ASK? A LOT OF US THINK IT ISN'T.
Kid's Voice Up
I WANT TO GROW UP IN A PLACE WHERE PEOPLE DON'T SPRAY GRAFFITI OVER OUR WALLS.
AND MY DAD (fade) CAN LEAVE HIS (MOTOR) WITHOUT THE RADIO GETTING NICKED.

PHONE 01-200 1000 FOR YOUR FREE COPY NOW PLEASE.
(Phone number is supered and remains until logo.)
Kids (Five or six quick cuts)
PLEASE. PLEASE. PLEASE. PLEASE. PLEASE. (Fade)
Voice Over
CRIME. TOGETHER WE'LL CRACK IT.

Prepared for the Home Office by the Central Office of Information 1988 Printed in the UK for HMSO HOME J08153J

CRIME
TOGETHER WE'LL CRACK IT

Advertising Campaign 1988

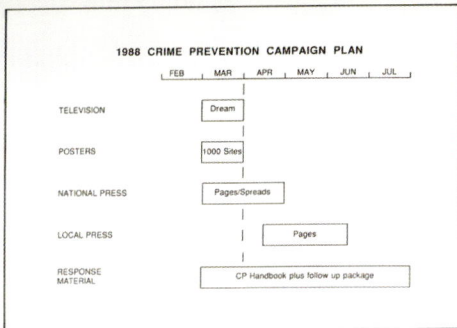

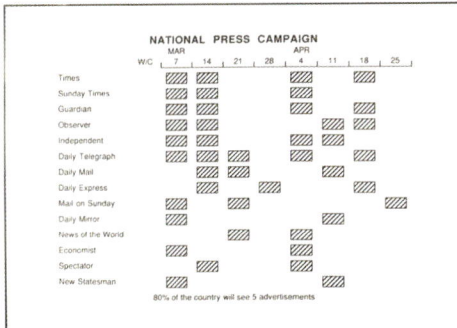

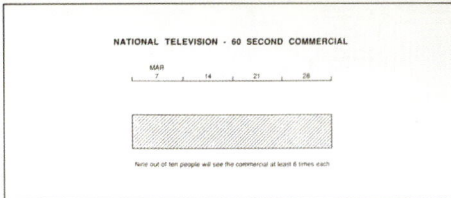

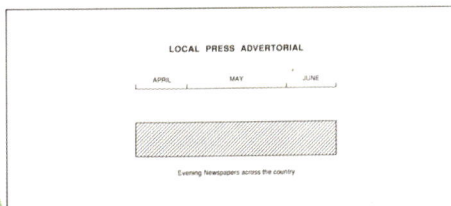

1988 CRIME PREVENTION CAMPAIGN PLAN

	FEB	MAR	APR	MAY	JUN	JUL
TELEVISION		Dream				
POSTERS		1000 Sites				
NATIONAL PRESS		Pages/Spreads				
LOCAL PRESS			Pages			
RESPONSE MATERIAL		CP Handbook plus follow up package				

NATIONAL TELEVISION - 60 SECOND COMMERCIAL

MAR
7   14   21   28

Nine out of ten people will see the commercial at least 8 times each

NATIONAL POSTER CAMPAIGN

MARCH

1000 POSTER SITES

LOCAL PRESS ADVERTORIAL

APRIL   MAY   JUNE

Evening Newspapers across the country

NATIONAL PRESS CAMPAIGN

	MAR 7	14	21	28	APR 4	11	18	25
Times		▨	▨		▨			
Sunday Times		▨	▨		▨			
Guardian		▨	▨		▨			
Observer		▨	▨			▨		
Independent		▨	▨		▨		▨	
Daily Telegraph		▨	▨		▨		▨	
Daily Mail		▨	▨		▨			▨
Daily Express		▨	▨		▨			▨
Mail on Sunday		▨						▨
Daily Mirror		▨					▨	
News of the World				▨	▨			
Economist		▨			▨			
Spectator		▨			▨		▨	
New Statesman		▨				▨	▨	

80% of the country will see 5 advertisements

17

TOOLED UP? THEN YOU'VE GOT TROUBLE

There's a new law against carrying knives.
Or any other offensive weapon.
Penalty: £400 or prison.
Hand them in at any police station now.

KNIVES AMNESTY. NO QUESTIONS ASKED. NO NAMES TAKEN.

attempted to drown themselves – fortunately they did not succeed – they were so happy at having been left alive that they went about cheering up everybody'. Supporting the government and the COI, Herbert Hughes (Wolverhampton West) concluded that: 'Is not the declared purpose of this film a good deal more patriotic than the object of Conservative propaganda, which is to make things appear worse?'[18] For what was an innocuous short film parodying the familiar complaint 'the country is going to the dogs', it is quite extraordinary that it should have caused such controversy in the House of Commons. However, such exchanges were typical of sustained attacks by (mainly Conservative) MPs on the activities of the COI. In many ways, it was remarkable that it continued until 2011.

The COI was unique among government departments in being staffed largely by journalists, artists, television and film directors, designers and publicity technicians. An extraordinary group of artists worked at some stage for the COI. These included: Rowland Hilder, Milner Grey, John Minton, Topolski, Edward Ardizzone, Abram Games, Ashley Havinden, F.H.K. Henrion, Hans Unger, Tom Eckersley, Laurence Scarfe, James Fitton, Ronald Searle, Edward Bawden, Andre Amstutz, Charles Tunnicliffe, Reginald Mount, Eileen M. Evans, Norman Thelwell, Royston Cooper, and the Crosby/Fletcher/Forbes group. Working for the whole range of ministries in an area susceptible to policy changes and creative and technical developments, the COI's staff had to demonstrate remarkable artistic dexterity and sensitive political skills. Much of the day-to-day work undertaken by the COI consisted of mounting campaigns aimed directly at the public. For example, the 'Protect and Survive' campaign for the Home Office, the 'Don't Drink and Drive' campaign for the Department of Transport and the 'AIDS' campaign launched by the Department of Health. In 1988, following the Criminal Justice Act, the Conservative government launched a 'Crime Prevention' campaign that involved all the media, and that would run for six months (Figs. 1a and b, and 2). It is often forgotten that the COI had to co-ordinate its campaigns, which required considerable strategy and planning. It is often too easy to see a COI poster, pamphlet or television commercial in isolation.

The range of work included producing articles, books, speeches, briefing materials, films, television commercials and exhibitions, and arranging tours for overseas. All of this involved input from journalists, artists and designers, translators and researchers. At its height, the COI was producing 3,000 publications annually (Fig. 3). Objectives were stressed: 'The sponsoring department takes the lead and calls on the advice and common services of the COI to provide raw material.' Prime Minister Harold Wilson, writing in the *Institute of Public Relations* journal, put it more succinctly, 'The Information Officer's duty is to give facts, either on his own initiative or more frequently, in response to enquiries from the press or the public. ... It is no part of his duties to engage in political propaganda... .'[19]

---

2. *Tooled Up? Then You've Got Trouble* (1988). The Criminal Justice Act 1988 contained a list of prohibited martial arts-style weapons and made it an offence to carry an article with a blade or sharp point in a public place. Following this Act, the Home Office launched an advertising campaign entitled 'Together We'll Crack It', which included a knives amnesty. This poster encourages people to hand them in at a police station: 'No questions asked. No names taken.' (BL, PP/HOME/1/32/88A)

By 1995 the size of the COI had been reduced to 900 staff, of which half were information officers, mostly specialists recruited from the private sector. The COI either created material itself or arranged for commercial agencies to do so. Press and television advertising campaigns were undertaken by advertising agencies and films were made by film companies under contract. The COI was headed by its Director-General assisted by a deputy Director-General. There were four groups: three production groups covering home and overseas work, each headed by a director and each subdivided into specialised services; and in addition there was a client service director, who oversaw day-to-day relations with customers. The original structure and functions would, over the years, be modified, but it's original organisational manifestation remained largely the same.[20] The COI handled advertising campaigns for most departments on a repayment basis. It advised departments on advertising methods, made recommendations on the cost-effective deployment of funds available, briefed the agency appointed to handle the campaign and monitored day-to-day work. Recruitment advertising for the armed services, police, nurses, teachers, etc., accounted for a large proportion of the total expenditure of more than £100 million a year.[21]

Relations between the COI and the media were complex. The press assumed a rather ambivalent attitude, largely as a consequence of the MOI's often insensitive censorship of news management during and immediately after the war. When the government established the News Distribution Unit (NDU), the press were initially critical, but eventually it was largely accepted on the understanding that the NDU had no editorial function and operated simply as a channel between departments and the press. Relations with the British Broadcasting Corporation (BBC) were more cordial. The BBC's Director-General, Sir William Haley, viewed the corporation as an essential conduit of communication between the government and the people and therefore favoured co-operation with the information services – particularly during the transitional post-war period.[22] Television was not a major medium at that stage, but the COI maintained close relations with the cinema newsreel companies (*British Movietone News*, *Gaumont-British News*, *Pathé News* and Rank Organisation's *This Modern Age* – a British version of *The March of Time*). The COI supplied footage and operated a pool system (for a time, at least) similar to that used by the MOI during the war. The government could show films and mount displays and exhibitions outside the commercial cinema through the lectures service of the COI.[23]

The COI also boasted an important Overseas Film and Television Division. After the Crown Film Unit was disbanded in 1952 as an economic measure, the COI no longer had a camera team of its own and instead commissioned documentary films from film and television companies for both the home and overseas audiences. As a result, the longer-format public information film all but disappeared. The COI continued to acquire films for its Central Film Library, which made 'informational' (as

---

3. *Take Care on the Farm.* When Prime Minister Harold Wilson stated that information officers working for the COI should not engage in political propaganda, this 1963 safety poster for the Ministry of Agriculture and Fisheries in Scotland is presumably what he had in mind. But this was only half the story. Still, it is always wise to be 'careful' when working on or visiting a farm! (BL, PP/179/43A)

Take care
on the farm

Prepared for the Department of Agriculture and Fisheries for Scotland by the Central Office of Information 1963
PRINTED IN SCOTLAND FOR H. M. STATIONERY OFFICE BY ALLEN LITHO KIRKCALDY Wt. 7668

opposed to entertainment) films available to the public for hire or sale, with some films remaining free (the charges being paid by sponsors). The change from free issue to hire, which occurred in 1952 (again for reasons of economy), led inevitably to a decline in output – but, surprisingly, usage actually increased steadily throughout the 1950 and 1960s, with industry and school and local education authorities being the biggest borrowers. In the 1960s, films such as *Smoking and You* (an anti-smoking film made by the COI for the Health and Education Departments) and *Lifting Patients* (a nursing training film made for the Department of Health) proved popular, as did *Critical Path*, a 1963 training film sponsored by Richard Costain, which demonstrated the benefits to industry and management of critical path analysis. Contrary to expectations, the spread of television into almost every home in the 1960s had been followed by an increase in the circulation of films for showing to groups. In 1968–69, for example, the Central Film Library distributed 100,000 issues, with a gross annual income of £120,000, compared with just over £27,000 in 1953–54, when charges were first imposed.

Some of Britain's most distinguished documentary directors, such as Lindsay Anderson, Karel Reiz, John Krish and Don Levy, made films for the COI. Indeed, Sir John Grierson, the pioneering documentary maker, was controller of the film division between 1948 and 1950. For the home departments, the COI produced material for four purposes: to inform the general public on matters affecting their well-being, such as safety, health and welfare; to aid recruitment to the public services (including the armed forces); to advise and encourage exporters; and to instruct specialised audiences on the latest techniques in science, industry, nursing, agriculture, etc. Although by the 1960s television had become the most important medium, there were still large areas of the world, especially Africa, the Middle East, Southeast Asia and parts of Latin America, where cinema-going continued to be a regular habit.

For television, the COI produced both short public service films for showing during breaks on BBC and Independent Television (both of which allocated free time for this purpose) and 'commercials' for showing on Independent Television during paid time. Perhaps the most famous (and effective) of all the subjects treated in this way were the campaigns on children's road safety and 'Don't Drink and Drive'. As television services for overseas were being recast in the 1960s and 1970s, this shift was being reflected in the COI's budget, with overseas television services representing in 1969–70 two-thirds of the budget. In 1968–69 the COI's London Television Service supplied some eighty-five countries with television material either in the form of 'newsbriefs' (short news items on recent events and developments) and general magazine programmes ('cinemagazines'), which were issued at regular intervals, often in colour, such as *This Week in Britain* (largely for the English-speaking Commonwealth), *London Line* (for the United States and Canada) and *Aqui Londres* (for Latin America). Prestige documentary films for special showings were occasionally produced for invited audiences as well as for cinemas and were intended to illustrate wider aspects of British life and achievements. *Atomic Energy* (1956) was a highly acclaimed film that told the story of Britain's work in harnessing atomic power for peaceful purposes. It was distributed to eight-five countries, shown to cinema audiences of nearly half a million and got eighty-nine television screenings with a total estimated television audience of over ten million. *Seawards the Great Ships*, written by John Grierson, chronicled the shipbuilding on the Clyde during the early 1960s and won an Academy Award in 1962, and in 1967 *Opus*, an impressionistic survey of the arts in Britain, premiered in the British pavilion at Montreal's Expo 67 and was chosen to inaugurate Mexico's first colour television service. The award-winning film was eventually seen in over 100 countries. These films reached an apex in the transitional period of the 1960s and were intended to provide a kaleidoscopic vision of British culture and innovation by projecting a modern Britain onto the screens of the world and encourage international trade. The COI's Adaptation Unit produced foreign-language versions of film and television programmes in over sixty languages, and in 1968 produced over 700 foreign-language versions of 270 films.[24]

World War II arguably changed the relationship between the state and the people in Britain. The war penetrated the lives of ordinary citizens more intrusively than had been the case in World War I. In part as a reward for the sacrifices made in wartime, and in part as a step towards the realisation of a 'New Jerusalem', the post-war Labour government under Clement Attlee acted on the reforms recommended during the war by the Beveridge Report. By identifying five issues that could be defeated by state action (Want, Disease, Ignorance, Squalor and Idleness), Beveridge had provided the British people with a domestic focus for victory. The war had generated a huge confidence in the potential positive influence of the state. By establishing the Welfare State, Labour offered a glimpse of a new Britain in which everyone, no matter what class, would be clothed and fed, and care would extend from the cradle to the grave. Peter Hennessy has said of the new ministers in the administration that they really did think 'that Jerusalem could be built here'.[25]

Moreover, the Labour government felt it was obligatory to provide information about its vision of this 'brave new world'. After the MOI was abolished, its residual functions were passed to the new Central Office of Information. This optimistic vision of the post-war world (workings of the government) was to be disseminated by the COI through the continued use of government propaganda (or information and instruction). Revealingly, throughout the COI's existence, few people were, or have been, aware of it – or if they were, its activity has been associated with domestic safety campaigns or with health advice. The COI was regarded as harmless from a propaganda point of view; its officials were 'information officers' whose work involved 'publicity' designed primarily to benefit not the source but the recipient. If it was regarded at all, the COI was seen as a conduit for a state functioning responsibly in the democratic context of informing citizens for their own good. Such a benign view (of its activities) was encouraged by all governments and was a consciously constructed self-delusion. In reality such propaganda was used to justify greater government intervention in the lives of ordinary people and as a tool to engineer consent. But more of this later. ♛

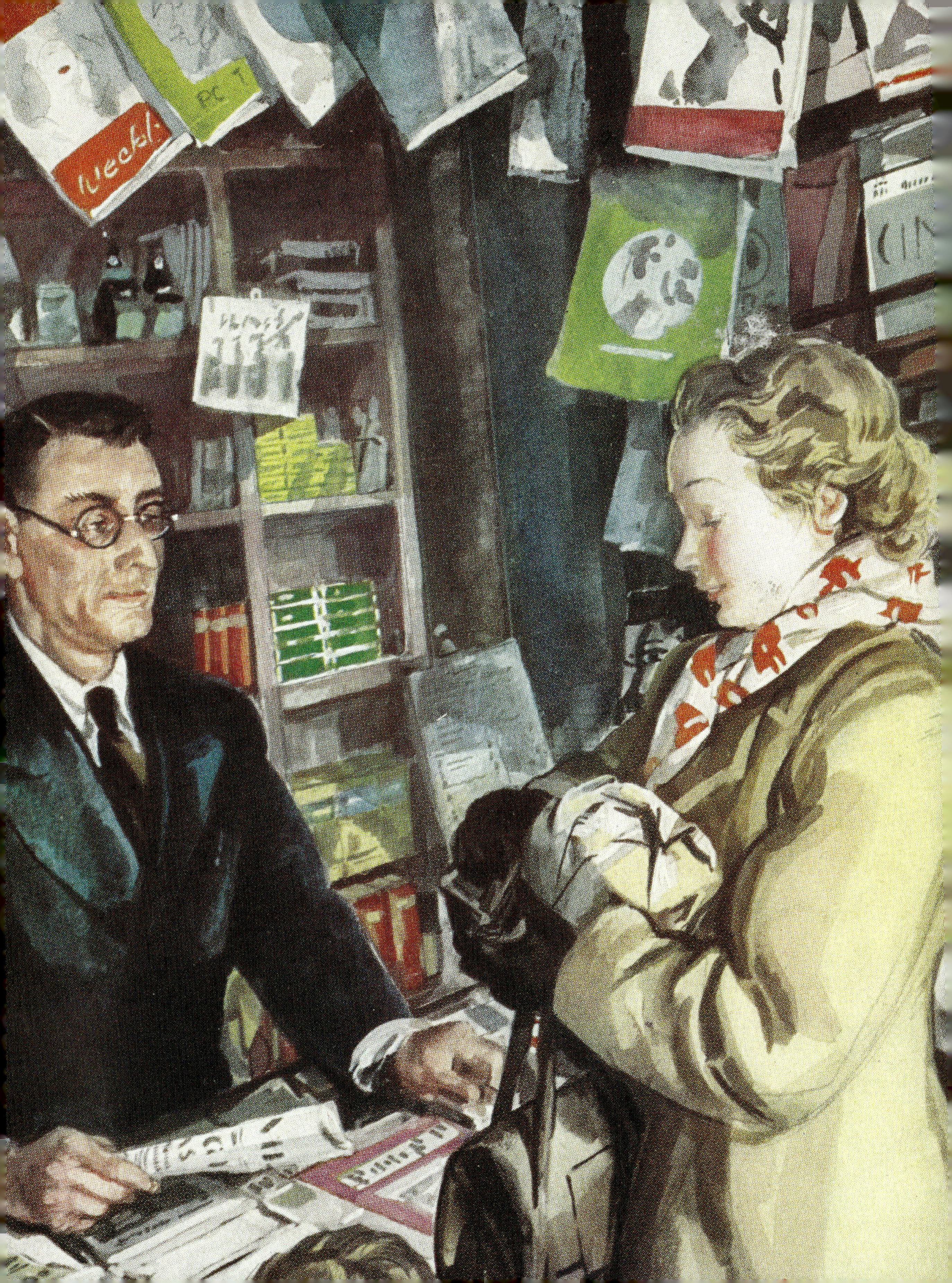

CHAPTER TWO

THE 'NEW JERUSALEM': BRITAIN IN THE 1940s AND 1950s

World War II changed people's lives and attitudes. After the war, in a bold attempt to make Lloyd George's earlier promise of a 'land fit for heroes' a reality, the newly elected Labour government launched a series of radical social and economic reforms intended to build a 'New Jerusalem' for its citizens. Labour had been elected to bring about a Socialist Commonwealth of Great Britain that was 'free, democratic, progressive and public spirited, its material resources organised in the service of the British people...'.[1] Together with concerns about the state of the British economy, health was a major post-war preoccupation. In terms of health, the vicissitudes of modern warfare, such as bombing raids on the major urban conurbations, forced the government to provide healthcare to civilian casualties such as they had never experienced before. In the years immediately after the war, a consensus had agreed on two priorities: top of the list was post-war recovery, closely followed by a desire on the part of the state to improve the health of the nation, which led directly to the formation of the National Health Service (NHS).

A HEALTHIER BRITAIN:
LAUNCHING THE NATIONAL HEALTH SERVICE

The overwhelming Labour victory in the July 1945 General Election allowed the Attlee government to implement its election promises unencumbered by political controversy and establish the comprehensive welfare programme that the Beveridge Report of 1942 had set out for the future of post-war Britain. Implicit in the creation of Labour's Welfare State was its promise of shared citizenship. An extensive raft of welfare measures followed, culminating in the establishment of the National Health Service (NHS). The Minister for Health, Aneurin Bevan, was given the task of introducing (and 'selling') the service.

The Attlee government was the first British government to fully engage with the dilemma of how a government communicates with its citizens to sustain a credible democracy. To do this it established the modern machinery of government communication and used the mass media extensively. The role of the Central Office of information (COI) in preparing and explaining the NHS to the people of Britain is one of the earliest examples of an idealistic vision of helping to develop an informed electorate through the pragmatic use of information as a means of persuasion and a tool for engineering consent.

From 1946 until its closure sixty-five years later in 2011 the COI was responsible for the UK government's marketing and communications, and largely responsible for commissioning and disseminating health propaganda. In 1946 the COI's aim was simple: to use its communications expertise to help the government achieve policy objectives. The mass-media campaigns under the aegis of the COI have shaped the debate about the maintenance of good health and have suggested a 'contract' of sorts whereby the state has provided scientific information and advocated certain changes in behaviour, with the individual citizen expected to follow the advice uncritically (what the state would view as 'informed consent').

In promoting and maintaining good health, can the state continue to expect an 'acquiescent public'? During the course of this book, I shall look at a number of health campaigns disseminated by the COI in order to subject these questions to critical examination. Most notably, in the 1960s and 1970s the government injunction not to drink and drive and to stop smoking, and then in the 1980s and 1990s the campaign to inform the public of the danger of AIDS.

However, in the immediate post-war years the Labour government had the more-pressing problem of introducing to the British people the most seismic shift in public health in the nation's history. In its 1945 General Election manifesto *Let Us Face the Future*, Labour stated its commitment to a National Health Service:

> By good food and good homes, much avoidable ill-health can be prevented. In addition the best health services should be available free for all. Money must no longer be the passport to the best treatment.
> In the new National Health Service there should be health centres where

the people may get the best that modern science can offer, more and better hospitals, and proper conditions for our doctors and nurses. More research is required into the causes of disease and the ways to prevent and cure it.

Labour will work specially for the care of Britain's mothers and their children – children's allowances and school medical and feeding services, better maternity and child welfare services. A healthy family life must be fully ensured and parenthood must not be penalised if the population of Britain is to be prevented from dwindling.

The COI was to play a crucial role in explaining and achieving these objectives. The NHS was officially launched on 5 July 1948, but a whole range of services, benefits and charges came into effect between 1944 and 1948. The Education Act (1944) had introduced free secondary education; in 1945 the Family Allowances Act provided families with financial support, while in 1946 the Industrial Injuries Act extended benefits to those injured at work, and in 1948 the Children's Act mandated council provision of housing and care to all children 'deprived of a normal home life' and the National Insurance Act extended a benefits safety net for the unemployed and the sick.

The National Health and National Insurance schemes are often viewed as being part of a unified scheme of social security (largely because they would eventually be run by a single department). However, in 1948 this was not the case. The NHS was launched, to modest fanfare by Health Secretary Aneurin Bevan, at the Park Hospital in Manchester on 5 July 1948. It was a hugely ambitious programme that brought together for the first time hospitals, doctors, nurses, pharmacists, opticians and dentists under one umbrella organisation to provide a range of services that were free for all at the point of delivery. The key principle underpinning the Welfare State was that it was universal, would be free of stigma and discrimination, and paid for by everyone through National Insurance payments. The National Insurance scheme was compulsory, and was a rationalisation and extension of existing systems of social insurance.

The COI, which was responsible for the dissemination of all (or at least most) of the publicity, was hampered by the fact that the departments concerned, the Ministry of Health (MOH) and the Ministry of National Insurance (MNI), maintained no formal machinery for liaison and in addition the Minister for Health, Aneurin Bevan, insisted that separate publicity campaigns be maintained.[2] There was therefore no single unified campaign of official propaganda that the COI might have co-ordinated. Indeed, the differences between the two pieces of legislation required substantially different thematic approaches to publicity. What had been agreed was that the 'Appointed Day' for the introduction of the new National Health Service would be 5 July 1948.

An initial problem facing the COI was that it was dealing with such a radical break from previous healthcare provision that it needed to be carefully explained. A further problem was that different aspects of the new provision were viewed differently by

sections of the population. Therefore a certain amount of 'selling' was necessary. On the one hand the COI had to inform the country what the new health service provided and on the other how it was to be paid for. The introduction of the NHS was vociferously opposed by the British Medical Association (BMA), which threatened non-co-operation over issues of responsibilities and pay. Doctors disliked the idea of becoming employees of the state and were in an extremely powerful position, because without them the NHS could not operate. Feelings undoubtedly ran high; 'We have not fought and won a war against dictatorship only to submit to it disguised as democracy of the Soviet pattern', protested J.S. Laurie, a general practitioner in Fitzwilliam, Yorkshire.[3] The government believed, however, that the NHS was enthusiastically anticipated by the working class.[4] Nevertheless, the government was forced to make a number of concessions to the doctors.[5]

The NHS was launched as a single organisation based on fourteen regional hospital boards, with an annual budget of £437 million. There were three parts: hospital services; family doctors, dentists, opticians and pharmacists; and local authority health services, including community nursing and health visiting. The NHS took over control of 2,751 hospitals containing 533,000 beds, many of them in large mental institutions. For the first time, consultants and senior physicians were paid like other staff and no longer honorary and entirely dependent on private patients for a living. Right from the start, the NHS belonged to the people.

The planning for the publicity campaigns started in 1947 and it was decided that in the first instance the COI would address three themes: explaining the new health service to the public and the medical professions; encouraging the public to register with a doctor before the 'Appointed Day'; and answering questions from the public and medical professions. The MNI's campaign started first and by December 1947 the COI had distributed posters to public buildings and factories on various aspects of social insurance, such as increased pension contributions and family allowances. Faced with the problem of ensuring the registration of three or four million new entrants to National Insurance, the MNI wanted to concentrate on persuading new entrants to insurance to register *before* the 'Appointed Day', and to get over the detailed instructions needed to ease the administrative burden and to minimise misunderstandings. The MNI had suggested that there should also be a free national distribution of a 'popular' pamphlet to explain the new legislation, rather than the usual practice of public sale.

By March 1948 a complete calendar of the publicity programmes for the two campaigns had been produced,[6] and consequently in the immediate period leading up to 5 July 1948 the COI launched a torrent of propaganda – leaflets and pamphlets, radio broadcasts, film, advertising and lectures – explaining and justifying the new welfare arrangements. In fact, the NHS campaign really began in May 1948, with a substantial display at the exhibition organised by the COI to celebrate the centenary of the 1848 Public Health Act. 'Health of the People' (Fig. 4) was opened by

---

4. *Health of the People.* This exhibition ran from May to June 1948 and was an attempt by the COI to communicate the positive difference that it was anticipated the new NHS would make in the future compared with public healthcare provision in the past. (Wellcome Collection)

Princess Elizabeth at Marble Arch and was an ambitious attempt to provide a history of public health and to demonstrate the difference that the new NHS would make.

The exhibition was used by the BBC as an opportunity to broadcast a discussion of the NHS in 'What's Your Worry?', a slot in *Woman's Hour*, on 16 May.[7] The role of broadcasting was vital to the COI publicity campaigns. As early as January 1948, the BBC had agreed to make the NHS the subject of a number of its flagship programmes (such as *Can I Help You?*, *Woman's Hour*, *Radio Newsreel* and *Focus*), as well as a major broadcast to the nation just prior to its launch by the Prime Minister, Clement Attlee, that would explain and link the two schemes.[8] The BBC felt that its contribution to publicity for the schemes would be most effective after the so-called 'Appointed Day', but it was willing to be flexible in the face of the strong preference from the representatives of the government and in fact concentrated most of its coverage in the period immediately before the official launch.[9] The growing tensions between the MOI and the BMA surfaced in February in a radio discussion, 'The National Health Service' in the BBC's *Friday Forum* series. In an acrimonious debate between Dr R. Cockshut of the BMA and Dr Stephen Taylor, Labour MP for Barnet and a member of the Socialist Medical Association, the former threatened that doctors would not co-operate with the NHS, adding 'you can't bring in the troops…you know!'[10]

Not surprisingly, in such a febrile atmosphere, the press had a field day. The *Daily Mail*, in its editorial of 3 July, set out the momentous changes that were about to take place and implied (not without a hint of criticism) that the state would now be responsible for an individual's welfare from 'cradle to grave':

> On Monday morning, you will wake up in a new Britain – in a State which 'takes over' all citizens six months before they are born, provides cash and free services for their birth, for their early years, their schooling, sickness, workless days, widowhood, and retirement. Finally, it helps defray the cost of their departure… You must begin paying next Friday… Everyone, from duke to dustman, earl to errand boy, must pay, even if they decline the free services or scorn the cash allowances…[11]

The *Manchester Guardian*, on the other hand, praised the NHS as a symbol of 'the advance of equalitarianism', and the *Daily Mirror* boasted 'we are leading the whole world in Social Security,' adding: 'Our State belongs to the people – unlike so many countries where the people belong to the State – and Social Security converts our democratic ideal into human reality.'[12] Opposition came, predictably, from Lord Beaverbrook's *Daily Express*, which vociferously warned that the whole exercise was a waste of taxpayers' money and *The Times* posed the question whether the next generation would be able to 'reap the benefits of a social service State while avoiding the perils of a Santa Claus State'.[13] Happily for the government, it could count on sympathetic support of the women's magazines, ranging from *Woman* at one end of the market spectrum to *Vogue* at the top end.

First get a recommendation from your family doctor that your eyes need testing. Then hand that recommendation to any doctor with special qualifications (lists will be available) or to any ophthalmic optician taking part in the new service. If you need glasses, these will be provided without charge. For re-testing you can go direct to any of the doctors with special qualifications, or to an ophthalmic optician.

The National Health Service will provide several kinds of spectacles of different types. For specially expensive types you will have to pay the extra cost.

Deafness   Specialist ear clinics will be established as resources allow. At them you will get not only an expert opinion upon deafness but also, if necessary, a *new hearing aid* invented by a special committee of the Medical Research Council. Production of these aids is now going on, but will not meet all demands at once. They will be supplied free, when ready, together with a reasonable allowance of maintenance batteries.

Home Health Services   Your local County or County Borough Council will, as soon as it can, make special provision for: (1) advice and care of expectant and nursing mothers and children under five (for particulars ask your doctor, health visitor, or Welfare Centre); (2) midwifery (ask your doctor or Welfare Centre); (3) home nursing where there is illness in the family (ask your doctor); (4) all necessary vaccination or immunisation (through your doctor or Welfare Centre); and (5) a health visitor service to deal with problems of illness in the home, especially tuberculosis.

Health Centres   Special premises known as Health Centres may later be opened in your district. Doctors may be accommodated there instead of in their own surgeries, but you will still have "your own doctor" to give you personal and confidential treatment. He will still come to your home as necessary. At the Health Centre he will be able to use equipment supplied from public funds. These Centres may also offer dentistry and other services on the spot.

WHAT TO DO NOW

1. Choose your doctor.
2. Get application forms from him or from the Post Office, Public Library, or office of the local Executive Council.
3. Fill one in for each member of the family.
4. Hand them to the doctor.

ACT AT ONCE

PREPARED BY THE CENTRAL OFFICE OF INFORMATION FOR THE MINISTRY OF HEALTH

(53077) Wt. 3016a 2/48 E.w.

THE NEW
NATIONAL
HEALTH
SERVICE

*

Your new National Health Service begins on 5th July. What is it? How do you get it?

It will provide you with all medical, dental, and nursing care. Everyone—rich or poor, man, woman or child—can use it or any part of it. There are no charges, except for a few special items. There are no insurance qualifications. But it is not a "charity". You are all paying for it, mainly as taxpayers, and it will relieve your money worries in time of illness.

5. *The New National Health Service.* 'Your *new* National Health Service begins on 5 July. What is it? How do you get it?' An extraordinarily simple design, with no fancy advertising aids, to herald arguably the most significant development in British medical health provision. (BL, PP/40/25A)

As the COI prepared to launch its propaganda campaigns in the lead-up to the 'Appointed Day', it was further encouraged that public opinion as a whole was broadly supportive. According to a Gallup poll in March 1948, 61 per cent saw the NHS as a 'good' idea and only 13 per cent as 'bad'.[14] Although Bevan continued to insist that the two schemes should not be linked in the respective publicity campaigns, the idea proposed by the MNI of a free 'popular' pamphlet to explain the schemes was taken up by the MOH. However, because of the continuing uncertainty over the final provision of the NHS caused by the opposition of the BMA, Thomas Fife Clark, the Chief Information Officer of the MOH (and later Director-General of the COI), decided that any such pamphlet should contain only the 'essential facts'.[15] Consequently, the MOH pamphlet on the NHS consisted of four pages whereas the MNI's contained thirty-two pages of detailed information intended to ensure the registration of millions of new entrants to National Insurance. Both had print runs of

THE

NATIONAL
HEALTH
SERVICE

*

WHO CAN USE THE NATIONAL HEALTH SERVICE?

Civilians resident in this country can use it, or any complete part of it.   No insurance qualifications are necessary.

Visitors from overseas who are taken ill or sustain an accident after their arrival in the country may also use the Service, but overseas residents who come here to seek treatment are expected to pay for it.

14 million copies.[16] The MNI document was simply called *Social Security in Britain*, which it referred to as a 'charter'…. 'an expression of the community to the individual. By his work and his social conduct the individual helps the community… and in return the community helps him when he is in need…'. Referring back to Britain's wartime experience and mindful of the promises made after World War I, the pamphlet proclaimed: 'The main burden of the war was being carried by ordinary men and women, and it is for them that the social security charter is devised.' The government was determined that it did not wish to return to the 'fear and insecurity' of the 1930s that had 'marred so many lives… this time the promises made to those who were doing the fighting and the suffering should be kept'.[17]

The MOH's four-page leaflet was much simpler; it was entitled *The New National Health Service* and printed on white paper (Fig. 5). The COI was given the brief to produce concise information that would set out unambiguously the aims and objective of the new service. Nevertheless, from a contemporary perspective, it strikes one as quite extraordinary that, in the new age of media management, Labour should decide on such a dull, bland leaflet to launch possibly the most radical, life-transforming and exciting development in British medical history.

The first point to make is the reference to a 'new' health service, something that Labour had promised in its post-war General Election campaign. The publication starts with two questions: 'What is it?' and 'How do you get it?' Under the heading 'What is it?', the opening paragraph proclaims that 'Everyone – rich or poor, man, woman or child – can use any part of it' without charge and there are no insurance qualifications. But it goes on to state that it is not a 'charity' for 'you are all paying for it…mainly as taxpayer', and it would 'relieve your money worries in times of illness'. The pamphlet, which is stark and to the point, had no illustrations but contained information grouped under nine subheadings: choosing a doctor, maternity services, hospital and specialist services, medicines, drugs and appliances, care of teeth and eyes, deafness, home health services, and health centres. A second leaflet (*The National Health Service*), which included a further section on the new ambulance service, would swiftly follow (Fig. 6).

The main concern for the government and the MOH, especially in light of the opposition to the new service by the BMA, was to encourage citizens over sixteen years old to register with a doctor:

> *Choose a doctor now – ask him to be your doctor under the new arrangements. Many will choose their present doctors. Any doctor can decline to accept a patient. If one doctor cannot accept you, ask another, or ask to be put in touch with one by the new 'Executive Council' which has been set up in your local area…. Your dealings with your doctor will remain as they are now: personal and confidential…. The difference is that your doctor*

---

6. *The National Health Service.* 'Who Can use the National Health Service?' The second edition in blue remains just as simple as the original document. The COI would, however, use other media, such as the cinema, to explain and justify the launch of the NHS. (BL, PP/40/25A)

will be paid by the Government, out of funds provided by everybody...Help to have the Scheme ready by 5 July by choosing your doctor at once.

The COI also used film propaganda for these purposes. In 1948 to help launch the NHS a number of short films were produced. *A Healthier Britain* was a special edition of *Pathé News* and was shown in all cinemas. It anticipates the leaflet that had been produced by the Ministry of Health to explain the benefits of the new NHS and which was posted to all homes and distributed to municipal buildings such as public libraries: 'It's coming' ... 'It's on its way' ... 'Look out for it' ... This leaflet is coming through your letterbox one day soon. Or maybe you've already had your copy. Read it carefully. It tells you what the new National Health Service is and how you can use what it offers.' The film then takes the cinema-viewer through the substance of the leaflet and ends with a number of important immediate actions that citizens need to take. To emphasise their importance the actions needed are projected onto the screen in capital letters: 'Choose Your Doctor Now' ... 'Ask your doctor now if he will look after you under the new scheme. If he can't accept you, ask at the Post Office for the address of the Executive Council, where you'll be given the names of other doctors in your area who are taking part in the new service' ... 'Don't forget – choose your doctor now'.[18]

Choose Your Doctor (sometimes referred to as *Doctor's Dilemma*) was a short public information trailer shown in cinemas in the lead-up to the inauguration of the NHS, and it provided guidance on how to register with a GP. Before the NHS, surgeries were run as private enterprises, and consultations, treatment and prescriptions had to be paid for upfront. This film, like much of the multi-media campaign, juxtaposed bold, simple visuals with the narrator's step-by-step instruction on how to sign up with a general practitioner. The final message is an unambiguous one: 'DON'T FORGET. CHOOSE YOUR DOCTOR NOW.' At the time, such an insistent campaign must have instilled a sense of urgency on all those who had yet to complete a registration form.[19]

The COI also commissioned a number of short animated films from John Halas and Joy Batchelor who had worked for the MOI during World War II. These films features 'Charley', a post-war cartoon star created for the Central Office of Information by Halas and Batchelor. Charley was Britain's Joe Public and acted as a conduit through whom the public could learn about the various reforms that were being undertaken in Britain to help the country get back on its feet after World War II.

There were eight 'Charley' films in total, looking at the new towns, The Education Act (schooling), the National Health, building up exports and working for heavy industry. Charley had his own chirpy theme tune, and opening titles in which he would ride across the screen on his bicycle, writing out his name. Each film was billed as being part of an ongoing series, so film audiences knew there were others to view and learn from. The format would begin with chipper Charley on his pushbike, exploring post-war Britain and commenting on social developments. He would interact with an unseen commentator, who would answer his questions, correct and educate him. Charley could often be reluctant to reform, and would need some cajoling to get into the spirit of things.

Charley was used to explain the post-war Labour government's new legislative reforms, and to coincide with the 'Appointed Day' two films were produced: *Your Very Good Health* (Fig. 7) for the MOH and *Charley's March of Time* for the MNI. In *Your Very Good Health*, Charley demystifies the new state-funded National Health Service, detailing the benefits which a free-at-the-point-of-delivery health service will offer to everyone in England. Charley aims to show the public how the main services would affect an ordinary family, including Charley's wife ('Mrs Charley') – even if he did consider her always fit and well because she was as 'strong as a blooming horse!' The script of the film is as follows:

> **Commentator:** *In the past we've had all sorts of public health services, such as main drainage and water supply. Everyone makes use of these services and everyone pays for them! Refuse disposal is another of these services – and so is street cleaning. These are all public health services, but the new Health Act proposes to organise 'PERSONAL' health services in the same way. There have been many personal health services, but different kinds of financial arrangements.*
> **Charley:** *Morning George.*
> **George:** *Morning Charles.*
> **Commentator:** *Morning. Some people could afford them, others could not. Some places were well off for hospitals, others were unlucky. This new health service will be organised on a national scale as a public responsibility. The cost of the service will be met from rates, taxes and National Insurance – and so everyone will pay for it.*
> **Charley:** *Huh! Thought there was a catch in it.*
> **Commentator:** *And everyone will benefit from it. When you're ill you won't have to pay for treatment.*
> **Charley:** *I don't have to pay the doctor now! I'm on the panel.*
> **Commentator:** *Yes, that's true. But your wife and children aren't. The panel system covers only half the population. And it doesn't cover hospital treatment or a lot of other things, does it? Now suppose – just suppose – you fall off your bike. Suppose your brakes give out. You might have concussion as well. You'd be carted off in an ambulance, which might cost a couple of quid, and then you'd have to pay the hospital too. All right! [Whistle sound.]*
> **Charley:** *Whew! Glad that's over.*
> **Commentator:** *The new health service would cover all this. Now let's consider it from the family viewpoint. Suppose your wife falls ill suddenly.*
> **Charley:** *But my ol' woman never is ill – strong as a blooming horse she is!*

7. *Your Very Good Health* (1948). Four black-and-white stills from the film's original colour print, each showing a different aspect (clockwise, from top left): Charley and his wife at the table discussing the merits of the new National Health Service; Old George, Charley's sceptical neighbour, who needs convincing of the scheme; a patient receiving excellent care in a new hospital; and Charley and his wife on their bike exploring social developments in post-war Britain. (BFI)

PHOTOS FROM 4

11) CHARLEY and family, cartoon characters created by Halas and Batchelor for Your Very Good Health a Government Information film that is examined in Flashback, Channel 4's exploration of film and TV's concept of the family, Wednesday 21 March, 6.30 pm.

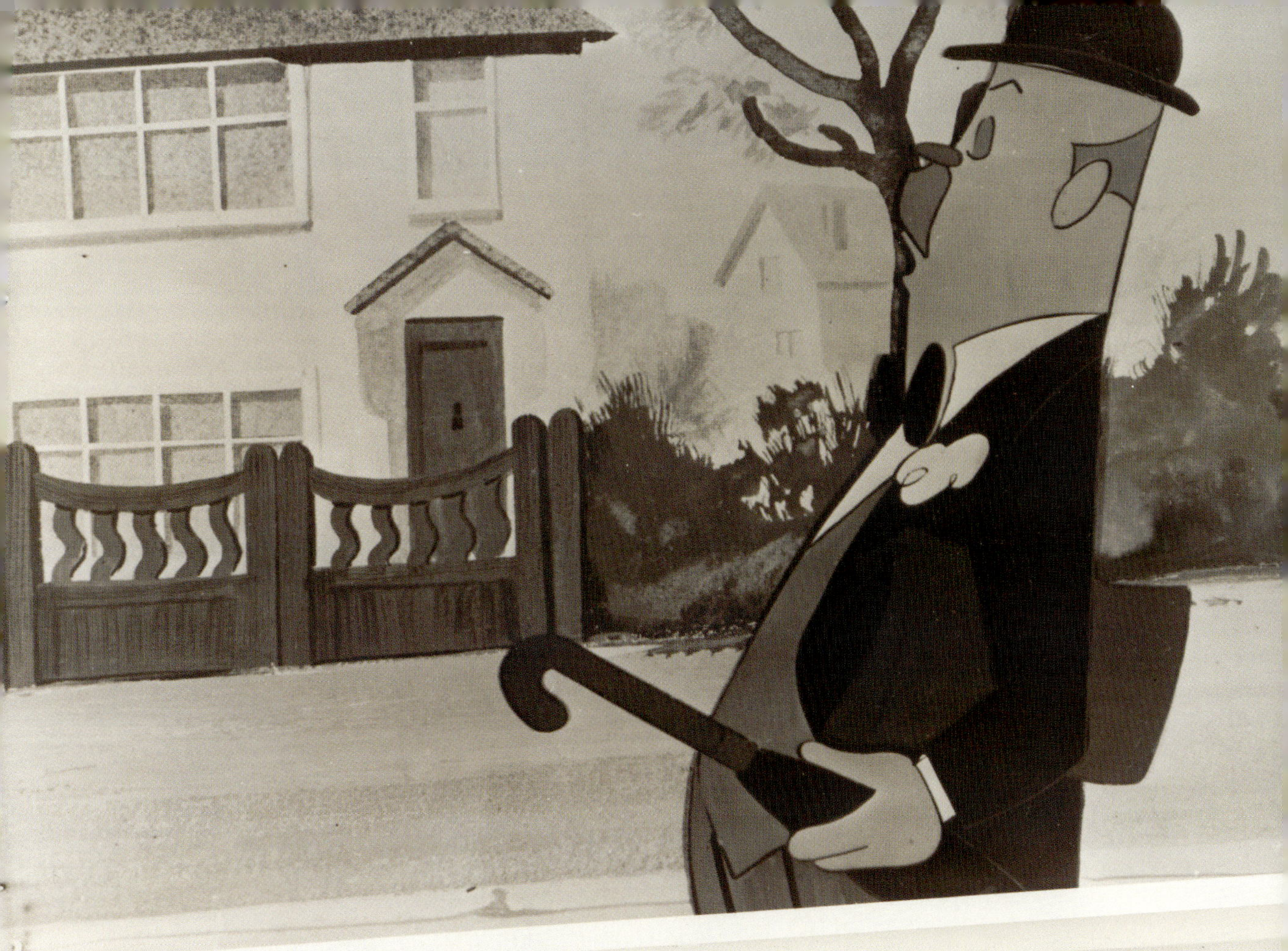

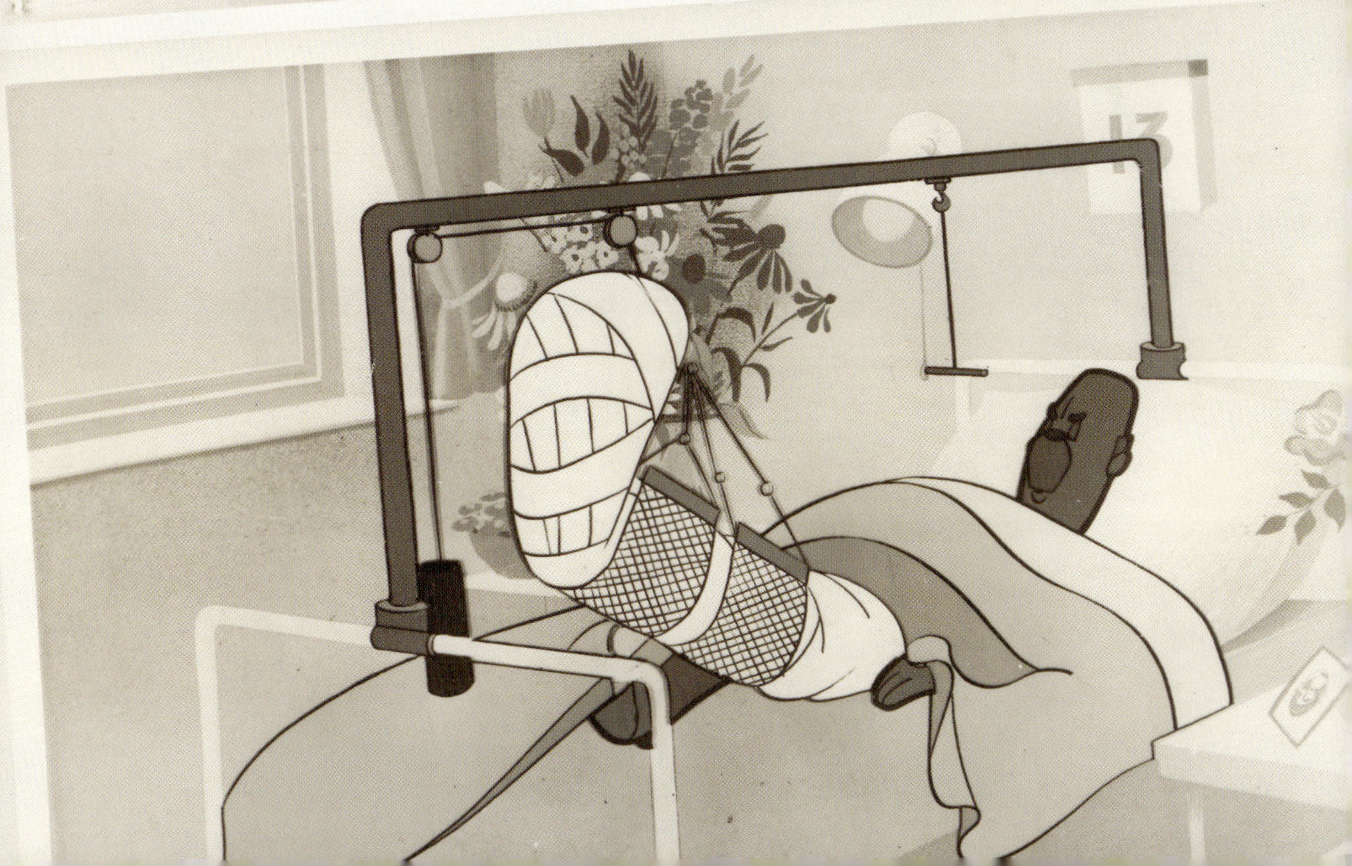
13

Mrs Charley: *We mothers can't afford to be ill – I'm not insured. Just a minute, ducks. And besides I can't take time off from my job!*

Commentator: *Well that's just it. Now let's see how the new Health Act will actually help you. The local council will have a new duty to provide home nursing, health visiting, and home help services. And you'll be able to call on them. Maternity and child welfare services will be improved. And, finally, to prevent illness, you'll have the advice of your own doctor. If you are ill, you'll have specialist services if you need them, without worrying about the cost.*

Mrs Charley: *That's more like it.*

Charley: *How does the whole scheme work?*

Commentator: *Well, suppose we see how it is at present. Hospitals were built haphazardly, according to the varying foresight and resources of many different authorities, with extremely patchy results. Reorganising will take time, but at the end of it the country will have the sort of hospitals and other services it needs, where they are needed. The family doctor will usually work in his own surgery as he does now, but special Health Centres will gradually be established as building allows. He will be backed up, your doctor I mean, by organised hospital and specialist services for the really difficult cases, a lesson we learnt during the war.*

Charley: *Sounds a bit of all right to me. But – just a minute. Where do I come in?*

Commentator: *Right here! Let's have a practical demonstration. Off you go to the doctor. You have some unusual illness, which can't be diagnosed. He'll no doubt wish you to see a specialist. In hospital you'll be under observation. This will include X-ray if it's found necessary. They may decide you need special drugs. Or blood transfusion. And they'll be able to make use of the path lab, to find out what's wrong and how best to make you well.*

Charley: *Whew, glad that's over! But look here. How about the people who don't want to use this service. Take Old George up the road for instance. Bet you a pound to a penny HE won't want to have anything to do with it.*

Commentator: *Well, let's find out.*

Charley: *Morning George. Busy? Here, what's your opinion of this new Health Act?*

George: *No use to me, old man.*

Charley: *Now wait a minute. Just suppose, only suppose mind you, you fell off that ladder? What would happen?*

George: *I should call my doctor and have a private ward at the local hospital.*

Charley: *All right, George, if you want to pay private fees that's your look out. No one's forcing you to use this service. But suppose instead of a simple broken leg you have a complicated break. And suppose you have to spend months off, sick. And suppose you don't need just one doctor but a number of experts' opinions. What's the answer to THAT?*

George: *Ruin.*

Charley: *With this new Act, you're covered against things like that.*

George: *I say, thanks a lot old man.*
Commentator: *It's all yours whenever you want it with your own choice of doctor. And that goes for the whole family. The scheme is comprehensive. It's not only to help you when you are ill, but to help to keep you well. And of course the younger generation will stand to gain the biggest benefits of all.*[20]

Under the National Health Service Act (1946) it was the duty of the Minister for Health to 'promote the establishment ... of a comprehensive Health Service designed to secure improvement in the physical and mental health of the people of England and Wales, and the prevention, diagnosis and treatment of illness', according to a detailed booklet entitled *The National Health Service* produced by the Ministry of Health and the COI six months after the launch of the NHS (Fig. 8). Unlike the free leaflet in July that launched the NHS, it cost sixpence to buy. The thirty-six-page booklet was intended for 'people at home and overseas who are interested in the National Health Service, how it was planned, what it has set out to do, and how it is operated; and for those who are workers in the Service, without whose understanding and whole-hearted effort it cannot succeed'.

The document contained a detailed explanation of why the new universal health service had been introduced and a restrained celebration of its immediate impact. The comprehensive nature of the provision and the complexity of the organisational structure of the NHS is set out in a double-page diagram in the middle of the booklet.

Given the resistance to the introduction of the NHS, the government was concerned to spell out that people still had a choice and that private healthcare remained an option. The Act, according to the booklet, accomplished these radical reforms while fully maintaining the freedom of the individual: 'Members of the public can use the Service or not, as they wish...'. The document is, however, quick to point out that in the six months since its launch, it has been an overwhelming success. 'In place of ... multiplicity there is now a unified Service available for the medical care of all citizens, regardless of class or income.'[21] 'In fact,' the booklet proclaims, '19 out of 20 people very quickly chose their doctors and decided to use the family practitioner service; and nine out of ten doctors and dentists, and nearly all the specialists, pharmacists and opticians are taking part. The National Health Service has been launched—with remarkable smoothness. Now Parliament, Press, public and professions have the task of helping the Government to ensure that it is developed on the best possible lines and used in the right way.'[22]

BUILDING THE NEW SERVICE

The Act was 'only the means of getting the new deal started'. The pamphlet makes clear that the nation would now need to build on this new service: 'In what direction will the new partnership of the professions and the "consumers" work to carry out their purpose of meeting the medical needs of the people adequately, everywhere?' (Revealing that patients are being referred in marketing terms – as if

THE 'NEW JERUSALEM'

The National Health Service

HIS MAJESTY'S STATIONERY OFFICE   6d. NET

HOSP

BOARDS OF GOVERNORS

Teaching Hospitals
and Specialists

HOSPITAL MANAGEMENT COMMITTEES

Hospitals

This diagram gives a broad vie
omits or simplifies some of the

KEY ———— Direct re
Responsib
.... Doctors a
Medicines
++++++++++++ Temporar
Hospital

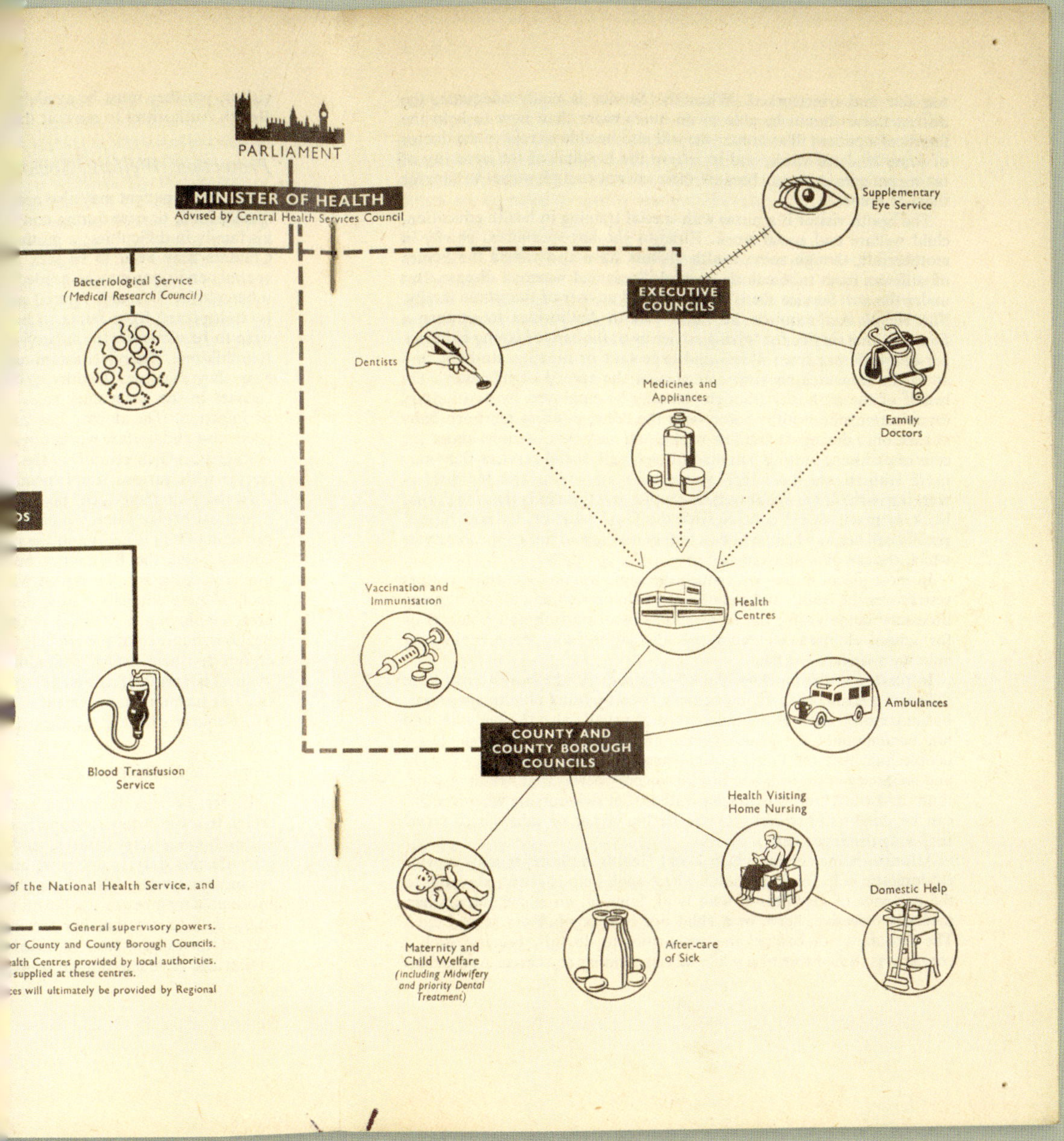

PARLIAMENT

MINISTER OF HEALTH
Advised by Central Health Services Council

Bacteriological Service
(Medical Research Council)

Supplementary
Eye Service

**EXECUTIVE
COUNCILS**

Dentists

Medicines and
Appliances

Family
Doctors

Vaccination and
Immunisation

Health
Centres

Ambulances

Blood Transfusion
Service

**COUNTY AND
COUNTY BOROUGH
COUNCILS**

Health Visiting
Home Nursing

Domestic Help

Maternity and
Child Welfare
(including Midwifery
and priority Dental
Treatment)

After-care
of Sick

of the National Health Service, and

———— General supervisory powers.
or County and County Borough Councils.
alth Centres provided by local authorities.
supplied at these centres.
ces will ultimately be provided by Regional

8. *The National Health Service.* The organisational structure of the NHS in 1948. (BL, PP/40/34A)

they were entering into some sort of purchasing transaction.) The first thing was to: '...get the Service into good running order and to keep on improving its efficiency. All big social changes start with a certain amount of uncertainty ... this Service cannot be comprehensive in the fullest sense until the country is farther along the road to prosperity and a rising standard of life.'

When Prime Minister Attlee made his speech to the nation on Sunday 4 July, he first placed the schemes in an historical perspective by linking them to the Atlantic Charter and to the wartime all-party support for the Beveridge Report. He also warned the public not to expect too much to start with, and pointedly linked both schemes firmly to productivity. Attlee's implementation of William Beveridge's blueprint for a post-war Welfare State was based partly on an implicit assumption made by Beveridge that a national health service would make the nation healthier and thus reduce health costs. This proved unfounded as demand exceeded all expectations. As early as December 1948, Bevan was warning his colleagues that the original estimate of £176 million for the NHS's first nine months was going to be overshot by almost £50 million.[23] Moreover, the provider of the social security safety net, the National Assistance Board, discovered that far more people qualified for benefits than had been anticipated, largely because the benefits paid out under the national insurance schemes were insufficiently high. 'From 842,000 recipients in July 1948, the National Assistance Board found itself with a million on its books by 1949 and 1,800,000 by 1954.'[24] In a climate of radical social change, environmental reconstruction and austerity that still included rationing of certain goods and foods, increased productivity would be needed to pay for these new health reforms.

Having justified the need for change to Britain's health provision (what *The National Health Service* booklet refers to as 'the new deal in medical care'), the MOH document asks what this 'new deal' will look like in ten years' time? To answer this question, it sets out the six main aims of the NHS. They include: up-to-date material resources; adequate human resources; better distribution of resources; greater teamwork in serving the patient; encouragement of variety and experiment; and encouragement of a preventive and 'positive' outlook on health. The booklet concluded that the advent of a new universal health service 'offers a chance – and a challenge – to build the most efficient health service in the world, and one which as the years go by will add steadily to the nation's fitness, happiness and working capacity.'[25] A few weeks after the NHS had been launched, the Olympic Games (the so-called 'Austerity Games') were opened at Wembley Stadium on 29 July while rationing was still in force in Britain. Fifty-nine nations took part in the Olympics, but the defeated powers of Germany and Japan were excluded. Remarkably, given the prestige associated with staging such a major sporting event, the COI was conspicuous by its absence.

Fitness, happiness and working capacity were positive words that chimed with rising expectation following victory in the war. However, little more than a year after its inception, the NHS was already facing criticism. Some complained that it was a 'National Ill-Health Service', too focused on the 'free provision of corsets, free wigs, and false teeth to all and sundry, and caring for the unhealthy at the expense of the healthy'. According to the *Manchester Guardian*, the NHS was already encouraging 'social parasitism'.[26] Others grumbled about 'abuse' of the health service by 'foreigners' (claims echoed in our own ongoing debates about access to the NHS). Immediately there was a huge surge in demand for medical care from people who had previously been denied access to free treatment. Hospital waiting lists soon reached 500,000. There were 19,000 GPs, almost all of them male, working alone from their own homes. In the first month of the NHS more than 90 per cent of the population signed on with a GP. Dr John Marks qualified as a doctor on the day that the NHS began: 'Nobody realised how much unknown sickness there was until the NHS began. So many people just could not afford to go to the doctor. The new service uncovered a huge cavern of unmet need. There was an unprecedented rush to the GPs with problems people had been putting off for years. Before the NHS, healthcare in this country was a disaster, particularly if you were poor.'[27]

Nevertheless, writing in her regular column in *The New Yorker* in January 1949, Mollie Panter-Downes conceded that there was a general feeling in Britain that 'the Service is not working out as chaotically as was expected by its critics' and that 'the bitter blood between the Minister of Health and the medical men has diminished'.[28] In April 1949, Mass Observation conducted a series of interviews across England on the public's reaction to the NHS and reported that 'unqualified approval was nearly twice as common as approval hedged in with reservations'. Service users, at least, certainly had good cause to celebrate: in its first year, the new NHS had provided patients with 27,000 hearing aids; 164,000 surgical and medical appliances; 6,800,000 dental treatments; and 4,500,000 pairs of glasses – and these figures did not include items supplied through general practice, hospital dental treatments or the hospital eye services. Ilford, a photographic supply company, even bid for an additional £1 million in new capital on the back of the National Health Service's voracious appetite for X-ray films.[29]

One aspect of the new health provision that the Ministry of Health wished to highlight was the blood transfusion service. The experience of the war had demonstrated the importance of blood, both in terms of supply and treatment. The MOH was particularly keen to publicise the new Regional Transfusion Centres and persuade people that since the war the need for more blood is greater than ever. In 1948 the COI produced a booklet entitled *Life Blood* (Figs. 9a and b), which argued the need for blood did not finish with the war: '...between 400,000 and 500,000 donations will be needed during the next twelve months – this is more than half as much as we collected in 1944 – the year of the Invasion of Europe.' The booklet clearly targeted the younger generation. '... during the war...the middle aged and elderly gave willingly three of four times a year...it is now the turn of the younger generation to take their place.'[30]

As well as improving and modernising existing services, such as these Regional Transfusion Centres, a fundamental shift in healthcare thinking was taking place that prioritised *preventative* healthcare. A basic tenet underpinning the reforms

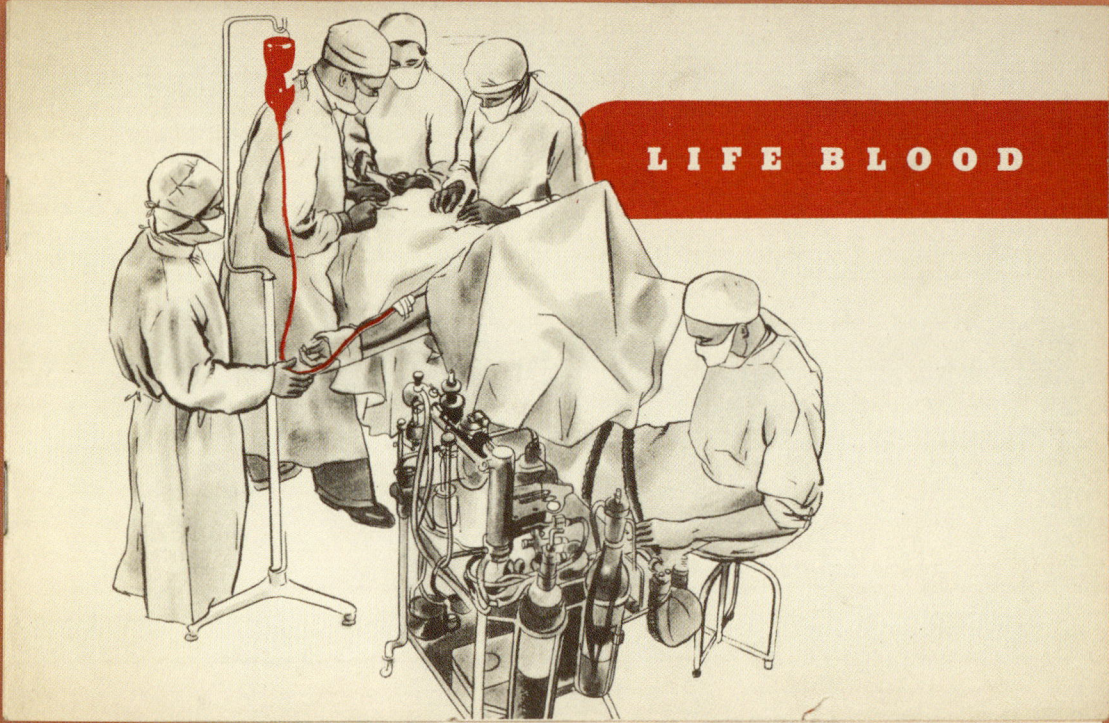

LIFE BLOOD

TEA AND BISCUITS FOR THE DONOR

44

was that if the public was better educated and had ready access to health provision then health in general would improve and people would eventually have less recourse to NHS facilities. As we have seen, this proved unfounded. Nevertheless, in the immediate period following the introduction of the NHS considerable resources (and propaganda) went into publicising the need for ordinary citizens to take more responsibility for their health.

Two examples can be cited to illustrate this: the importance of healthy teeth and the desirability of a balanced, healthy diet. The experiences during World War II had demonstrated that if citizens were forced, under the exigencies of war, to adopt more-healthy lifestyle choices then, in fact, their health (and productivity) would improve. In *The National Health Service* booklet the government stated that the expenditure on the NHS could only be justified on the basis that the 'essential aims of the Service and all who work in it, must be to *prevent* illness'. The document estimated that loss of production due to absenteeism through sickness costs the country at least £3,000,000,000 a year (a figure that did not include reduction of working capacity due to poor health and bad eyesight). 'Much of absenteeism and impaired capacity was preventable.'[31]

KEEP SMILING THE HAPPY SMILE

With the establishment of the NHS, dental examination and treatment was, for the first time, made available free. Immediately, the demand for dental services was overwhelming, with about eight million cases a year, twice the expected level. One-third of patients treated needed dentures, an indication of the alarming state of the nation's teeth. As demand surged, the expense of this service was soon felt, with budgets stretched beyond initial estimates. The MOH launched a campaign intended to educate parents and children on sound oral hygiene. Four posters – *THEIR, TEETH, REALLY, MATTER* – formed the nucleus of a concerted campaign that attempted to link the regular brushing of teeth with a healthy diet of foods 'which exercise the teeth' (Figs. 11a, b, c and d). Interestingly, and presumably to appeal to the vanity of children growing into adolescence, the recurring phrase on all four posters – 'sound teeth mean good health' – is addended with 'and good looks'. With a waspish turn of phrase that suggested (to adults at least) that failure to abide by these rules would result in the need for dentures (which in fact was the case), the final poster in the series ends with, 'Be true to your teeth and they won't be false to you!'

The COI's campaigns promoting oral hygiene in the 1940s and 1950s – largely in the form of posters – offered some top tips for keeping teeth and gums healthy,

---

9. *Life Blood.* A booklet produced by the COI that stressed the vital importance of blood to ensure life and to encourage citizens to donate blood in the aftermath of the setting up of the new NHS. Blood donation was one way in which citizens could make their own personal contribution and the COI launched numerous campaigns over the years to encourage individuals to help in this way. 'Tea and biscuits for the donor' proclaimed the booklet, and implored readers: 'Help us still further by telling your friends how easy it is, and that the giving of blood does no harm to the health. Tell them that blood is needed for accidents on the road, in the pit and factory; for patients undergoing severe operations; for those with anaemia who cannot make their own blood; for people with severe burns; for newly born babies and mothers in childbirth; and for many others. Encourage your friends to be blood donors.' (BL, PP/78/16A)

TAKE CARE OF YOUR CHILDREN'S TEETH

(1) TEACH YOUR CHILDREN TO CLEAN THEIR TEETH EVERY MORNING AND ALWAYS LAST THING AT NIGHT.

Particles of food—especially soft, sweet, sticky foods—between the teeth and gums cause decay.

(2) MAKE SURE THAT YOUR CHILDREN VISIT THE DENTIST REGULARLY.

HOW DECAY SPREADS

1. Decay begins in a little pit or crack in the hard outer covering, where food and germs have collected.

2. The decay reaches the softer inner substance of the tooth and begins to undermine the outer shell.

3. The outer shell breaks away, and the decay spreads towards the pulp of the tooth. Poison enters the mouth through the open sore.

4. The decay reaches the pulp or "nerve" and spreads. An abscess forms at the root of the tooth and poison is absorbed in the blood.

Teeth need regular care and attention; give the dentist a chance to stop decay at the first sign.

SOUND TEETH MEAN GOOD HEALTH

PLEASE TURN OVER

③ GIVE YOUR CHILDREN THE RIGHT FOODS.

Nourish the teeth with—

MILK . BUTTER . MARGARINE
EGGS . CHEESE . TOMATOES
ORANGES & ORANGE JUICE
FISH . COD LIVER OIL
DRIPPING

Exercise and clean the teeth with—

CARROTS . CELERY
LETTUCE . APPLES . NUTS
BREAD CRUSTS . TOAST
RUSKS

An expectant mother should eat the right foods too and take her welfare foods—milk, orange juice, Vitamin A & D tablets. A baby's first teeth are very important and need special care. They begin to form 7 months before birth.

④ SWEETS AND SNACKS BETWEEN MEALS ARE BAD FOR TEETH—THEY SHOULD NEVER BE ALLOWED AFTER CLEANING THE TEETH AT NIGHT.

SOUND TEETH MEAN GOOD HEALTH

Issued by the Department of Health for Scotland.   Printed in Great Britain for H.M. Stationery Office by J. & J. Gray, Edinburgh.

10. *Take Care of Your Children's Teeth* (circa 1949). A double-sided leaflet addressed to parents (and expectant mothers) providing four rules for healthy eating and for dental hygiene. Following the launch of the NHS, the Ministry of Health appeared obsessed with healthy teeth – almost as if it represented an outward manifestation of the success (or otherwise) of the NHS itself. Both sides of the leaflet contain the widely disseminated slogan, 'sound teeth mean good health'. (BL, PP/40/17L)

and generally centred on what to eat, when to brush and the importance of regular dental checks. A free, double-sided leaflet *Take Care of Your Children's Teeth* (Figs. 10a and b) combined information on healthy eating that would promote strong teeth with tips on dental hygiene.

These early dental health campaigns, however, proved disappointing and failed to improve tooth decay in children. In part, this was exacerbated by the introduction of dental charges. The fees paid to dentists were cut in 1952 and at the same time a universal £1 charge was introduced to contribute to the escalating costs of dental treatment on the funds of the NHS.[32] The end of rationing in 1954 had brought about a massive increase in sugar consumption that resulted in the rapid reduction of children without any evidence of tooth decay from 22 per cent in 1948 to just 13 per cent in 1958. As a result, in the late 1950s and 1960s the Ministry of Health stepped up its oral health propaganda. One example was the 'Happy Smile' campaign in the 1960s. The 'Happy Smile' consisted of four rules: 'Eat good food no sticky mush'; 'Both morn and night, please use the brush'; 'An apple's best your meal to end'; 'And see the dentist – he's your friend!' The launch of a concerted dental health campaign sought to reverse the increase in poor dental health, encouraging the adoption of a *preventive* rather than curative approach to dental health. By utilising eye-catching visuals the 'Happy Smile' campaign promoted the value of good oral health and nutrition in a fun and novel way. It similarly emphasised the visual positioning of children within a wider public health campaigning focus.

A HEALTHY DIET

Together with the dental health education campaigns in the 1940s and 1950s, Britain's post-wartime economy brought about a reappraisal of the nutritional value of foods and COI propaganda of this period not only reflected this theme but also promoted the link between good looks and good health. Despite the stresses of wartime, the health of the nation – especially that of the poor – improved during World War II. Goods essential to health were distributed more fairly; prices for food and other essential items were pegged at a standard rate. This controlled pricing meant that the poor could afford to buy them, which resulted in a more-balanced diet and drinking less. People were encouraged to eat protein, carbohydrates, pulses, and fruit and vegetables. Babies, pregnant women and the sick were allocated additional nutrients such as milk, orange juice, and cod liver oil. Luxuries, including fish, alcohol and cigarettes, were not officially rationed but were limited and expensive, as factories focused on the war effort. Therefore the rich and the poor were eating almost the same diet. The Ministry of Food reported that people had lost weight, but were generally healthier for it. As a result, the population of Britain remained healthy throughout the war – in many ways, healthier than it has been before or since.[33]

11. *THEIR, TEETH, REALLY, MATTER.* The campaign launched in the late 1940s and claimed 'Sound teeth mean good health and good looks'. (BL, PP/40/23A)

SOUND TEETH MEAN GOOD HEALTH AND GOOD LOOKS.

Teach your children to rinse their mouths after meals, and to clean their teeth regularly every morning and always last thing at night.

THEIR

* Brush the top teeth downwards and the bottom teeth upwards. This removes the bits of food between the teeth.

* Do not eat anything—or have a sweet, milky drink— after the last toothclean.

* Besides daily personal care, teeth need to be seen regularly by a dentist, too.

SOUND TEETH MEAN GOOD HEALTH

Sweets and snacks between meals cause tooth decay, then bad breath and toothache. Soft, sticky foods are the worst.

TEETH

HOW DECAY SPREADS:

1. Germs in the decaying food left between the teeth attack the hard outer covering of a tooth.

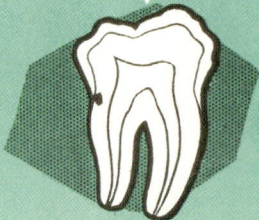

2. The hole gets larger, decay spreads inside the tooth, reaches a nerve — result, TOOTHACHE!

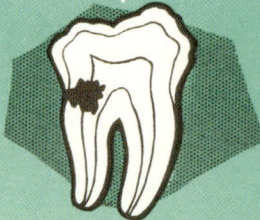

3. An abscess forms at the root. There is swelling and more pain. Poison is absorbed in the body and affects general health.

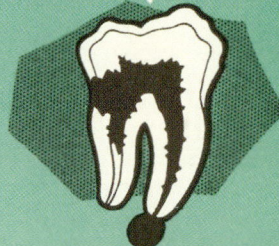

SOUND TEETH MEAN GOOD HEALTH

FOODS WHICH BUILD THE TEETH—
Milk, butter, eggs, cheese, margarine, dripping, meat, tomatoes, oranges, orange juice, fish, cod liver oil.

REALLY

FOODS WHICH EXERCISE THE TEETH—
Raw carrots, celery, lettuce, apples, nuts, crusts and toast.

SOUND TEETH MEAN GOOD HEALTH

MATTER

Sound teeth mean good health and good looks. Be true to your teeth and they won't be false to you!

PREPARED FOR THE MINISTRY OF HEALTH AND THE DEPARTMENT OF HEALTH FOR SCOTLAND BY THE CENTRAL OFFICE OF INFORMATION.

Printed in Great Britain for Her Majesty's Stationery Office by M.M.P. Ltd. D.d.167322-1/65-7687

Rationing continued after the end of World War II and people were encouraged to produce their own food in back gardens and allotments – just as they had in the war. Bread rationing had actually been introduced by the Labour government in 1946 with the slogan 'Eat Less Bread'. Following a global shortage of wheat and rice, the British people were informed by the COI 'Bread means lives. Don't waste a crumb' and posters advised 'Go easy with bread. Eat potatoes instead'.[34] The severe shortages of most consumer products prompted the continuance of the wartime 'make-do-and-mend' culture. Indeed, by the early 1950s sugar, butter, cheese, margarine, cooking fat, bacon, meat and tea were all still rationed (Fig. 12). Fourteen years of food rationing in Britain ended at midnight on 4 July 1954 when restrictions on the sale and purchase of meat and bacon were lifted.[35] Members of the London Housewives' Association held a special ceremony in Trafalgar Square to mark Derationing Day.[36]

In 1945 the Ministry of Food and the COI published the first *Manual of Nutrition* (still going to this day). Originally the work of Dr Magnus Pyke, it has become a standard work and grew out of Pyke's wartime researches at the Ministry of Food. The COI also published a leaflet for expectant mothers on the importance of the Welfare Food Scheme.[37] The Welfare Food Scheme, or Service, was introduced by the Ministry of Food in December 1941 to supplement wartime rations for all children, expectant and nursing mothers, and also certain elderly people. The foods concerned were cod liver oil, concentrated orange juice and vitamin tablets. A National Milk Scheme to ensure, with Treasury aid, the supply of milk for mothers and babies had already been introduced in July 1940. During the post-war period, the Welfare Food Scheme continued for young children and mothers while rationing was in force. The leaflet focused on 'Before baby is born' and urged mothers to take advantage of Welfare Foods regularly: 'That's the only way you can share them with your new baby...remember they are foods, not medicine.' What 'they' are and how to receive them is outlined in the rest of the leaflet (Figs. 13a and b, 14 and 15).

Following the end of rationing a number of food campaigns were launched in 1954. Posters in particular played a prominent role and were issued by various government ministries and departments with a view to making life better for Britons. The campaigns sought to influence numerous areas of everyday life, including health, hygiene, holidays, food, work, pensions, savings and crime. One poster, titled *The Seven Rules of Health*, reminds citizens how to keep clean and healthy by exercising, getting enough sleep and washing. Published by the Ministry of Health in the early 1950s, it advises people to put clean underwear on once a week. It also urges them to wash all over every day, claiming 'it takes a bit of time but it's worth it, and so refreshing'.

Posters were certainly prominent in the COI food campaigns. The footballer Jimmy Hill fronted an 'Energy Foods' campaign, which encouraged people to eat more fats, starch and sugar (Fig. 17). This message is very much at odds with contemporary nutritional advice, but it does explain why the amount of energy the population derived from fat reached a peak of 40 per cent during the 1950s,

Britain's bread hangs by Lancashire's thread

COTTON needs more workers, more output more exports to buy food for us all

WHAT COTTON EXPORTS BUY:
An Example

One dress length sold abroad will bring Britain

1 lb. of Sugar *and* 7 1-lb. Loaves *and* ½ lb. of Tea *and* 1 lb. of Cocoa

and 1 lb. of Jam *and* ¼ lb. of Bacon *and* 7 oz. of Butter *and* 4 oz. of Cheese

Prepared for the Ministry of Labour and National Service and the Board of Trade by the Central Office of Information.
1816-12794 - P.7722-100 M - 5/48 (T4 P.)

12. *Britain's Bread Hangs by Lancashire's Thread* (1948). With certain foods still rationed and to increase the nation's exports, the government launched campaigns – making the point with leaflets like this one – to lure workers (mainly women) into export industries such as wool and cotton. (BL, PP/164/40L)

Before baby is born

GIVE HIM *or her* A GOOD START IN LIFE

Besides keeping you going, the food you eat during these next few months is building your baby's bone, muscle and blood. So eat all your rations yourself. That's the only way you can share them with your new baby.

And for your baby's sake, as well as your own, be sure to take your Welfare Foods regularly. Remember they are foods, not medicines. What they are and how to get them is described on the other side of this leaflet.

PLEASE TURN OVER

13. *Welfare Food Service leaflet* (circa 1949). 'And for your baby's sake, as well as your own, be sure to take your Welfare Foods regularly. Remember they are foods, not medicines.' (BL, PP/95/6A)

What the WELFARE FOOD SERVICE offers you and your baby

MILK for growth, bones and teeth

Milk contains nearly all the materials needed for building your baby's body. It is specially important for making baby's teeth and bones, and for preserving your own teeth during pregnancy, too.

For you, milk is supplied at a specially low price–a daily pint of ordinary milk for 1½d. Just hand your milkman the registration card which the Food Office will give you. Ask your Food Office about getting cheap milk while on holiday.

ORANGE JUICE to help keep you healthy

Ordinary diet, even with extra milk, doesn't contain enough vitamin C for expectant mothers. You need vitamin C to keep your gums sound and your skin fresh and clear. Orange juice gives it to you.

Your grey ration book enables you to get a bottle of concentrated Orange Juice for 5d. every 9 days. Your Food Office will give you the address of your nearest distribution centre.

VITAMINS A and D

You need more of these vitamins, too. Vitamin A helps you to resist diseases of the eyes, nose, throat and chest. And without enough vitamins A and D the milk you drink can't do its job of building baby's bones and teeth.

A packet of vitamin A and D tablets (or a bottle of Cod Liver Oil if you prefer it) are free to you every 6 weeks. Your grey book enables you to get them at the centre where you get the Orange Juice.

EXTRA MEAT

Besides these Welfare Foods your grey ration book entitles you to an extra half ration of meat every week, because it is such an important body-building food.

Some points to remember

1. If you take a special grade of milk that costs more than ordinary milk, you pay the difference yourself.

2. Ask your Food Office how you can continue to get Welfare Milk while on holiday, or if you move to a new address.

3. You can get Orange Juice and Cod Liver Oil (or vitamin tablets) for the next ration period in advance – but you cannot make up for any you have missed.

4. Don't forget to renew your grey ration book by the date shown on page 3.

5. If 1½d. a pint for milk, or 5d. a bottle for Orange Juice, is beyond your means, ask your Food Office if you can have them free.

Prepared by the Ministry of Food (in conjunction with the Ministry of Health and the Dept. of Health for Scotland) and the Central Office of Information.   W.F.S.2

52-1459

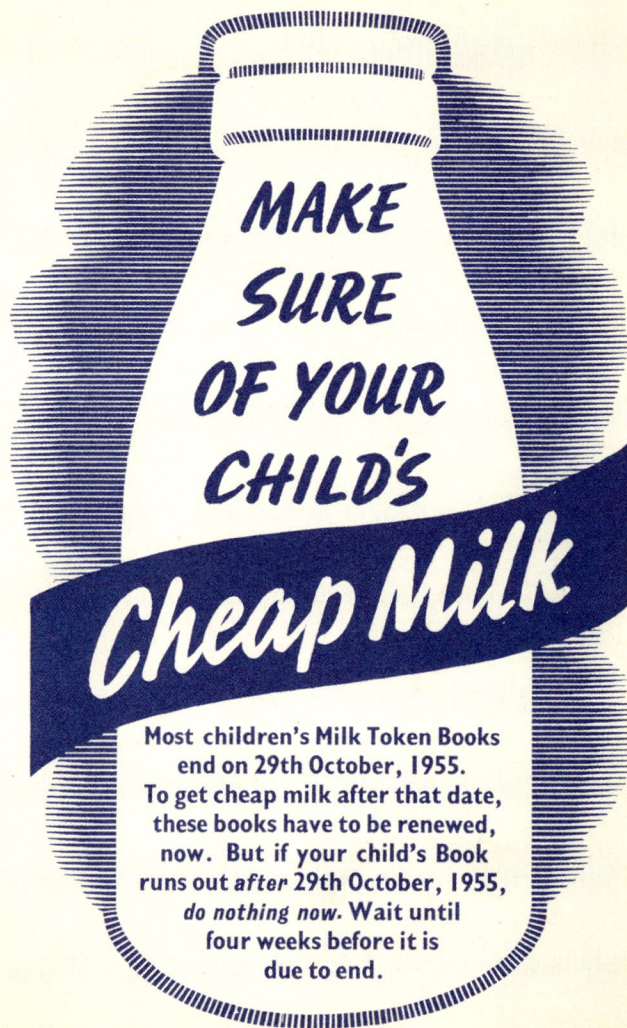

SEPTEMBER 1955   LEAFLET W.F.S.1

WELFARE FOODS SERVICE

MAKE SURE OF YOUR CHILD'S

Cheap Milk

Most children's Milk Token Books
end on 29th October, 1955.
To get cheap milk after that date,
these books have to be renewed,
now. But if your child's Book
runs out *after* 29th October, 1955,
do nothing now. Wait until
four weeks before it is
due to end.

PLEASE TURN OVER

---

14. *Make Sure of Your Child's Cheap Milk* (1955). Universal free school milk was introduced by the Labour government in August 1946. This leaflet reminded parents that from 29 October the weekly milk token book (for free powder, formula or liquid milk) was coming to an end. (BL, PP/71/8A)

15. *What to Do Before Your Baby is Born.* A guide to 'correct eating' for mothers-to-be, who the government wanted to ensure were aware of 'priority foods'. (BL, PP/71/1L)

WHAT TO DO

BEFORE YOUR BABY IS BORN

A guide to correct eating for the Mother-to-be with details of Priority Foods and Recipes

Protective Foods 1

MINISTRY OF
AGRICULTURE, FISHERIES
AND FOOD

These foods contain VITAMIN A

for
Growth and
Eyesight

These foods contain VITAMIN D

for
Strong Bones
and Teeth

remaining at this level until the 1990s, when the proportion began to fall, reaching 36 per cent by 2005. Another poster campaign, of a young boy holding above his head a football, drew parents' attention to 'Body Building Foods' consisting of calcium, protein and iron (Fig. 18). Other campaigns focused on 'Protective Foods' that stressed the importance of vitamins for 'growth and eyesight', 'for strong bones and teeth', and 'for good appetite, good digestion and sound nerves' (Fig. 16). It was only with the Education Act (1944) that the state took responsibility for the nutrition of children, and the provision of free school meals and milk became a statutory duty. By 1951 (by which time a small charge was introduced, except for those in real need), 49 per cent of children were having school meals. Campaigns such as 'Body Building Foods', promoting the balanced diet necessary for growing boys and girls, meant that the health of the nation was much better in 1950 than it had been before. In fact, it is surprising, and perhaps shocking, to discover that a 1999 study by the Medical Research Council, which compared the diet records of 4,600 children aged four in 1950 with similar records taken in 1992, concluded that children in the 1950s were healthier than their 1990s' counterparts[38] (Fig. 19).

After the immediate-post-war spike in birth rates (referred to by one historian as a 'birth quake'), nursing homes (this was before the NHS) had to cater for a sudden and unprecedented increase in the number of babies. As those children progressed to school age, they placed a strain on classrooms and teachers. In fact, birth rates in England and Wales had dropped dramatically by the early 1950s.[40] Nevertheless, even in the period prior to the establishment of the NHS, the government felt compelled to provide guidance for first-time parents on how to bring up children correctly. The COI produced a series of films that reveal contemporary attitudes to child-rearing, dealing with topics such a pregnancy, birth, parenting, child development and child psychology. *Your Children and You* (1946) provided practical advice for caring for babies and young children, and actually urges parents to encourage a child's natural curiosity. *Children Growing Up with Other People* (1947) is one of two 'companion' films about child psychology made by the Australian director Margaret Thomson (the other being *Children Learning by Experience*, 1947). Thomson's gently observational film about childhood and adolescence was made at the behest of the Ministry of Education. *Your Children's Meals* (1947) adopts a non-confrontational approach (compare it with the recent work of TV chef Jamie Oliver) by cautioning parents to be firm but not to make a fuss because that may encourage bad behaviour. In *Charley's Junior Schooldays* (1949), sumptuous Halas and Batchelor colour animation is used to explain the workings of the new, radical, Education Act. The films of this period, which are gently imbued with liberal values, are important historical – as opposed to cinematic – documents, and unquestionably capture the evolving optimism of a freshly forged post-war Britain.

While the health of the nation improved in the 1950s with the introduction of the NHS (and full employment, which ensured that people had the financial means to be

16. *Protective Foods 1* and *Protective Foods 2*. These two posters use a cross-section from society (train driver, ballerina, soldier and children) to promote a balanced diet containing the essential vitamins A, B, C and D. (BL, PP/212/9/8A and BL, PP/212/9/9A)

Protective Foods 2

MINISTRY OF AGRICULTURE, FISHERIES AND FOOD

These foods contain VITAMIN B Complex

for
Good Appetite,
Good Digestion,
Sound Nerves

MILK

LIVER

LEAN BACON

These foods contain VITAMIN C

for Vitality,
Clear Skin,
Healthy Gums

SALADS

Blackcurrants

Energ

These f

---

17. *Energy Foods.* This poster, for a campaign of the same name, features the Fulham footballer Jimmy Hill (before he became a national figure), and promotes fat, starch and sugar as positive elements in a diet. (BL, PP/212/9/6A)

18. *Body Building Foods.* A healthy looking schoolboy profiting from foods containing calcium, protein and iron. (BL, PP/212/9/7A)

Body Building Foods

MINISTRY OF
AGRICULTURE, FISHERIES
AND FOOD

These foods contain · · ·

CALCIUM
for Bones
and Teeth

MILK

SARDINES

PROTEIN
for
Muscular
Tissue

Milk
BEANS
PEAS
HERRINGS

IRON
for
Blood

LIVER
POTATOES
MEAT

better fed), the COI and the Ministry of Health continued to produce a steady stream of health education propaganda, some of which was a continuation of themes employed during the war. 'Coughs and Sneezes Spread Diseases', for example, was an extension of the highly successful propaganda first used by the Ministry of Information in World War II, intended to educate the public about the dangers of contagion. COI-sponsored film shorts played an important role in this respect – often using humour to get a serious message across. Five of the most amusing public health films in the immediate post-war era include: *Coughs and Sneezes* (1945), a Halas and Batchelor animation *Modern Guide to Health* (1946–47), *Don't Spread Germs* (1948), *Jet-Propelled Germs* (1948) and *Another Case of Poisoning* (1949).

With labour shortages in the 1940s and 1950s and the need to raise productivity, the campaign was widely used to combat absenteeism at a time when a healthy workforce was critical. Variations of such posters conveyed the same message for over sixty years: use a handkerchief (later a tissue) to stop the spread of germs (Figs. 20 and 21). The publicity was designed to show how thoughtlessness helps to spread not only the common cold, but also many other diseases. The simple combination of words and image has led to its enduring appeal for the Ministry of Health and was last used in 2007 as part of attempts to reduce the spread of influenza.

Another Case of Poisoning (1949) is typical of the approach adopted by the COI. It lasted for 14 minutes and was produced by Richard Massingham, who is principally known for starring in public information films made in the 1940s and early 1950s. In the best tradition of health campaigns, the film aimed to shock cinema audiences into paying attention to its message, in this case the vital importance of food hygiene to prevent food poisoning. The synopsis is as follows:

Mr Norris *who works in a food factory falls victim to a near fatal food poisoning. The doctor examining him asks a number of searching questions....*

Doctor: *You've got a very responsible job, you may do a great deal of damage.*
Mr Norris: *Oh, we've got plenty of rules and regulations*
Doctor: *...but do you carry them out?...Did you use the lavatory yesterday?*
Mr Norris: *Yes, I was a little on the loose side. I didn't feel too good.*
Doctor: *And you washed your hands before leaving?*
Mr Norris: *I must have done, it's one of the rules of the factory.*
Doctor: *You don't seem too certain. It's most important. Are there notices up in the lavatories?*

---

19. *Food Calendars* (1951). To supplement information on the benefits of eating healthy foods with the right amount of nutrients, fats and vitamins, the Ministry of Food (via the COI) published a weekly press guide *Food Facts* and monthly *Food Calendars* provided housewives and mothers with seasonal recipes to try out.[39] They included 'autumn miscellany', 'summer variations' and 'all-in-one oven meals'. These calendars were to foster a more-imaginative approach to preparing food – one that would incorporate as wide a variety of meat, vegetables and sweets as possible. For example, in the 1951 October–November calendar there is a recipe for 'Mock Goose' – using rabbit! The guides and calendars were just one more attempt in the early 1950s to move away from post-war austerity, although the use of substitutes would have been familiar to anyone who had lived through World War II. (BL, PP/35/10L, 35L, 12A, 13A, 8A and 9L)

MINISTRY OF FOOD

PP/35/10L

Cookery Calendar DEC 1951 JAN 1952

Suggestions for Entertaining

Christmas and New Year Parties often need just that touch of planned inspiration that a last-minute hunt through the cookery books cannot supply. The following suggestions may come in handy. Your cakes and puddings are probably already made but, if not, there are recipes in the Oct./Nov. Calendar.

GIBLET PATTIES

Giblets from a fowl or turkey
4 oz. onion, chopped
1 bay leaf
1 pint water
1 level teaspoon salt
Pinch of pepper
4 oz. scraps from the fowl, chopped
¼ pint thick sauce (*see below*)
2 teaspoons lemon juice
Rough puff pastry, using 8 oz. flour

Place the giblets, onion, bay leaf, water and seasoning in a pan, cover and cook gently until the giblets are tender; drain, keeping the liquor. Remove the meat from the neck and chop with the rest of the giblets. Mix the meats, sauce and lemon juice. Roll out the pastry and cut into rounds to line and cover 9 to 12 patty pans (using a 2¼" cutter and a 2" patty pan). Fill the lined patty pans with the meat mixture and cover with the remaining pastry rounds. Flute up the edges, brush with milk and make a small hole in the centre of each patty. Bake in a very hot oven for 20 minutes.
Sauce:—1 oz. margarine, 1 oz. flour, ⅛ pint giblet stock, ⅛ pint milk, salt and pepper to taste.

DEVILLED PINWHEELS

6 oz. plain flour and
3 level teaspoons baking powder
or 6 oz. self-raising flour
Pinch of salt
2 oz. cooking fat
Cold water to mix
4 oz. luncheon meat
1 teaspoon of a worcester sauce
1 level teaspoon grated horseradish
1 level teaspoon made mustard
1 tablespoon salad dressing

Sift the flour, baking powder (if used) and salt and rub in the fat. Mix to a soft dough with the water and roll out to a rectangle, ¼" thick. Mash the luncheon meat, mix with the other ingredients and spread thinly over the dough. Roll, swiss roll fashion, into a long roll and cut into slices ½" thick. Place on a greased tin and bake in a hot oven for 15 minutes. Serve while warm. N.B. 4 oz. finely diced ham may be used in place of the luncheon meat.

SOME SUGGESTIONS FOR FILLINGS AND SPREADS

1. Grated cheese mixed with grated horseradish and chopped or grated beetroot.
2. Grated cheese mixed with chopped pickle and salad dressing.
3. Cream cheese with chopped dates and walnuts.
4. Cream cheese and diced pickled onion.
5. Chopped hard boiled egg with diced chicken or turkey and salad dressing.
6. Anchovy paste and chopped olives.
7. Mashed sardines and diced celery.
8. Flaked fish with tartare sauce.

ALL QUANTITIES FOR 4

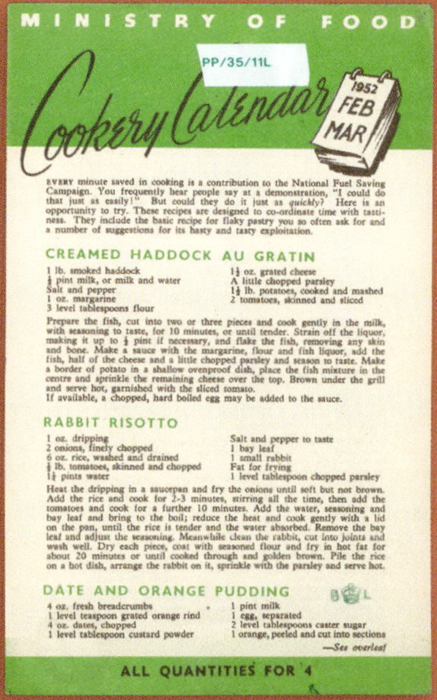

MINISTRY OF FOOD

PP/35/11L

Cookery Calendar 1952 FEB MAR

EVERY minute saved in cooking is a contribution to the National Fuel Saving Campaign. You frequently hear people say at a demonstration, "I could do that just as easily!" But could they do it just as *quickly?* Here is an opportunity to try. These recipes are designed to co-ordinate time with tastiness. They include the basic recipe for flaky pastry you so often ask for and a number of suggestions for its hasty and tasty exploitation.

CREAMED HADDOCK AU GRATIN

1 lb. smoked haddock
½ pint milk, or milk and water
Salt and pepper
1 oz. margarine
3 level tablespoons flour
1½ oz. grated cheese
A little chopped parsley
1½ lb. potatoes, cooked and mashed
2 tomatoes, skinned and sliced

Prepare the fish, cut into two or three pieces and cook gently in the milk, with seasoning to taste, for 10 minutes, or until tender. Strain off the liquor, making it up to ½ pint if necessary, and flake the fish, removing any skin and bone. Make a sauce with the margarine, flour and fish liquor, add the fish, half of the cheese and a little chopped parsley and season to taste. Make a border of potato in a shallow ovenproof dish, place the fish mixture in the centre and sprinkle the remaining cheese over the top. Brown under the grill and serve hot, garnished with the sliced tomato.
If available, a chopped, hard boiled egg may be added to the sauce.

RABBIT RISOTTO

1 oz. dripping
2 onions, finely chopped
6 oz. rice, washed and drained
½ lb. tomatoes, skinned and chopped
1½ pints water
Salt and pepper to taste
1 bay leaf
1 small rabbit
Fat for frying
1 level tablespoon chopped parsley

Heat the dripping in a saucepan and fry the onions until soft but not brown. Add the rice and cook for 2-3 minutes, stirring all the time, then add the tomatoes and cook for a further 10 minutes. Add the water, seasoning and bay leaf and bring to the boil; reduce the heat and cook gently with a lid on the pan, until the rice is tender and the water absorbed. Remove the bay leaf and adjust the seasoning. Meanwhile clean the rabbit, cut into joints and wash well. Dry each piece, coat with seasoned flour and fry in hot fat for about 20 minutes or until cooked through and golden brown. Pile the rice on a hot dish, arrange the rabbit on it, sprinkle with the parsley and serve hot.

DATE AND ORANGE PUDDING

4 oz. fresh breadcrumbs
1 level teaspoon grated orange rind
4 oz. dates, chopped
1 level tablespoon custard powder
1 pint milk
1 egg, separated
2 level tablespoons caster sugar
1 orange, peeled and cut into sections

—*See overleaf*

ALL QUANTITIES FOR 4

MINISTRY OF FOOD

PP/35/12A

Cookery Calendar 1950 JULY AUG

PICNIC MEALS

Picnic meals should be appetising, sustaining and of high nutritive value. The suggestions made here contain body building foods and energy foods and, with the addition of salads and fruit, they make a complete meal.

PRACTICAL SUGGESTIONS

Cream the butter or margarine used for spreading—it goes further and spreads easily. If preferred, mix it with grated cheese or mashed boiled egg or similar filling.

Make all sandwich fillings moist.

Press sandwiches well before packing.

To keep sandwiches fresh, wrap them in waxed or greaseproof paper, then in plastic material or a damp cloth. Wrap different kinds separately or the flavours will mix.

Pasties are an excellent way of carrying meat, fish or even fruit. They are easy to serve and easy to eat. Salad is easy to carry in a screw top jar.

Remember to wash salad vegetables and fresh fruit before you pack them.

Pack a can of fruit juice in your basket but remember to take a can opener.

If you are taking milk don't forget to bring the bottle home. Your milkman needs the empties to keep your daily supply of milk going.

RABBIT AND POTATO PASTIES

Short pastry using 6 oz. flour
8 oz. cooked rabbit, chopped
4 oz. grated raw potato
1 hard boiled egg, chopped
1 tomato, skinned and chopped
2 tablespoons stock or milk
Salt and pepper to taste

Divide the pastry into four and roll each piece into a circle about 6" in diameter. Mix all the other ingredients and divide the mixture between the pastry rounds. Damp edges of the pastry and fold into pasty shapes. Bake in a hot oven for 20 minutes.

ALL QUANTITIES FOR FOUR

MINISTRY OF FOOD

PP/35/13A

Cookery Calendar 1951 JUNE JULY

SUMMER VARIATIONS

In early summer we can begin to get more variety on the menu. Here are a few ways to take advantage of what the season offers.

FISH FILLET AND MUSHROOM ROLLS

2 tail fillets cod or haddock (approx. 12 oz. each)
Salt and pepper
Stuffing:
2 oz. mushrooms, washed and finely chopped
½ oz. shredded suet
1 oz. breadcrumbs
Grated rind of ½ lemon
1 teaspoon lemon juice
Salt and pepper to taste
Grated lemon rind and parsley sprigs to garnish
Sauce:
1 oz. margarine
2 oz. mushrooms washed and quartered
⅛ pint water
1 teaspoon lemon juice
Salt and pepper to taste
1 oz. flour
½ pint milk

Wash the fillets and cut them in half lengthwise. Roll up each piece fairly loosely and place it, on its side, in a greased ovenproof dish. Mix the stuffing ingredients well together and fill the centre of each roll with the mixture. Cover the dish with a piece of greased paper and bake in a moderate oven for 20-25 minutes. Put the margarine, mushrooms, water, lemon juice and a little seasoning into a small saucepan and cook very gently until the liquid has evaporated. Mix in the flour and add the milk. Bring to the boil, stirring all the time, and boil gently for 5 minutes. Pour the sauce round the fish and serve immediately, sprinkled with grated lemon rind and garnished with small sprigs of parsley.

FLAKY CHEESE SALAD SLICES

6 oz. flour
½ level teaspoon salt
Pinch of pepper
1½ oz. fat
½ teaspoon of a Worcester sauce
Cold water
3 oz. cheese, grated
1½ oz. cream cheese, or other unrationed cheese (optional)
2 tomatoes, skinned and sliced
Salt and pepper to taste
Outer leaves of a lettuce, shredded and mixed with 2 tablespoons salad dressing

Sift the flour, salt and pepper together and rub in the fat. Mix to a stiff dough with the sauce and cold water and roll out the pastry to an oblong. Divide the grated cheese into 4 portions, and sprinkle a quarter over ⅔ of the pastry. Fold over into three, roll out again, sprinkle with another portion of cheese and fold in three again; allow to stand in a cool place for 10 minutes. Repeat the addition of cheese and the rolling and folding twice and cool once more. Roll the pastry to an oblong, 10" × 8", and knock the edges with the back of a knife. Brush the top with a little egg or milk and bake in

ALL QUANTITIES FOR FOUR

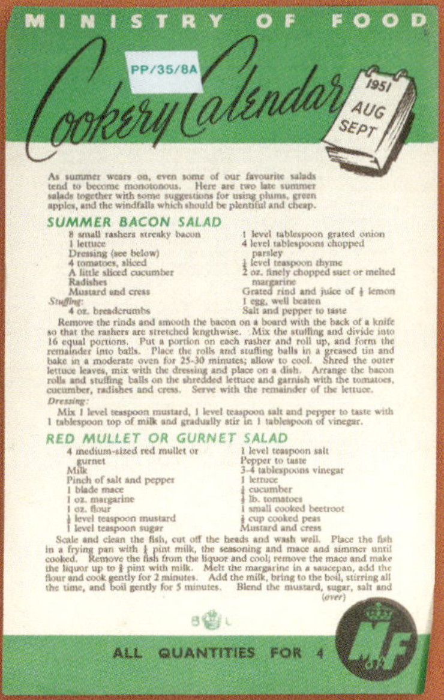

MINISTRY OF FOOD

PP/35/8A

Cookery Calendar 1951 AUG SEPT

As summer wears on, even some of our favourite salads tend to become monotonous. Here are two late summer salads together with some suggestions for using plums, green apples, and the windfalls which should be plentiful and cheap.

SUMMER BACON SALAD

8 small rashers streaky bacon
1 lettuce
Dressing (see below)
4 tomatoes, sliced
A little sliced cucumber
Radishes
Mustard and cress
Stuffing:
4 oz. breadcrumbs
1 level tablespoon grated onion
4 level tablespoons chopped parsley
½ level teaspoon thyme
2 oz. finely chopped suet or melted margarine
Grated rind and juice of ½ lemon
1 egg, well beaten
Salt and pepper to taste

Remove the rinds and smooth the bacon on a board with the back of a knife so that the rashers are stretched lengthwise. Mix the stuffing and divide into 16 equal portions. Put a portion on each rasher and roll up, and form the remainder into balls. Place the rolls and stuffing balls in a greased tin and bake in a moderate oven for 25-30 minutes; allow to cool. Shred the outer lettuce leaves, mix with the dressing and place on a dish. Arrange the bacon rolls and stuffing balls on the shredded lettuce and garnish with the tomatoes, cucumber, radishes and cress. Serve with the remainder of the lettuce.
Dressing:
Mix 1 level teaspoon mustard, 1 level teaspoon salt and pepper to taste with 1 tablespoon top of milk and gradually stir in 1 tablespoon of vinegar.

RED MULLET OR GURNET SALAD

4 medium-sized red mullet or gurnet
Milk
Pinch of salt and pepper
1 blade mace
1 oz. margarine
1 oz. flour
½ level teaspoon mustard
1 level teaspoon sugar
1 level teaspoon salt
Pepper to taste
3-4 tablespoons vinegar
1 lettuce
½ cucumber
½ lb. tomatoes
1 small cooked beetroot
½ cup cooked peas
Mustard and cress

Scale and clean the fish, cut off the heads and wash well. Place the fish in a frying pan with ½ pint milk, the seasoning and mace and simmer until cooked. Remove the fish from the liquor and cool; remove the mace and make the liquor up to ½ pint with milk. Melt the margarine in a saucepan, add the flour and cook gently for 2 minutes. Add the milk, bring to the boil, stirring all the time, and boil gently for 5 minutes. Blend the mustard, sugar, salt and (*over*)

ALL QUANTITIES FOR 4

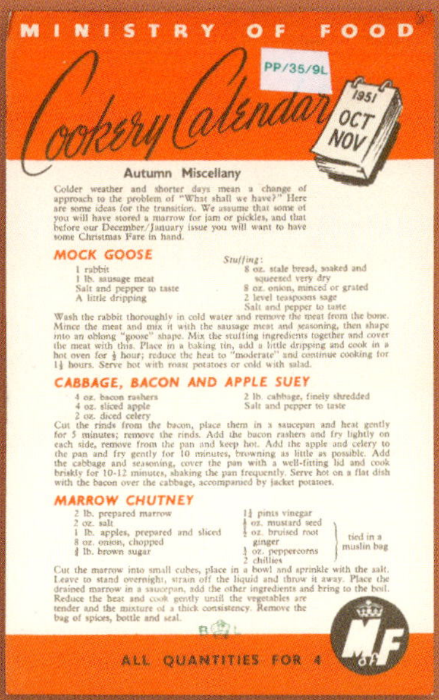

MINISTRY OF FOOD

PP/35/9L

Cookery Calendar 1951 OCT NOV

Autumn Miscellany

Colder weather and shorter days mean a change of approach to the problem of "What shall we have?" Here are some ideas for the transition. We assume that some of you will have stored a marrow for jam or pickles, and that before our December/January issue you will want to have some Christmas Fare in hand.

MOCK GOOSE

1 rabbit
1 lb. sausage meat
Salt and pepper to taste
A little dripping
Stuffing:
8 oz. stale bread, soaked and squeezed very dry
8 oz. onion, minced or grated
2 level teaspoons sage
Salt and pepper to taste

Wash the rabbit thoroughly in cold water and remove the meat from the bone. Mince the meat and mix it with the sausage meat and seasoning, then shape into an oblong "goose" shape. Mix the stuffing ingredients together and cover the meat with this. Place in a baking tin, add a little dripping and cook in a hot oven for ½ hour; reduce the heat to "moderate" and continue cooking for 1½ hours. Serve hot with roast potatoes or cold with salad.

CABBAGE, BACON AND APPLE SUEY

4 oz. bacon rashers
4 oz. sliced apple
2 oz. diced celery
2 lb. cabbage, finely shredded
Salt and pepper to taste

Cut the rinds from the bacon, place them in a saucepan and heat gently for 5 minutes; remove the rinds. Add the bacon rashers and fry lightly on each side, remove from the pan and keep hot. Add the apple and celery to the pan and fry gently for 10 minutes, browning as little as possible. Add the cabbage and seasoning, cover the pan with a well-fitting lid and cook briskly for 10-12 minutes, shaking the pan frequently. Serve hot on a flat dish with the bacon over the cabbage, accompanied by jacket potatoes.

MARROW CHUTNEY

2 lb. prepared marrow
2 oz. salt
1 lb. apples, prepared and sliced
8 oz. onion, chopped
¾ lb. brown sugar
1½ pints vinegar
¼ oz. mustard seed, ½ oz. bruised root ginger, ¼ oz. peppercorns, 2 chillies — tied in a muslin bag

Cut the marrow into small cubes, place in a bowl and sprinkle with the salt. Leave to stand overnight, strain off the liquid and throw it away. Place the drained marrow in a saucepan, add the other ingredients and bring to the boil. Reduce the heat and cook gently until the vegetables are tender and the mixture of a thick consistency. Remove the bag of spices, bottle and seal.

ALL QUANTITIES FOR 4

COUGHS AND SNEEZES SPREAD DISEASES
He's a
PUBLIC ENEMY
TRAP YOUR GERMS
IN A HANDKERCHIEF
C.S. 03
Prepared for the MINISTRY OF HEALTH by the Central Office of Information
C.P. Ltd.

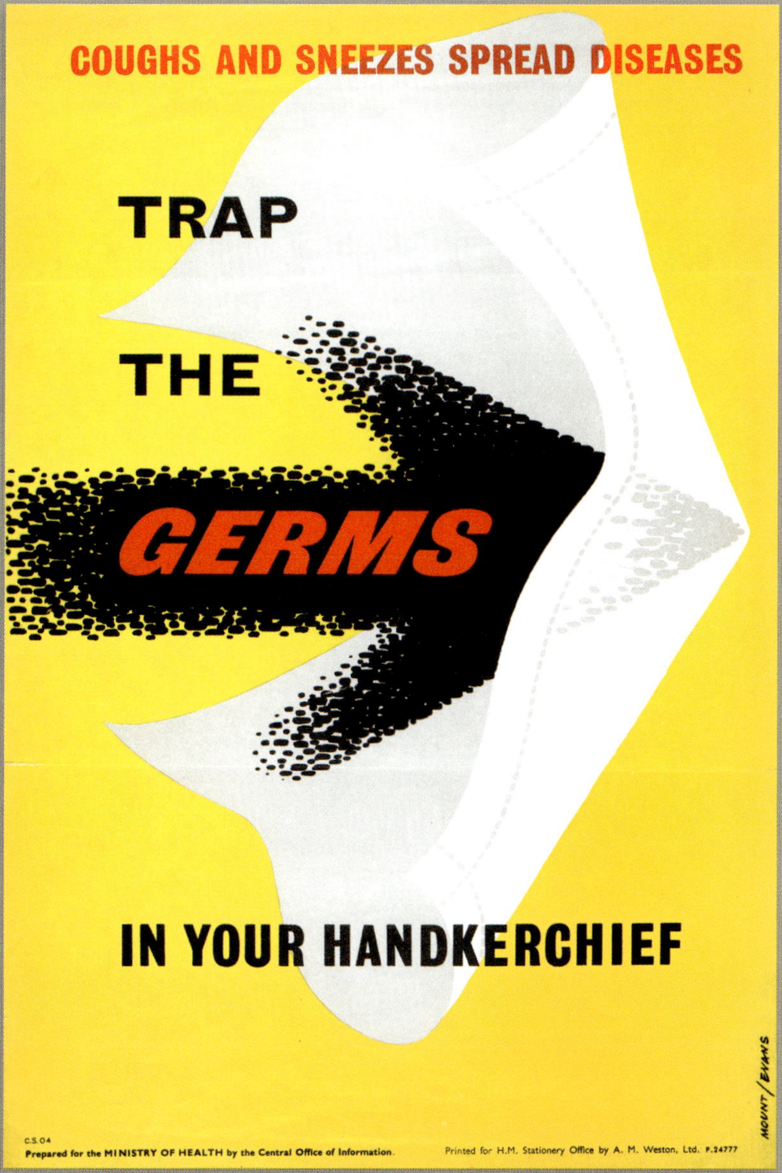

COUGHS AND SNEEZES SPREAD DISEASES

TRAP

THE

GERMS

IN YOUR HANDKERCHIEF

C.S.04
Prepared for the MINISTRY OF HEALTH by the Central Office of Information.   Printed for H.M. Stationery Office by A. M. Weston, Ltd. P.24777

MOUNT/EVANS

20. He's a Public Enemy. Another Ministry of Health poster for the 'Coughs and Sneezes Spread Diseases' campaign. The aim of the campaign was to convince people that unprotected sneezing and coughing without covering one's mouth were inherently anti-social. (BL, BS/81/19)

21. Trap the Germs. A late 1940s Ministry of Health poster for the 'Cough and Sneezes Spread Diseases' campaign, combating the evils of sneezing. Handkerchiefs were in the front line of defeating the spread of germs. This poster was designed by Reginald Mount and Eileen Evans. The Mount/Evans studio in the 1950s and 1960s became closely associated with the Central Office of Information campaigns, producing characteristically precise and humorous designs for a wide variety of government agencies. (BL, BS/81/19)

Mr Norris: *Yes, you can't miss them.*
*[By means of a flash-back we see Mr Norris coming out from a cubicle with
a cigarette in his mouth, he combs his hair and in spite of a notice in front
of him which reads 'Cleanliness prevents Diseases. Wash Your Hands' he
ignores the message.]*
Doctor: *A lot of people don't like these rules or think they are unnecessary...*

The film then takes the audience through Mr Norris's day and shows how ordinary
people are oblivious to food hygiene: the food factory he works at, where the girls
on the production line sneeze and toss their hair over the cream buns; the local
restaurant, where flies (Fig. 22) and mice roam the kitchens and cutlery stands in
rancid water; the cook telling his young kitchen-hand, 'Don't pick your nose, it is so
very dirty'; the butcher who handles a dog and a cat before preparing the meat
(while wearing a bloody bandage); the barmaid in the evening who polishes a dirty
glass with a licked finger; even Mr Norris's wife, whose kitchen is a paradise for germs.
The film ends with the doctor looking directly at the camera and warning: 'Now Don't
Just Go Home and Forget about This. Food Poisoning is serious. And YOU can Help to
Prevent It!'

Like the slogan 'Coughs and Sneezes', the film demonstrates the power of
endurance of a relatively simple combination of image and words. Improvements
in national health also owed much to the introduction of antibiotics, which gradually
eradicated many diseases that had been major killers, like tuberculosis (TB). In
1950 there were 50,000 cases of TB in the UK, but the number began to decline with
better nutrition and housing, and the pasteurisation of milk and antibiotics. Highly
contagious diseases like diphtheria and poliomyelitis remained major killers in the
1950s. Continuing the theme of preventing infection, health education played an
important role in encouraging parents to get their children immunised against them.
The poster designed by the COI to help combat diphtheria is particularly striking.
It shows a small baby pointing to his parents, 'Hey! Time I was immunised against
Diphtheria' (Fig. 25). In 1940 more than 61,000 cases were reported, resulting in over
3,000 deaths. The campaign proved successful – so much so that in 1957 there
were just thirty-eight cases of diphtheria and six deaths. However, the incidence
of poliomyelitis increased until 1951 and many children were disabled by it before
a vaccine was developed. Routine immunisation with inactivated poliomyelitis
vaccine, which was discovered in the US in 1952 (Salk's IPV), was introduced in the
UK through the NHS in 1956. (This was replaced by live attenuated oral polio vaccine
[Sabin's OPV] in 1962.) The introduction of polio immunisation was accompanied by
mass campaigns in the media and wider society ('Polio can cripple even the fittest')
targeted at all individuals below the age of forty. The poster (Fig. 23) announced the
extension of the polio vaccine to adults.[41] The artist Reginald Mount, who worked for

22. *Prevent Food Poisoning. Cover Food Against Flies* (circa 1950). A simple but stark image of a fly, intended to
drive home the message that flies carry germs and therefore food must be covered at all times. The housefly
can transmit over thirty bacterial and protozoan diseases to human food. (Wellcome Collection)

PREVENT FOOD POISONING

COVER FOOD AGAINST FLIES

Flies carry germs which can
infect uncovered food.

Issued by the Ministry of Health and the Department of Health for Scotland

POLIO

can cripple — even the fittest

**THE BEST DEFENCE
IS VACCINATION
IT'S** *NOW* **AVAILABLE FREE
TO ALL UP TO AGE ~~45~~ 40**

**Ask your local health department,
clinic or family doctor for details**

ISSUED BY THE MINISTRY OF HEALTH

P.03. Prepared by the Central Office of Information   Printed for H.M. Stationery Office by M.M.P. Ltd. London. Wt P 79108-2/60-6289

23. *Polio can Cripple – even the Fittest.* Health education played a role in encouraging people to vaccinate. This poster is announcing the extension of polio vaccine to adults 'up to age 40' in 1960. (Wellcome Collection)

24. *Polio.* Reginald Mount's striking 1950s' poster design to encourage citizens to be vaccinated against polio. A grief-stricken young girl on crutches wearing calipers (notice the 'O' framing her head for dramatic affect). The tragic figure is depicted in the dark, denoting ignorance, with just the half-face revealing her hapless state.

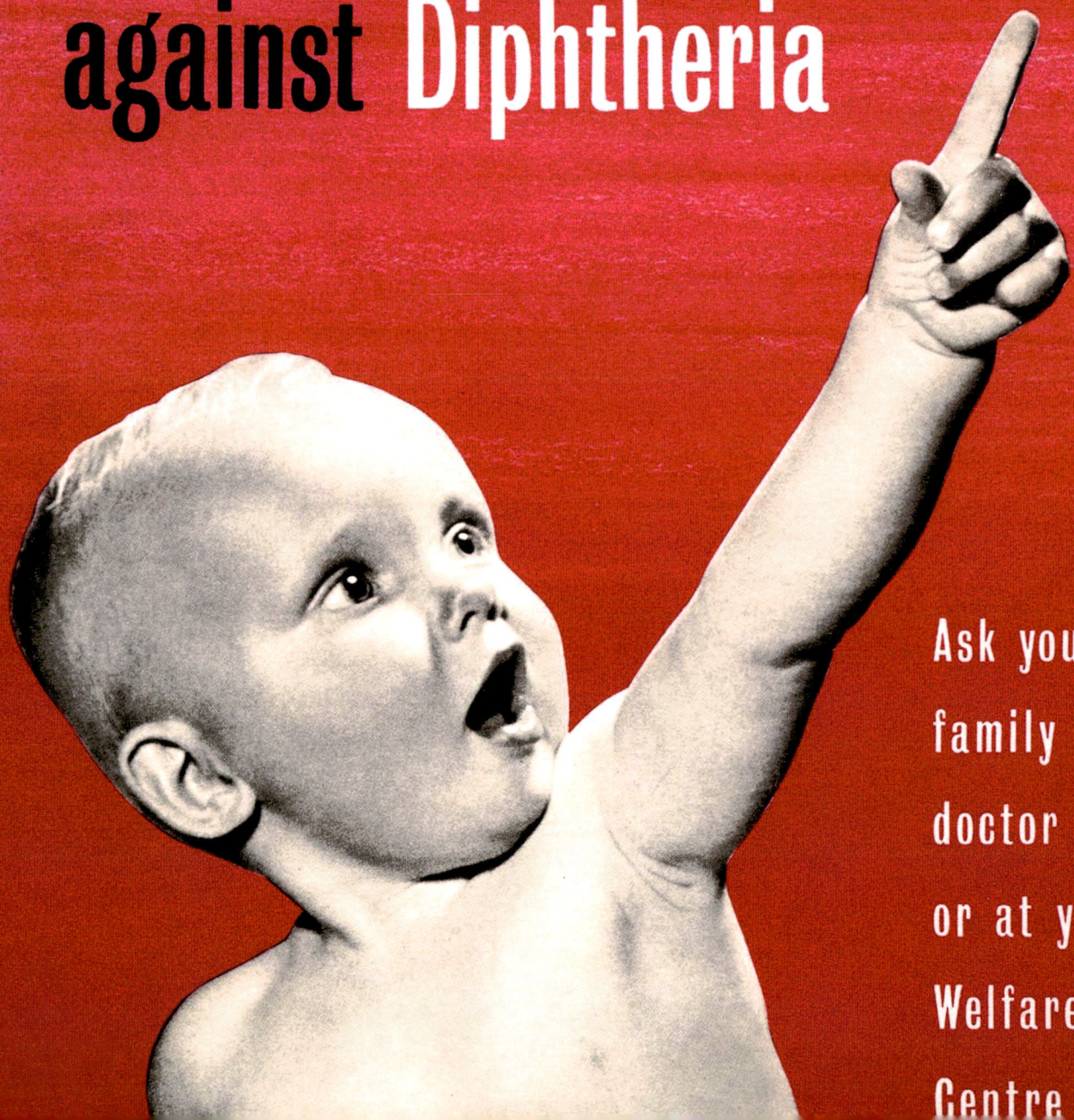

Hey! time I was immunised against Diphtheria

Ask your family doctor or at your Welfare Centre

both the MOI and the COI, also produced a more emotional and shocking poster (for the time) that showed a grief-stricken young girl on crutches wearing calipers (notice the 'O' framing her head for dramatic affect, Fig. 24).

THE ONSET OF THE COLD WAR AND BRITAIN'S CHANGING ROLE

The creation of the free National Health Service in 1948 improved the quality of medical care, especially for the elderly, women and the poor, but at a cost that rapidly led to the introduction of charges for dentistry and prescriptions. Posters, leaflets and pamphlets were widely employed by the COI in an attempt to sensitise the (adult) population to the dangers posed by epidemics, endemic diseases and other chronic public health issues. While such health propaganda was clearly helpful, it alone could never hope to singly modify habits and behaviour patterns that governments believed needed to be changed.[42] Set against the achievements of immunisation, there was also a rapid increase in cancer, strokes and especially heart disease: the three major killers of Britons in the later twentieth century. Nevertheless, the NHS proved unquestionably popular following its introduction and remains so to this day. When Gallup asked patients in 1956 'how they felt about the service', 90 per cent answered favourably and only 3 per cent unfavourably. Indeed, 64 per cent accepted as 'fair' the prescription charge of one shilling per item that had been introduced by the Conservatives in 1952.[43] The popularity of the NHS, which rapidly gained the status of 'national treasure', explains why it has proved such a political hot potato for any government to reform or even (whisper it) to privatise. The achievement of Britain's post-war Welfare State should not, however, be exaggerated. By 1950 Britain's combined expenditure on healthcare and social security (partly shaped by the broad-based popularity of the NHS) was lower than that of war-devastated West Germany – and it soon slipped behind that of most Western European countries.[44]

The reason for this was that the Attlee government, despite receiving $2.7 billion ($1 billion more than western Germany) under the United States' European Recovery Program (ERP), also known as the Marshall Plan, was determined to remain a major military and political power and was prepared to allocate much of the ERP to its defence and rearmament budget in order to achieve this aim (even though in 1949 over 13 per cent of all imports were financed by aid from the Marshall Plan). This was somewhat ironic for a Labour Party traditionally opposed to militarism. Nevertheless, in 1950, Britain spent 6.6 per cent of its GDP on defence: more than any major country except the Soviet Union. In 1952 Britain became the world's third nuclear power when it detonated an atomic bomb off the coast of Australia.

The standard rate of income tax was nine shillings in the pound – an extremely high percentage by today's standards. Consequently, most Britons had little surplus

25. *Hey! Time I was Immunised Against Diphtheria.* This striking poster from the 1950s is encouraging parents to get their children vaccinated against diphtheria. (TNA, INF 13/292/28)

money and even less to spend it on. In order to justify this, the COI took a leaf out of the book of the wartime MOI and produced a series of booklets (priced at threepence) that provided a detailed breakdown of the post-war Labour budgets. One of the first in the series was *The Budget and Your Pocket* (Figs. 26a, b, c, d, e and f), which basically attempts to answer the questions posed on the front cover by a group of citizens – 'Why must taxes be so high?' and 'When are things going to get better?' Inside the blue booklet is an interesting comic strip entitled 'Story without an End', consisting of a series of social vignettes intended to demonstrate the complexity of a modern economy and its competing demands. The last strip is of a cloth-capped man scratching his head and proclaiming: 'Blow me. Where does this end?' The booklet adopts a simple but transparent explanation to 'John Citizen', demonstrating how we pay and what we get for it ('the truth about taxes'). There is even the ubiquitous national budget cake to show what people pay and what they get in return, with a warning that the country must not live beyond its means ('why are we no better off?'). To coincide with the *The Budget and Your Pocket*, the COI produced a short film, *Pop Goes the Weasel*, which informed the country how everyone's taxes were being spent; a simple explanation was given to how the money raised by taxation was divided among the various existing wartime commitments and services that the government provided for the public's benefit. Not appearing too preachy, and no doubt to engage the 'ordinary man', the explanation was given by an affable park-keeper.

The 1950–51 budget is in a new pull-out format and appears to be free (Figs. 27a and b). Printed in yellow, it consists of two sides and is generally slicker – very much the product of contemporary advertising techniques. The cover juxtaposes a galloping money box (stuffed with notes and labelled 'REVENUE') and the Houses of Parliament, accompanied by the question 'What happens to the money?' In this budget, the new Chancellor Hugh Gaitskill capped NHS spending and charges for dental work and glasses. The section 'What it all adds up to' demonstrates clearly that in terms of the national 'cake', defence expenditure far outstripped spending on the NHS. The former accounting for four shillings and one pence in the pound (£781 million) compared to spending on health, which was two shillings in the pound (£396 million). It is perhaps not surprising that even as early as 1950, two years after its inception, the NHS was providing new services and becoming increasingly effective, but it was also becoming more expensive. The Conservatives won the 1951 General Election, giving them their first chance to run the National Health Service. They remained in power until 1964. One of their main priorities was to cut taxes but the rising cost of the NHS made this difficult; it was politically sensitive to attack the basic principles of the system. However, there were many proposals to introduce charges for aspects of NHS treatment, such as prescriptions and dental care. These were introduced through the National Health Service Act of 1952.

---

26. *The Budget and Your Pocket.* This 1948–49 booklet is explaining the Labour government's taxation policy 'Taking Away and Giving Back'. (BL, PP/91/11A)

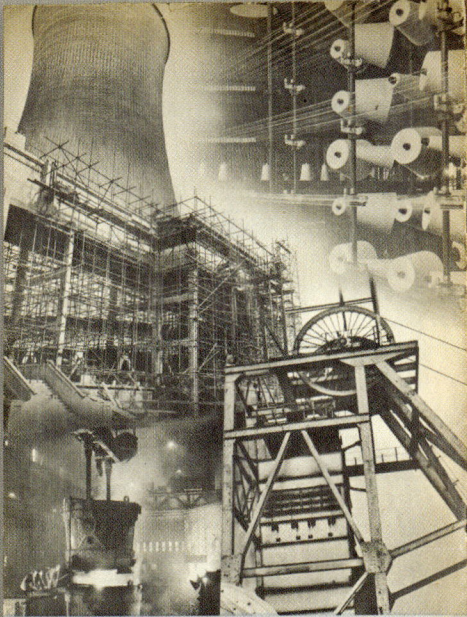

New factories, farms, foundries, mines, power-houses—our real "Recovery Programme", the makings of our future prosperity. We are spending over a fifth of our whole national income to build these things and keep existing ones in good repair. The Budget surplus helps to pay for them, and in their turn they will build up our future incomes, so that the tax burden will weigh more lightly upon us.

PUBLISHED BY HIS MAJESTY'S STATIONERY OFFICE.

The Budget and your Pocket

Why must taxes be so high?

Why is money so tight these days?

When are things going to get better?

3d NET

STORY WITHOUT AN ENDING

This fable and its characters are imaginary. So are the wage applications it depicts. In order to tell the story, it has been necessary to use workers in real industries as examples. They could be from almost any industry —the choice of the three below has no special significance.

Furniture

WITH A FEW MORE BOB IN THE PAY PACKET I COULD MANAGE IT

Jim is getting married. He wants to buy a bedroom suite. Here's a nice job at £40.

NICE WORK, JIM. WE'VE GOT OUR RISE

Jim and his mates (we'll suppose they're textile workers) decide to press for a rise.

PAYING MORE WAGES NOW, OLD BOX HAVE TO PUT MY PRICES UP. SORRY!

Up goes the wages bill. Jim's employer gets on the phone to his customers.

THAT'S A STIFF PRICE TO PAY

Sam the miner wants a new suit. Cloth has gone up. Sam's suit costs more.

ANY AGAINST? NO! MOTION CARRIED!

The miners decide they must have an increase to meet the rising cost of living.

THEY'VE PUT UP THE PRICE OF COAL NOW. I CAN'T MANAGE ON WHAT YOU GIVE ME, TOM

The cabinet-maker's wife is finding it harder to make ends meet.

AN EXTRA FIVE BOB IS THE LEAST WE CAN DO WITH

Tom the cabinet-maker can only see one answer to that problem—more pay.

Furniture

BLOW ME, WHERE DOES THIS END?

£45

Jim comes back for his bedroom suite. New price, £45. Jim is back where he began.

Suppose that, in the present condition of the country, several million people working in many different industries took Jim's line. What would happen then? Or what would happen if companies used the same sort of argument for raising their dividends? If you can answer that, you have understood the story.

Talking of Prices

The basket of shopping that cost £1 before the war now leaves only 4s. change out of £2. But incomes—on average—are nearly twice as high as they were. We are getting more money, but very little more for it: the value of money has fallen.

This almost always happens during wars. From 1940 onwards everybody was busy at work: some, in the Forces, making nothing; others, in industry, making things which the Forces would use up as fast as they could. So when the war ended there was plenty of money to spend, and not much to spend it on. But prices were up, and were still climbing. They would have gone up much more if price controls and subsidies had not been used to keep them down.

But the ruin and loss of war left great world shortages, and people with things to sell were asking higher prices everywhere. Many of them were things we could not do without—food we could not grow at home and materials for us to work on—so we had to pay higher prices for imports.

There was a tendency for wages and prices to continue rising: wages, so as to pay the prices; then prices, because wages had gone up; and so on. This was upsetting things at home and making it harder to sell our goods overseas. So in February last year, after many other attempts to check this upward spiral, employers and trade unions agreed with the Government to try to keep dividends and wage rates steady and to reduce prices where possible.

This attempt has had considerable success. In the following twelve months most firms—although making bigger profits—acted on the recommendation not to pay bigger dividends, and average wage rates and retail prices rose no more than 3 or 4 per cent. The prices of some goods actually fell.

Why are we no better off?

During this period production has been increasing. Total output of industry and agriculture in 1948 was one-fifth higher than in the years immediately before the war. But all this extra output cannot yet go into the shops. It is needed to repair the damage of war; to make up for lost time in re-equipping and expanding our industries; to provide the extra exports needed to pay for imports.

Only after these extra needs have been met can the little that is left of the extra output go into the shops—and there are now two million more of us to provide for than before the war. That is why, although there were more of some things last year (tobacco, for example, books and magazines, entertainment) and less of others (goods for the home, petrol for the car, clothes for ourselves), there was on average slightly less per head than in 1938.

Although the total of our personal incomes in 1948 exceeded £9,500 million—compared with under £5,000 million in 1938—we were on average no better off. More money without more goods to spend it on gets us nowhere. More goods without higher prices would really make us better off: so that must be the aim.

It may be asked why, since we want to avoid raising prices, things are made worse by high taxes. But *do* taxes make things worse? Most of the rest of this book is an answer to these two questions.

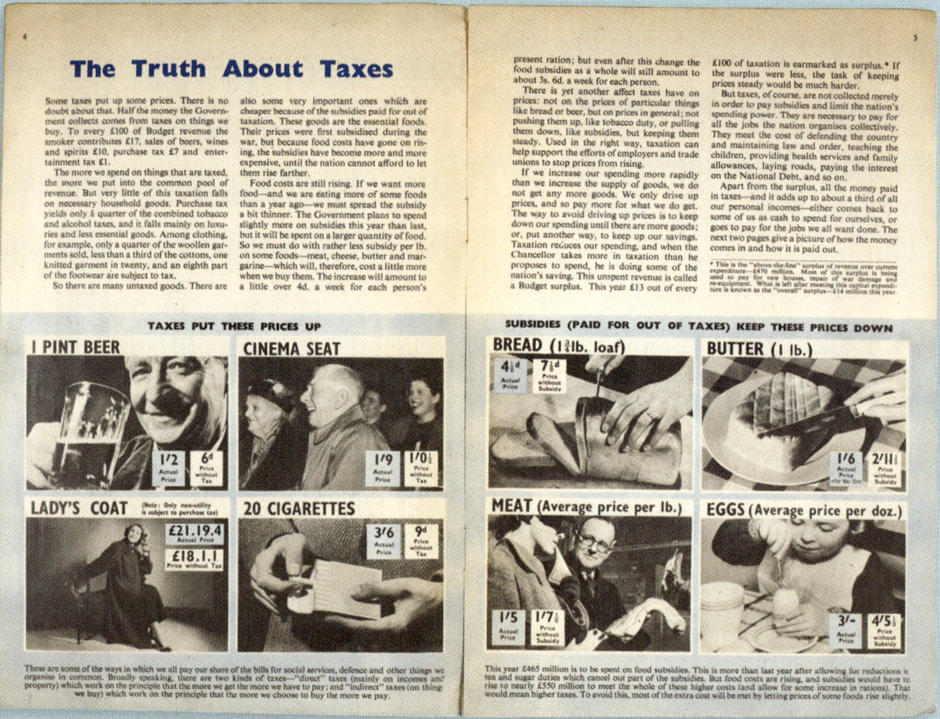

4

The Truth About Taxes

Some taxes put up some prices. There is no doubt about that. Half the money the Government collects comes from taxes on things we buy. To every £100 of Budget revenue the smoker contributes £17, sales of beers, wines and spirits £10, purchase tax £7 and entertainment tax £1.

The more we spend on things that are taxed, the more we put into the common pool of revenue. But very little of this taxation falls on necessary household goods. Purchase tax yields only a quarter of the combined tobacco and alcohol taxes, and it falls mainly on luxuries and less essential goods. Among clothing, for example, only a quarter of the woollen garments sold, less than a third of the cottons, one knitted garment in twenty, and an eighth part of the footwear are subject to tax.

So there are many untaxed goods. There are also some very important ones which are cheaper because of the subsidies paid for out of taxation. These goods are the essential foods. Their prices were first subsidised during the war, but because food costs have gone on rising, the subsidies have become more and more expensive, until the nation cannot afford to let them rise farther.

Food costs are still rising. If we want more food—and we are eating more of some foods than a year ago—we must spread the subsidy a bit thinner. The Government plans to spend slightly more on subsidies this year than last, but it will be spent on a larger quantity of food. So we must do with rather less subsidy per lb. on some foods—meat, cheese, butter and margarine—which will, therefore, cost a little more when we buy them. The increase will amount to a little over 4d. a week for each person's present ration; but even after this change the food subsidies as a whole will still amount to about 3s. 6d. a week for each person.

There is yet another affect taxes have on prices: not on the prices of particular things like bread or beer, but on prices in general; not pushing them up, like tobacco duty, or pulling them down, like subsidies, but keeping them steady. Used in the right way, taxation can help support the efforts of employers and trade unions to stop prices from rising.

If we increase our spending more rapidly than we increase the supply of goods, we do not get any more goods. We only drive up prices, and so pay more for what we do get. The way to avoid driving up prices is to keep down our spending until there are more goods; or, put another way, to keep up our savings. Taxation reduces our spending, and when the Chancellor takes more in taxation than he proposes to spend, he is doing some of the nation's saving. This unspent revenue is called a Budget surplus. This year £13 out of every £100 of taxation is earmarked as surplus.* If the surplus were less, the task of keeping prices steady would be much harder.

But taxes, of course, are not collected merely in order to pay subsidies and limit the nation's spending power. They are necessary to pay for all the jobs the nation organises collectively. They meet the cost of defending the country and maintaining law and order, teaching the children, providing health services and family allowances, laying roads, paying the interest on the National Debt, and so on.

Apart from the surplus, all the money paid in taxes—and it adds up to about a third of all our personal incomes—either comes back to some of us as cash to spend for ourselves, or goes to pay for the jobs we all want done. The next two pages give a picture of how the money comes in and how it is paid out.

* This is the "above-the-line" surplus of revenue over current expenditure—£470 million. Most of this surplus is being used to pay for new houses, repair of war damage and re-equipment. What is left after meeting this capital expenditure is known as the "overall" surplus—£14 million this year.

5

TAXES PUT THESE PRICES UP

I PINT BEER — 1/2 Actual Price; 6d Price without Tax

CINEMA SEAT — 1/9 Actual Price; 1/0½ Price without Tax

LADY'S COAT (Note: Only non-utility is subject to purchase tax) — £21.19.4 Actual Price; £18.1.1 Price without Tax

20 CIGARETTES — 3/6 Actual Price; 9d Price without Tax

These are some of the ways in which we all pay our share of the bills for social services, defence and other things we organise in common. Broadly speaking, there are two kinds of taxes—"direct" taxes (mainly on incomes and property) which work on the principle that the more we get the more we have to pay; and "indirect" taxes (on things we buy) which work on the principle that the more we choose to buy the more we pay.

SUBSIDIES (PAID FOR OUT OF TAXES) KEEP THESE PRICES DOWN

BREAD (1¾lb. loaf) — 4½d Actual Price; 7½d Price without Subsidy

BUTTER (1 lb.) — 1/6 Actual Price; 2/11½ Price without Subsidy

MEAT (Average price per lb.) — 1/5 Actual Price; 1/7½ Price without Subsidy

EGGS (Average price per doz.) — 3/- Actual Price; 4/5½ Price without Subsidy

This year £465 million is to be spent on food subsidies. This is more than last year after allowing for reductions in tea and sugar duties which cancel out part of the subsidies. But food costs are rising, and subsidies would have to rise to nearly £550 million to meet the whole of these higher costs (and allow for some increase in rations). That would mean higher taxes. To avoid this, most of the extra cost will be met by letting prices of some foods rise slightly.

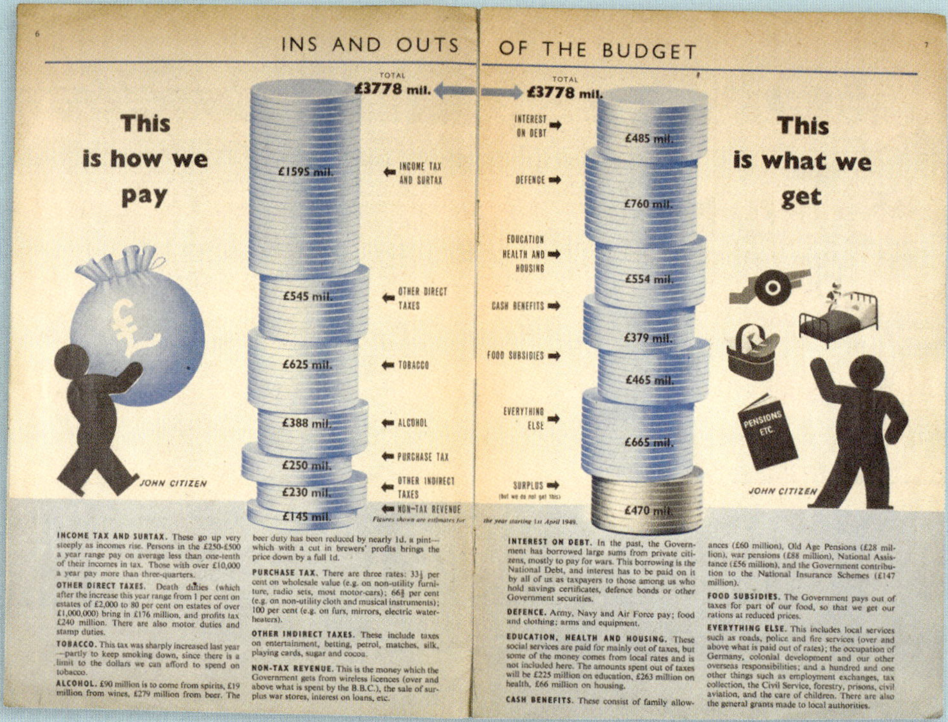

6

INS AND OUTS OF THE BUDGET

7

This is how we pay

TOTAL £3778 mil.

£1595 mil. — INCOME TAX AND SURTAX

£545 mil. — OTHER DIRECT TAXES

£625 mil. — TOBACCO

£388 mil. — ALCOHOL

£250 mil. — PURCHASE TAX

£230 mil. — OTHER INDIRECT TAXES

£145 mil. — NON-TAX REVENUE

JOHN CITIZEN

Figures shown are estimates for the year starting 1st April 1949.

This is what we get

TOTAL £3778 mil.

INTEREST ON DEBT — £485 mil.

DEFENCE — £760 mil.

EDUCATION HEALTH AND HOUSING — £554 mil.

CASH BENEFITS — £379 mil.

FOOD SUBSIDIES — £465 mil.

EVERYTHING ELSE — £665 mil.

SURPLUS (but we do not get this) — £470 mil.

PENSIONS ETC.

JOHN CITIZEN

INCOME TAX AND SURTAX. These go up very steeply as incomes rise. Persons in the £250-£500 a year range pay on average less than one-tenth of their incomes in tax. Those with over £10,000 a year pay more than three-quarters.

OTHER DIRECT TAXES. Death duties (which after the increase this year range from 1 per cent on estates of £2,000 to 80 per cent on estates of over £1,000,000) bring in £176 million, and profits tax £240 million. There are also motor duties and stamp duties.

TOBACCO. This tax was sharply increased last year—partly to keep smoking down, since there is a limit to the dollars we can afford to spend on tobacco.

ALCOHOL. £90 million is to come from spirits, £19 million from wines, £279 million from beer. The beer duty has been reduced by nearly 1d. a pint—which with a cut in brewers' profits brings the price down by a full 1d.

PURCHASE TAX. There are three rates: 33⅓ per cent on wholesale value (e.g. on non-utility furniture, radio sets, most motor-cars); 66⅔ per cent (e.g. on non-utility cloth and musical instruments); 100 per cent (e.g. on furs, mirrors, electric water-heaters).

OTHER INDIRECT TAXES. These include taxes on entertainment, betting, petrol, matches, silk, playing cards, sugar and cocoa.

NON-TAX REVENUE. This is the money which the Government gets from wireless licences (over and above what is spent by the B.B.C.), the sale of surplus war stores, interest on loans, etc.

INTEREST ON DEBT. In the past, the Government has borrowed large sums from private citizens, mostly to pay for wars. This borrowing is the National Debt, and interest has to be paid on it by all of us as taxpayers to those among us who hold savings certificates, defence bonds or other Government securities.

DEFENCE. Army, Navy and Air Force pay; food and clothing; arms and equipment.

EDUCATION, HEALTH AND HOUSING. These social services are paid for mainly out of taxes, but some of the money comes from local rates and is not included here. The amounts spent out of taxes will be £225 million on education, £263 million on health, £66 million on housing.

CASH BENEFITS. These consist of family allowances (£60 million), Old Age Pensions (£28 million), war pensions (£88 million), National Assistance (£56 million), and the Government contribution to the National Insurance Schemes (£147 million).

FOOD SUBSIDIES. The Government pays out of taxes for part of our food, so that we get our rations at reduced prices.

EVERYTHING ELSE. This includes local services such as roads, police and fire services (over and above what is paid out of rates); the occupation of Germany, colonial development and our other overseas responsibilities; and a hundred and one other things such as employment exchanges, tax collection, the Civil Service, forestry, prisons, civil aviation, and the care of children. There are also the general grants made to local authorities.

12

Taking Away and Giving Back

Taxes have one other very important function. In addition to paying for subsidies and schools, the Army and old age pensions, in addition to stopping us from spending too much and so driving up prices, they also go a long way towards levelling out our incomes. They do this partly by what they take away, partly by the way they give some of it back.

How taxes fall on different incomes

Taxes fall more heavily on large than on small incomes. From the £5-a-week income of a married couple with two children income tax takes nothing, while a single person with the same income pays 1s. 8d. in the £. At the £1,000-a-year level income tax takes 3s. 7d. in the £ from a married couple with two children and 5s. 3¼d. in the £ (that is, £265) from a single person. At the £10,000 level the single person pays 12s. 10d. in the £ and keeps £3,587 of his income, married people almost as much. There are average rates over the entire income of £10,000; for every £ earned over £15,000, as much as 19s. goes in tax.

Who pays Income Tax, and how much?

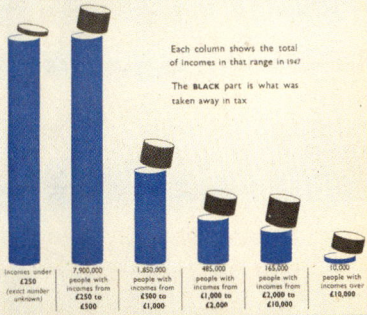

Each column shows the total of incomes in that range in 1947

The **BLACK** part is what was taken away in tax

incomes under £250 (exact number unknown)

7,900,000 people with incomes from £250 to £500

1,650,000 people with incomes from £500 to £1,000

485,000 people with incomes from £1,000 to £2,000

165,000 people with incomes from £2,000 to £10,000

10,000 people with incomes over £10,000

13

One result of this steep rise in rates is that there are now fewer than three hundred people in the country who receive, after tax, an income of over £5,000 a year. In 1938 there were about eleven thousand. Another result is that wage-earners, who in 1938 took 39 per cent of the total of personal incomes after tax, took 48 per cent last year. It may also be noted that incomes of £2,000 or more totalled £363 million after tax in 1947, and that this represented something like one-twentieth of the total of all personal incomes after tax that year.

THE SHARE-OUT OF INCOME AFTER IT HAS BEEN TAXED

How each £100 of personal income was shared

	1938	1948
Wages (of manual workers only)	£39	£48
Salaries (including pay of clerks, policemen, etc.)	£25	£21
Forces Pay	£ 2	£ 3
Profits, Interest and Rent (including professional earnings, farmers' income, profits of shop-keepers)	£34	£28
	£100	£100

In addition to the taxes on income, death duties take a higher proportion of large inherited estates. There has been an increase in duties on estates over £17,500, and those above £1 million now pay 80 per cent in tax. Previously the highest rate was 75 per cent, and that only on estates over £2 million. This year the contribution of death duties to the common fund will be nearly one-half the total of cash benefits paid out from the common fund.

Benefits vary according to needs

Taxation, therefore, takes more from those who have more to give. When it comes to giving back, in social services and cash payments, most is given to those who are most in need—the very young, the old, the sick and the disabled—while everybody, no matter how much he pays in taxes, benefits from food subsidies and from having things such as a good Police Force and good roads.

★ ★ ★

14

CUTTING THE CAKE

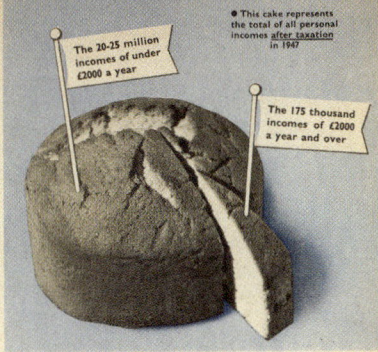

● This cake represents the total of all personal incomes after taxation in 1947

The 20-25 million incomes of under £2000 a year

The 175 thousand incomes of £2000 a year and over

THE SIZE OF THE CAKE

The levelling of incomes by taxation has gone a long way. The most obvious way to increase the real incomes of the less well off is by raising the total output of goods and services—increasing the size of the national cake. That means each of us doing all he (or she) can to increase his (or her) own output and to help other people increase theirs. This is the most important fact about our economic position, and it is easier to say "Yes" to it as a general statement than to act upon it, in real life, in our own jobs. There are two main ways to increase output: better methods, and better plant. There is great need for both.

There are many new and better methods of getting production jobs done, and any problems that may arise in introducing them are solved sooner and more happily by full and regular consultation between all concerned.

The other main way to increase output is more and better machinery, and more horsepower for industry. The most prosperous nations in the end are those with the

best factories and equipment: those which set aside the greatest proportion of their yearly production to increase their future capacity to produce, instead of using it up on things to enjoy today. That is the purpose of the investment programme, the most constructive and hopeful part of our whole recovery plan. Out of every £1 of wealth we produce we are setting aside over 4s., a very large part, to build houses and schools, improve factories and mines, and build new ones with modern, efficient machinery in them.

Savings pay for re-equipment

One of the most important things about the Budget is that it enables this investment programme to be carried out without inflation. If we are going to use a lot of our production to make such things as factories and machinery, which pay for themselves only over a long period, we have to save a corresponding amount of money and lend it to the Government or industry to pay for them. Otherwise the prices of everything will get driven up, because people will be trying to spend more money in the shops than we are making goods to be bought there.

There are three main ways the nation saves money. Firms do it by not distributing all their profits to the shareholders; last year, leaving aside the cost of keeping up existing machinery and buildings, firms did over a third of the nation's saving. The second way is through personal savings (insurance and friendly society payments, bank deposits, Savings Certificates, Defence Bonds and Post Office and Trustee Savings Bank accounts); last year they provided a seventh of the total, compared with two thirds in 1938. The third way is through the Budget. If the Government thinks that firms and individuals together are unlikely to save as much as is needed, it can make sure of the balance by taking more in taxation than it proposes to spend. This happened last year, and is happening again this year.

The more saving we are prepared to do personally, the less need is there for a Budget surplus. But so long as saving by individuals and companies is less than is needed, the Budget surplus is both a protection against higher prices and a guarantee that our investment programme will be carried out.

What it all adds up to

Now consider the whole story of this booklet. It may seem strange to keep some prices high by taxation, so as to raise money which is partly for a Budget surplus to keep prices down. But that is exactly what must be done. Without the surplus, there would at present be a risk of prices and wages chasing one another upwards and getting out of control. The effect of taxes on prices, however, is limited and under control. The final remedy will come when we are producing more, and producing it more efficiently so as to keep our prices down—earning more money, and getting more for it.

PREPARED FOR HIS MAJESTY'S GOVERNMENT BY THE ECONOMIC INFORMATION UNIT AND THE CENTRAL OFFICE OF INFORMATION

Crown Copyright Reserved

To be purchased directly from His Majesty's Stationery Office at the following addresses : York House, Kingsway, London, W.C.2; 13a Castle Street, Edinburgh 2; 39 King Street, Manchester 2; 2 Edmund Street, Birmingham 3; 1 St. Andrew's Crescent, Cardiff; Tower Lane, Bristol 1; 80 Chichester Street, Belfast; or through any bookseller.

Price 3d. net. S.O. Code Number 70-590

Printed in Great Britain by Sun Printers, Ltd., London, and Watford, Herts.

THE

NATIONAL BUDGET

1950/51

REVENUE

What happens to the money?

27. *The National Budget.* A pull-out leaflet for the 1950–51 budget, representing a new, contemporary, advertising approach to previous budget documents with a detailed breakdown of revenue and expenditure. (BL, PP/86/1A)

WHAT IT ALL ADDS UP TO

REVENUE

This is how the Government collects each £ of Revenue

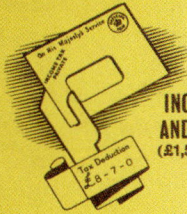

INCOME TAX AND SURTAX
(£1,508 million) — 7/9

DEATH DUTIES PROFITS TAX, etc.
(£465 million) — 2/5

ALCOHOL
(£384 million) — 2/0

PURCHASE TAX
(£303 million) — 1/7

TOBACCO
(£590 million) — 3/0

ENTERTAINMENTS BETTING, etc.
(£71 million) — 4d

EVERYTHING ELSE
e.g. motor duties, stamp duties and sale of surplus war stores, etc.
(£577 million) — 2/11

TOTAL = £3,898 million   **£1·0·0**

EXPENDITURE

This is how the Government spends each £ that it collects

DEFENCE
(£781 million) — 4/1

EDUCATION, HOUSING SUBSIDIES & other local services
(£438 million) — 2/3

HEALTH
(£395 million) — 2/0

FOOD SUBSIDIES
(£410 million) — 2/1

PENSIONS, ALLOWANCES, etc.
War and other pensions, Family allowances, Government Contribution to National Insurance
(£382 million) — 1/11

NATIONAL DEBT
Interest on war loans, savings certificates, defence bonds, etc.
(£490 million) — 2/6

EVERYTHING ELSE
Works, Buildings, etc. 4½d
Agriculture & Fisheries 3d
Foreign & Commonwealth Relations 4d
Irish Services 3d • Ministry of Supply —
Civil Expenditure 4d • Colonies 1½d
Employment Services 1½d • Broadcasting 1d
Research 1d • Civil Aviation 1½d • Rest 10d
(£559 million) — 2/11

SURPLUS
Helps towards financing house building, school building, war damage claims, etc.
(£443 million) — 2/3

£1·0·0   TOTAL = £3,898 million

THE 'NEW JERUSALEM'

Although health provision dominated the early post-war years, the country was also attempting to recover from the devastation of World War II while at the same time adapting to a peacetime footing. To this end, considerable hope and expectation was placed on the newly created United Nations as a global peacekeeping organisation. The UN, and particularly the leading role (allegedly) played by Great Britain, featured in early COI literature. In 1948, for example, the COI published a detailed thirty-six-page pamphlet entitled *Britain and the United Nations*, which claimed that 'at every stage in this movement for world-wide co-operation, Great Britain has played a leading role' (Figs. 28a and b). There were even daily radio broadcasts, including news bulletins and live debates from the United Nations and in 1952 the COI commissioned a notebook for secondary school teachers, of which the 'main object is to show the connection between the United Nations and the life of the pupil both within and without the classroom, to help him realise that the United Nations affect him personally'. To this end, teachers were informed that 'an intellectual as well as an emotional approach is vital'.[45] United Nations Day marks the anniversary of the UN Charter, which came into force on 24 October 1945. In 1971 the United Nations General Assembly recommended that the day be observed by member states as a public holiday. UK governments have never acceded to this, but until recent times the COI marked the day with a campaign that included leaflets, pamphlets and posters (Figs. 29a and b).

In the immediate post-war period, themes of renewal and harmony were to the fore in COI output. The 1950s saw Britain searching for a new, post-colonial identity and an important aspect of the work of the COI concerned overseas information, particularly to the United States and the Commonwealth. Propaganda for the overseas services accounted for about three-quarters of the COI's staff time (although less than half its total expenditure!).[46] Unlike work for the home services, where the COI served over twenty-five ministries at one time, in its overseas service it worked to the policy requirements of a single department, the Foreign and Commonwealth Office. It had been agreed immediately after the war that the COI's role should be restricted to that of a central national publicity agency serving the needs of Whitehall. This formula succeeded in diffusing any potential political opposition at home while enabling the Foreign Office to conduct the 'projection of Britain' abroad.[47] In 1946 it was stated that 'the basic object of British overseas information is to ensure the presentation overseas of a true and adequate picture of British policy, British institutions and the British way of life'.[48] The COI would have an important role to play in the pursuit of such aims, but, of course, this was precisely the kind of area in which the British Council excelled.

In its third annual report in 1950, the COI chose to inject a sharper note of self-justification for its existence and for the work it carried out overseas. It stated:

The overseas services are maintained in order that the people of other countries shall be kept informed of the kind of people the British are, and the kind of place they live in: in order also that the world shall learn more of the

British Commonwealth as a whole, and especially of the colonies. If accurate information of this kind is brought before the world, it is more difficult for misconceptions to arise of the kind that existed, for instance, on the Continent before the last war, and did something towards causing it.[49]

Film and (eventually) television played an especially important role in helping to promote a positive, often idealised, image of Britain and the COI mass-produced 'cinemagazines' – magazine-style programmes made specifically for overseas consumption. The COI's Colonial Film Unit also produced a number of longer films intended to present Britain and its people in a favourable light. Film propaganda and the printed media were employed by the COI to extol the virtues of British life and the virility of British business, creativity and enterprise. Some of the so-called 'patriotic' films were intended to encourage immigration, others to promote trade and to encourage the growth of British export markets. The reality of post-war austerity and reconstruction meant that Britain needed to expand its workforce. By showing overseas audiences how British people work, live and play, and the nature of British institutions, the COI's approach to promoting immigration was appropriately restrained. According to Tony Dykes, '...gentle persuasion rather than overt invitation was the order of the day. Tacit or not, the message conveyed by these films is unmistakable: come to Britain, they say; it's a peaceful, tolerant, inventive and flourishing place to live'.[50] The British Nationality Act of 1948 conferred the status of 'British citizen' on all subjects of the Commonwealth, enshrining in law their right to work and settle in the UK. In June 1948 the merchant vessel *Empire Windrush* arrived at Tilbury Docks carrying 492 workers from the Caribbean. They had come to Britain to assist with post-war reconstruction.[51]

One of the first films to be shown in this genre was an impressively constructed montage of Britain at leisure, entitled *Come Saturday* (1949). Made for the Foreign Office (FO), it was primarily directed at the United States. Having started to receive aid for reconstruction under the European Recovery Program, a key objective of propaganda for the FO was to demonstrate the cultural and political affinities between the two nations. 'Down tools, down telephones. It's Saturday. Work is over, the weekend has begun...' Carefully chosen images of workers enjoying their well-earned leisure conjured a Britain entrenched in the values of social democracy and enshrining the principles of freedom and liberty that Americans could identify with.

Similarly, in *An English Village* (1956), a film sponsored by the Colonial Office, idealised scenes of village life in the south of England are presented as evidence of tranquillity and stability, and it depicts a unique community spirit engendered by wartime adversity. The film is a skilfully, and highly romanticised, portrait of cosy village life: the socially inclusive composition of the parish committee, the companionability of the local pub and the friendly rivalry at the annual fruit and flower show. In 1958 the FO and the Commonwealth Relations Office (CRO) sponsored *Oxford*, a product of post-war efforts to attract overseas students to study in Britain. Like *An English Village*, the film extols the virtues of everyday life in

BRITAIN and the UNITED NATIONS

A.GAMES

HIS MAJESTY'S STATIONERY OFFICE · ONE SHILLING NET

COMMISSION FOR
CONVENTIONAL ARMAMENT

INTERNATIONAL
COURT OF JUSTICE

United Nations Organisation

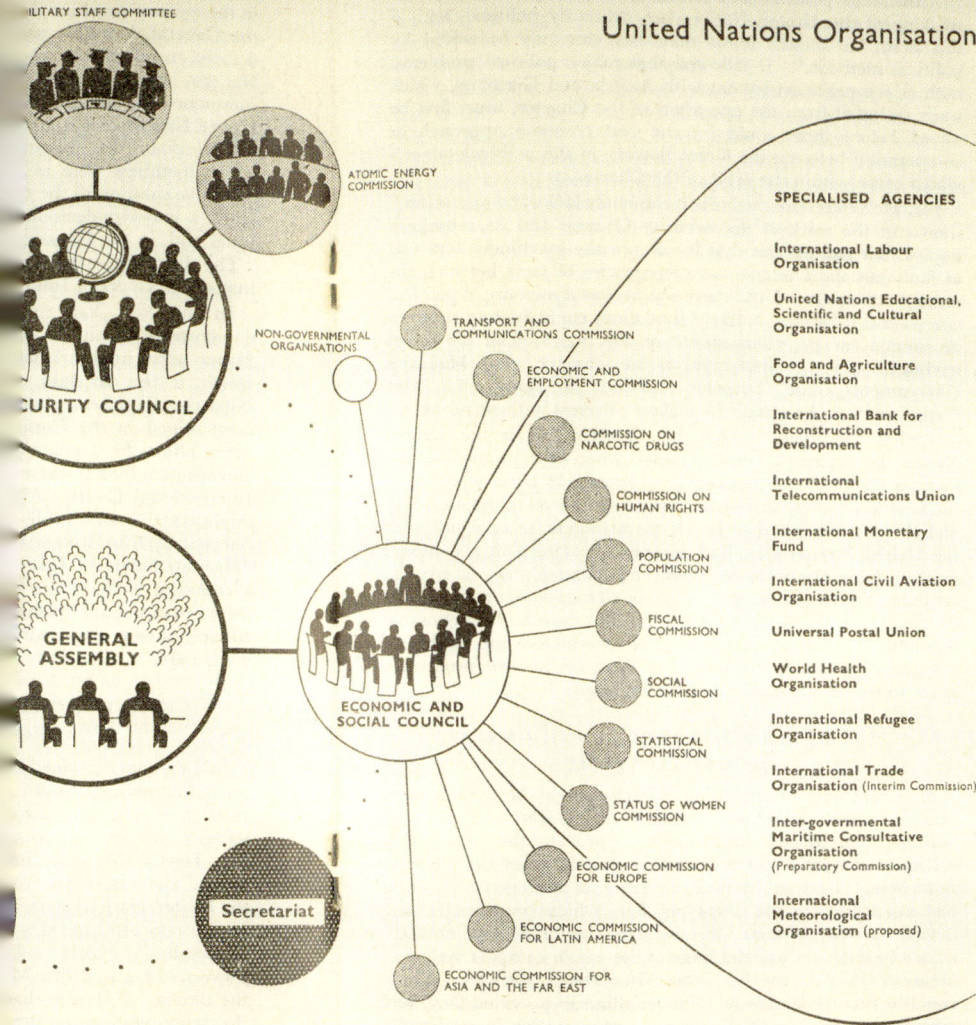

MILITARY STAFF COMMITTEE

ATOMIC ENERGY COMMISSION

SECURITY COUNCIL

GENERAL ASSEMBLY

Secretariat

NON-GOVERNMENTAL ORGANISATIONS

ECONOMIC AND SOCIAL COUNCIL

TRANSPORT AND COMMUNICATIONS COMMISSION

ECONOMIC AND EMPLOYMENT COMMISSION

COMMISSION ON NARCOTIC DRUGS

COMMISSION ON HUMAN RIGHTS

POPULATION COMMISSION

FISCAL COMMISSION

SOCIAL COMMISSION

STATISTICAL COMMISSION

STATUS OF WOMEN COMMISSION

ECONOMIC COMMISSION FOR EUROPE

ECONOMIC COMMISSION FOR LATIN AMERICA

ECONOMIC COMMISSION FOR ASIA AND THE FAR EAST

SPECIALISED AGENCIES

International Labour Organisation

United Nations Educational, Scientific and Cultural Organisation

Food and Agriculture Organisation

International Bank for Reconstruction and Development

International Telecommunications Union

International Monetary Fund

International Civil Aviation Organisation

Universal Postal Union

World Health Organisation

International Refugee Organisation

International Trade Organisation (Interim Commission)

Inter-governmental Maritime Consultative Organisation (Preparatory Commission)

International Meteorological Organisation (proposed)

THE 'NEW JERUSALEM'

28. *Britain and the United Nations* (1948). An extremely interesting cover design by Abram Games to this detailed thirty-six-page pamphlet (priced at one shilling), showing a singular figure on a global stage offering the hand of friendship and help to those who are prepared to extend their own hands of friendship. Inside, a detailed diagram of the structure of the UN, including its various commissions and agencies, 'many of them little known'. In a chapter 'The United Nations – "They" or "We"' the COI claims that 'the British Government has helped to set up the United Nations' and to extend its work into the fields of world food, world health, world trade and world education'. But the effectiveness of this work depends on 'the intelligent support of every practical man and woman in Britain for this new attempt to organise the world's peace and prosperity. The statesmen could not have gone even so far as they have gone without knowing that they had the British people behind them'. (BL, PP/91/12A)

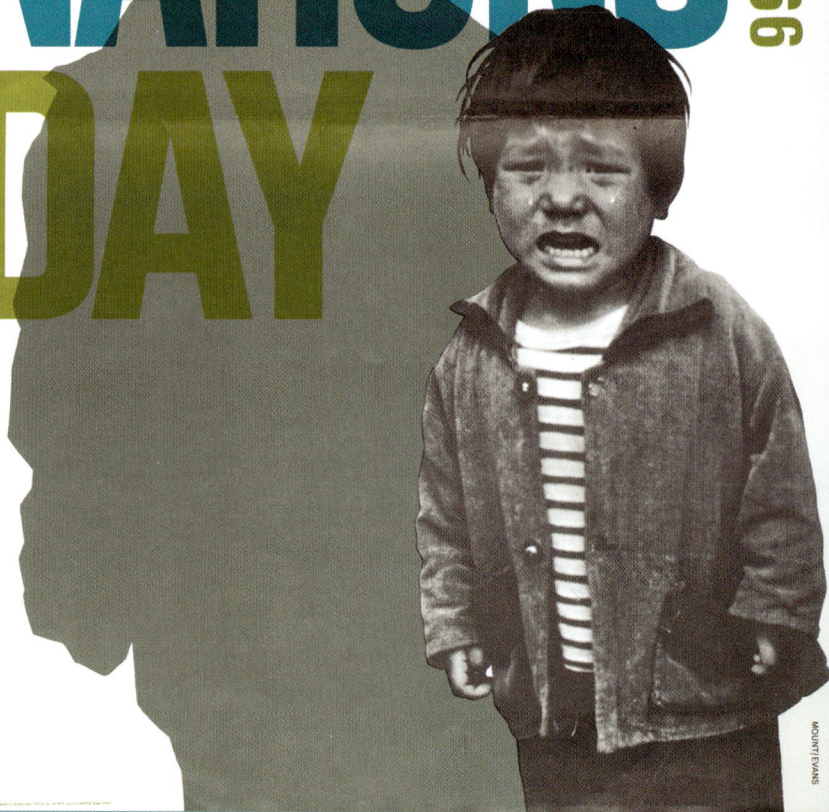

GIVE MORE TO HELP REFUGEES

UNITED NATIONS DAY

24 OCTOBER 1966

MOUNT EVANS

29. *United Nations Day* (24 October). Two examples of COI posters from 1966 and 1971, celebrating different aspects of the work carried out by the UN. (BL, PP/140/37A and 38A)

UNITED NATIONS DAY 24 OCTOBER 1971
The UN Second Development Decade 1971-80

Economic and
social progress
-a shared
responsibility

PREPARED FOR HER MAJESTY'S GOVERNMENT BY THE CENTRAL OFFICE OF INFORMATION 1971. Printed in England for Her Majesty's Stationery Office by U.D.O. (Litho) Ltd., London. Dd 621239 8/71

THE 'NEW JERUSALEM'

Oxford ('town') and the sequences of study in the university ('gown'), including its tradition, consciously include scenes of ethnic diversity.

Production of television material by the COI had more than doubled in 1958. *Look at London* (1958) was part of a wider magazine-type series called *Dateline Britain*. Intended for broadcast in Canada and Australia, the only Commonwealth countries with television networks at the time, the film was sponsored by the CRO and featured Canadian-born actor and broadcaster Bernard Braden (later famous for *On the Braden Beat,* ITV 1962–67, and *Braden's Week*, BBC 1968–72), who takes viewers on an idiosyncratic tour of London.

Printed material including books, pamphlets and leaflets supplemented 'patriotic' film propaganda. To this end, the COI's work occasionally overlapped with that of the British Council. Much of the COI material is rather mundane, but nonetheless contributed to projecting British values and the British way of life, not least in the promotion of British literature. In the immediate post-war years, the COI produced a regular monthly update for overseas book-buyers called *Books to Come* (Figs. 30a, b, c and d). These professionally produced booklets (costing threepence to the sterling area) featured a major author and contained detailed information on new books and publishers. The British Council often acted as a conduit for such publicity.

In a similar fashion, the British Council and the COI worked together with publishers to commission literature that reflected positive, idealised, images of life in Britain. For example, Longman's published a series for the British Council, 'The British People: How They Live and Work' (Figs. 31a, b and c). This included individual editions on *English Villagers*, *University Students* and *Ordinary People*.

The COI also published a far more sober monthly international review in a magazine format called simply *MIRROR* (Figs. 32a, b, c and d). In spite of a glossy tabloid cover, the contents were largely serious and of considerable intellectual magnitude. Prominent politicians, scientists and writers such as T.S. Eliot, Stephen Spender, Sir Kenneth Clark and Sir Stephen Tallents regularly contributed. The *MIRROR* was an international review 'with the object of furthering international co-operation through the mutual exchange of ideas'. It first appeared in six editions in nine European countries, printed in English, French, Norwegian, Dutch, Greek and German. Following the granting of independence to India and Pakistan, *MIRROR* was swiftly extended to the rest of the Commonwealth. In a high-minded editorial, it defined its purpose as 'furthering international understanding and friendship. In the realm of culture – the arts and the sciences – exists the common ground on which must be built the wider agreements of tomorrow. In the growth of knowledge lies our only hope of finding universal tolerance, that mutual accommodation to our differences which the facts compel'. Some editions were specifically targeted to a certain readership. In 1950, for example, there was a special edition (Figs.33a and b) aimed at China with the intention of allowing 'the Chinese reader to discern and

30. *Books to Come.* These COI booklets, here featuring (clockwise, from top left) Rebecca West, Nevil Shute, Graham Greene and Christopher Isherwood, provided advance information for overseas book-buyers and formed part of the propaganda drive to project British values and way of life. (BL, PP/104/31A, 8A, 41A and 5A)

British
BOOKS TO COME
No. 53   FEBRUARY 1949
PRICE SIXPENCE

REBECCA WEST, whose latest work, *The Meaning of Treason*, is listed on page 15 of this issue. A biographical note appears on page 8.

AN ADVANCE LIST FOR OVERSEAS BOOKBUYERS

NO. 92 · JUNE 1952
BOOKS TO COME

NEVIL SHUTE: See page 8

AN ADVANCE LIST FOR BOOKBUYERS

British
BOOKS TO COME
No. 58   MAY 1949
PRICE SIXPENCE

CHRISTOPHER ISHERWOOD. A new edition of his translation of Charles Baudelaire's *Intimate Journals* is listed on page 23.

AN ADVANCE LIST FOR OVERSEAS BOOKBUYERS

No. 82   AUGUST 1951   PRICE ONE SHILLING
BOOKS TO COME

GRAHAM GREENE: see page 6.

AN ADVANCE LIST FOR BOOKBUYERS

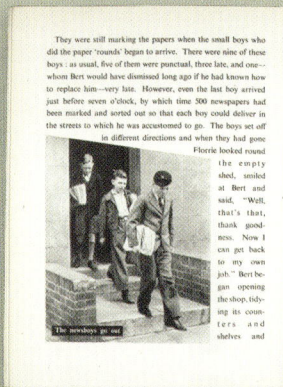

THE SHOP
ON THE CORNER

by
JOHN
CLARKSON

1/- NET

THE SHOP
ON THE CORNER

by
John Clarkson

Published for
THE BRITISH COUNCIL
by LONGMANS GREEN & CO. LTD.
London New York Toronto

The Smith family on Sunday afternoon

They were still marking the papers when the small boys who did the paper 'rounds' began to arrive. There were nine of these boys : as usual, five of them were punctual, three late, and one—whom Bert would have dismissed long ago if he had known how to replace him—very late. However, even the last boy arrived just before seven o'clock, by which time 300 newspapers had been marked and sorted out so that each boy could deliver in the streets to which he was accustomed to go. The boys set off in different directions and when they had gone Florrie looked round the empty shed, smiled at Bert and said, "Well, that's that, thank goodness. Now I can get back to my own job." Bert began opening the shop, tidying its counters and shelves and

The newsboys go out

Opening the shop

seeing that his goods were displayed in the way he liked: magazines hanging from rails above the counter, newspapers on the counter itself, more magazines on shelves at the side of the shop, tobacco and cigarettes on shelves at the back of the counter, bottles of ink, balls of string, reels of sewing cotton and packets of pins on shelves near the window, toys, games and children's books on top of a set of lockers, bottles of fizzy drinks under the counter, and ices in the refrigerator.

From sounds overhead, Bert knew that Florrie had already

7

31. The Shop on the Corner. This booklet was produced as part of 'The British People' series, published by Longman's for the British Council. Each booklet contained more than thirty illustrations and a descriptive commentary that today is faintly embarrassing. The corner shop is run by Bert and Florrie with the help of their 'paper boys' and features the Smith family, respectable figures in the local community. (BL, 010360.pp.1.6.)

32. MIRROR. Four examples of front covers from 1950–51 that illustrate the diversity of the digest – ranging from 'Beauty of Women Down the Ages' and 'Britain's Atomic Story' to 'Inside a Soviet Prison' and 'Ideals of the Commonwealth'. (BL, PP/100/17A, 22A, 28A and 24A)

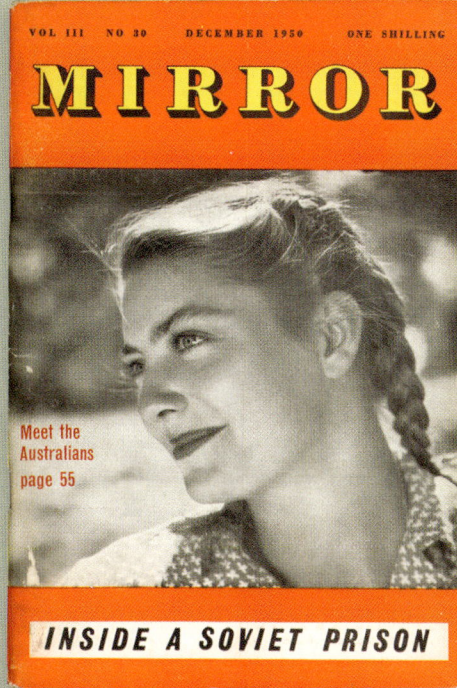

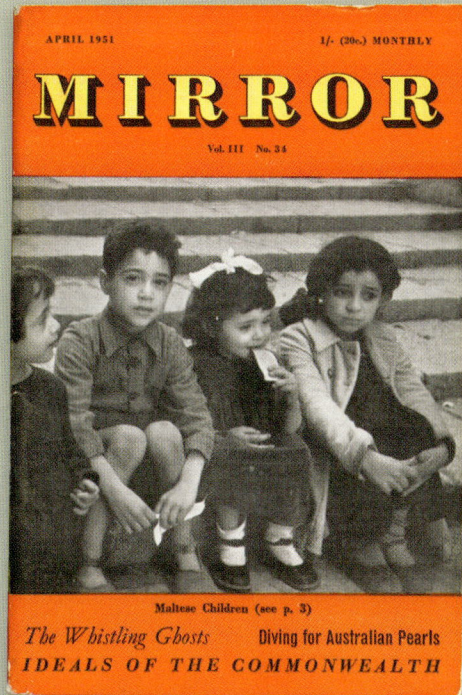

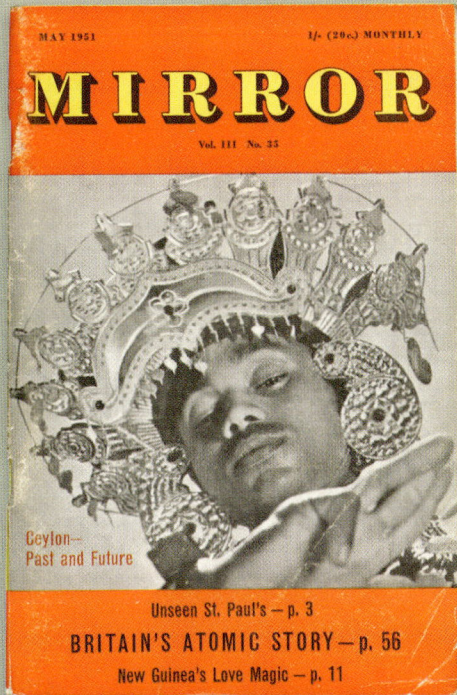

ONE SHILLING

MIRROR

Making the deaf hear (page 41)

BEAUTY OF WOMAN DOWN THE AGES

VOL. III   JULY 1950   NO. 25

VOL III   NO 30   DECEMBER 1950   ONE SHILLING

MIRROR

Meet the
Australians
page 55

INSIDE A SOVIET PRISON

APRIL 1951   1/- (20c.) MONTHLY

MIRROR

Vol. III No. 34

Maltese Children (see p. 3)

The Whistling Ghosts   Diving for Australian Pearls

IDEALS OF THE COMMONWEALTH

MAY 1951   1/- (20c.) MONTHLY

MIRROR

Vol. III No. 35

Ceylon—
Past and Future

Unseen St. Paul's – p. 3
BRITAIN'S ATOMIC STORY – p. 56
New Guinea's Love Magic – p. 11

MIRROR

is a monthly review presenting to Chinese readers a reflection of contemporary thought and activity in Europe, through articles, essays, stories and illustrations chosen from British and other European sources. Other editions are on sale in India, Pakistan, Burma, Siam and Indonesia.

MIRROR

reproduces factual articles giving information about progress in industry, agriculture, science, education, social welfare, literature, art and entertainment.

MIRROR

focuses the varied opinions of distinguished writers and journalists, historians and philosophers, scientists and artists, on the problems of our time.

MIRROR

reflects recent work in biography, fiction, poetry and art. In its surface the Chinese reader can discern and study a microcosm of European ideas, and see how far European traditions, values and hopes for the future can illuminate his own.

All correspondence relating to editorial or other matters should be addressed to:
MIRROR, Norgeby House, Baker Street, London, W.1.

M I R R O R

VOLUME 1 : NUMBER 1

Published by the Central Office of Information, London

原子能之和平用途

作者當系英國醫學研究所主任，他講原子能的有益用途，可以治海疾病及醫創的研究，他解釋原子素可在不同形態中與在固的原子的解重量而其此名回原子的同位素有的自然，在有的可能的恒人工廠生出的同位原素則他，不是有核子素已是能的原子作用作者又和原一種顯量的發展可使這不的一位原素那個同位原素在研究時可用以探索者有放射性的同位原素那個同位原素可以跟入化合的副狀態那個個原素的非常用以跟入化合的隱跟索劑原素的同位素的色素的一部

分之有缺貧的輸血循問以測未輸血機能的一部

原素在細胞愛子樣即可取得放射性的同位原素質慶在有價值的指局射線那樣增加原子素其他用途可在高透現愛克斯現在它的放射線在用以室驗研究有些典為有放射的研究入活中之同位原素的著作特殊當音各種沿染都可一個研究之同位原素的其的一個研究之同位原素的各的分子的分子的究竟都有一些用分子的分子的究竟都用分子的分之理用在有這個信侯系別原子分之理用在有這個原子分

所謂他的放射現那即在其有逼積化學作用的變化之機物中作用的及物理的研究放了許得知何遷化物用此即利用這各它所而性質可能性射線放的物質些遷化化學作用即是方物的物理的變化那得其光熱之變化我以研之作者特殊有可學而能利用所知識別物研放射化即世界全體倘或受重要的問題遷這若將科學之好其貢獻為可使世界全這些知識以為現在人類

PEACEFUL USES
OF ATOMIC ENERGY

By SIR HENRY DALE

FROM *THE LISTENER*

My theme is the uses of nuclear energy for purposes of a wholly beneficent kind; not on a very large but on a relatively small scale, and, for some purposes, in amount so minute as to require very delicate instruments for its detection and measurement. Radiant energy, liberated by the breakdown of the atomic nuclei of unstable elements can be used in the treatment of certain diseases and in medical and other researches. An element may exist in different forms, differing from one another by the weights of their atoms. These are termed isotopes of the element in question. Usually one of these is a common one, constituting nearly the whole of the element as we obtain it in nature; and the name "isotope" is most frequently used for other rarer forms of the same element. Some of these exist naturally, and others can now be produced artificially. The natural rarer isotopes are mostly not radioactive, being recognised and separated from the common ones only by the difference in atomic weight. The artificial ones, with which I am chiefly concerned, are made from ordinary elements by methods which the study of atomic energy has provided: and they are radioactive. That means that the nuclei of their atoms are unstable, and are always breaking down and emitting radiations, just as natural radium does. And I am going to tell you about a remarkable development which enables a radioactive isotope of almost any element, or even a stable one, to be used in research as a "tracer," enabling us to follow very closely the way in which the atoms of that element enter into chemical combinations, and how they pass from one combination to another.

Let me give you an example of one of the simpler uses of such a tracer element in a problem of human medicine. During the war transfusion of blood from a donor was all too often needed. It became

3

study a microcosm of European ideas, and see how far European traditions, values and hopes for the future can illuminate his own'. The edition was printed in both English and Mandarin.

Publications such as *MIRROR* reflected the reality of the onset of the Cold War. In March 1947 President Truman had announced his era-defining foreign policy, denouncing communism for its inherent expansionism and promising an 'enduring struggle' against it – both politically and economically. It was the so-called Truman Doctrine that provided the underpinning for the Marshall Plan – the massive programme of aid to restore the European economies – passed in 1948. The Truman Doctrine and the Marshall Plan – which have been referred to as 'two halves of the same walnut' – served the United States' political and economic interests, in that not only were they intended to contain communism, but in return recipient countries would be expected to purchase US goods and provide investment opportunities for American capital.[52] The Soviet response was to establish the Cominform (Communist Information Bureau) in September 1947. This provided the Soviet Union with the means to tighten its grip on the Eastern European satellite countries, which were expected to trade only with Cominform members. In April 1948 the Western European recipients of Marshall Plan aid established the Organisation for European Economic Co-operation (OEEC) to administer this aid, becoming one of the first instruments of Western solidarity in the Cold War. In April 1949 the North Atlantic Treaty Organization (NATO) brought together signatories from Western Europe and North America, who all pledged to regard an attack on one of them as an attack on them all. Predictably the Soviet leader, Joseph Stalin, responded to the creation of the OEEC by setting up the Council for Mutual Economic Assistance (Comecon) in January 1949 to co-ordinate socialist economic planning for Eastern Europe, and then in May 1955 with the Warsaw Pact, the Soviet Union's answer to NATO.

During the Cold War Europe was divided into two hostile and irreconcilable camps, sustained by different economic systems and protected by military pacts, which in turn led to an escalating nuclear arms race. The Cold War provided Britain with a formidable propaganda challenge, which was soberly pointed out in a Foreign Office briefing paper in December 1951:

> The 'cold war' is a struggle for men's minds. It is a struggle to determine whether the mass of mankind shall look for hope towards the Soviet Union or towards the Western democracies. This struggle, however, is not solely a conflict between two sets of ideas. Power enters into it, and a third factor is that intangible product of power and ideas which is called prestige.[53]

Prior to World War II, British power and prestige had been taken for granted. But

33. *Special Edition* (1950). Based on the original format of *MIRROR* and aimed at the Chinese intelligentsia, the content was intensely serious with little scope for lighthearted humour. Witness the first essay by Sir Henry Dale on 'Peaceful Uses of Atomic Energy'. (BL, PP/100/1L)

Britain was transitioning (sometimes painfully) from Empire to Commonwealth and its position as a global superpower was now behind it. In such circumstances, the COI was deeply involved in providing propaganda that supported the Western perspective on the Cold War and the mistrust of the Soviet Union. Much of its time was taken up with the issue of Civil Defence (more of this later), but equally important was the need to identify the nature of the new enemy (remember that the Soviet Union and what would soon become a communist China had been Britain's allies in World War II). In May 1947 Attlee chaired a Special Cabinet Committee on Subversive Activities, and in 1948 the government established the Information and Research Department (IRD), a covert anti-communist propaganda unit within the Foreign and Commonwealth Office with links to the COI. The IRD was formed as a direct response to increasingly hostile Soviet propaganda in the wake of the communist coup in Prague, the escalating blockade of West Berlin and mounting pressure on Finland.[54] When war, which involved almost 100,000 British service personnel, broke out in Korea in 1950, the fear of another major conflict had become very real[55] (Fig. 34).

Arguably nothing symbolised the ideological divide of the Cold War more than the so-called 'German Problem'. Having divided the German capital into occupation zones immediately after the war, Stalin attempted to blockade Berlin in June 1948. Following the lifting of the blockade in May 1949 by the US and British airlift, the Federal Republic of Germany (West Germany) was established. In October, the German Democratic Republic (East Germany) came into existence.

In 1952 the COI and the Foreign Office published *Germany's Place in the New Europe* (Fig. 35), which detailed these events together with Germany's financial and international obligations and concluded that the defence of Western Europe had to be undertaken in Berlin and western Germany. In September 1950 the Western Powers declared in New York that any attack against the 'German Federal Republic or Berlin, from any quarter, would be considered an attack upon themselves'. Interestingly, the booklet refers to the EDC (European Defence Community). The proposal for a mutual defence treaty had been signed by Belgium, France, Italy, Luxembourg, the Netherlands and West Germany on 27 May 1952, but failed to obtain ratification in the French parliament, and consequently never entered into force. Instead, West Germany was admitted to NATO in September 1953.

The fear of another war, of a Soviet occupation, haunted Europe and was constantly revived by communist provocations such as the Berlin Blockade and the coup in Czechoslovakia. W.E. John's 1952 book *Biggles Follows On*, which was

---

34. *The Communist Problem* (1957). In September 1954 the United States, France, Great Britain, New Zealand, Australia, the Philippines, Thailand and Pakistan formed the South-East Asia Treaty Organization, or SEATO. The purpose of the organisation was to prevent communism from gaining ground in the region. This booklet followed a SEATO seminar on 'Countering Communist Subversion'. SEATO was formally disbanded in 1977 following the ending of the Vietnam War in 1975. (BL, PP/113/9A)

35. *Germany's Place in the New Europe* (1952). The Soviet Union's blockade of Berlin[57] made it clear that 'the free world' needed to strengthen militarily in the face of a developing menace. The challenge was set out in striking detail by comparing the land forces in Europe available to each side. (BL, PP/113/26L)

Rebellion

The Party or, where there is no Party, individual Communists, must at all times try to interpret the current political situation with a view to determining whether there is, in Communist terminology, a "revolutionary situation" or a "period of retreat".

A "revolutionary situation" is one in which the Party considers it has every opportunity of seizing power. An examination of the occasions when Communist Parties have been able to take over control of the State shows that generally speaking there are three requisites for a "revolutionary situation". These are first: the ability of the Communists through their general penetration of the labour movement to bring the economy of the country to a standstill; second, the control of the Ministry of the Interior and the Police; and third, sufficient power over the armed forces, both to neutralize the Army's opposition and also the ensure that essential services in the country can be maintained without opposition from the masses . . . .

Subversion is violent or non-violent according to whether Communist Parties decide that there is or is not a "revolutionary situation" . . . . . . In South-East Asia in 1948 . . . . certain Communist Parties decided that there was a "revolutionary situation". It is generally believed that this interpretation was made at a so-called Youth Conference in Calcutta, and there is little reason to doubt this assumption.

The result was open rebellion in India, Burma, Indonesia and Malaya and an intensification of revolt in Vietnam and the Philippines . . . .

— Richard Thistlethwaite

Read these SEATO pamphlets for further information on Communist subversion:

The Communist Way to World Power
by RICHARD THISTLETHWAITE
Communism's Use of Armed Aggression
by ADMIRAL ARTHUR W. RADFORD
Communism in Decline: the Huk Campaign
by JESUS VARGAS and TARCIANO RIZAL
The Battle of Our Time
by DOUGLAS HYDE
Freedom or Communism?
by DR. LUANG SURIYABONGS
Trade and Aid in the Service of Communism
by PROFESSOR GEORGE E. TAYLOR

The Communist Problem

Over one hundred delegates attended the SEATO Seminar on Countering Communist Subversion, held at Baguio in the Philippines in November, 1957. The Seminar was the first of its kind; a forum in which all aspects of subversion and its basis in Communist doctrine were freely discussed. A number of contributions to the Seminar by leading experts in all fields of Communist philosophy and action have already been published by the South-East Asia Treaty Organization. In this pamphlet, direct quotations from the Seminar addresses illustrate some of the speakers' main points.

ECONOMIC AND MILITARY PARTNERSHIP

ICELAND
FINLAND
NORWAY
SWEDEN
DENMARK
EIRE
NETHERLANDS
U.K.
Berlin
BELGIUM
LUXEMBOURG
W. GERMANY
FRANCE
SWITZERLAND
AUSTRIA
YUGOSLAVIA
ITALY
ALBANIA
SPAIN
GREECE
PORTUGAL
TURKEY

Countries in the
E.D.C. and N.A.T.O.
(W. Germany in E.D.C. only)

Other countries in
N.A.T.O.

Comparative sizes of Land Forces

N.A.T.O. | U.S.S.R. & Satellites

N.A.T.O. excluding E.D.C.
E.D.C.
W. Germany

U.S.S.R.
Satellites

This
is
the
COMMONWEALTH

6ᵈ net

Heading the list of frequent Commonwealth Conferences are those of the Prime Ministers.

There were 26,425 Commonwealth students in the UK in 1958.

The Commonwealth gets together

All Commonwealth countries (except Canada) are members of the Sterling Area.

Commonwealth countries have 24 million tons of shipping.

You can get anywhere in the Commonwealth by air in 2½ days.

The Directorate of Overseas Surveys had photographed over 1,500,000 square miles of Commonwealth territory by 1959.

Over 1,250,000 words are carried on the Commonwealth telecommunications system daily; it is the largest network in the world.

253,000 miles of cable already connect Commonwealth countries and a new two-way cable is projected to cover the whole Commonwealth.

The Commonwealth Relations Office is the channel for communications between the UK and Commonwealth countries; the Colonial Office conducts relations with the UK Dependencies.

The Technical, Scientific and Educational representatives of Commonwealth countries work side by side in London to ensure full co-operation.

About 2,500 teachers go from the UK to the Commonwealth every year.

There are 77 official and voluntary organisations concerned with special aspects of Commonwealth affairs, ranging from Forestry to Student Welfare.

The Commonwealth Way

The Rule of the elected majority . . .

. . . taking into consideration the feelings of the minority.

Freedom for a man to speak his mind . . .

. . . so that views are aired and grievances ventilated.

The dignified and independent rule of law . . .

. . . where justice is openly and fairly administered.

Sport increasingly helps to knit the Commonwealth together . . .

. . . cricket is almost a Commonwealth monopoly.

Delegates from a dependency discuss the future of their country round a table in London . . .

. . . and citizens rejoice as a new nation of the Commonwealth is born

Reading List

Some United Kingdom Government Publications on the Commonwealth:

PICTURE OF THE COMMONWEALTH. A pictorial introduction to our great family of nations. 1/6 net.

QUEEN AND PEOPLE. By Dermot Morrah. An illustrated booklet on the development of the monarchy and its role in the Commonwealth today. 2/- net.

SPORT IN THE COMMONWEALTH. A fully-illustrated account of the many sports practised between Commonwealth countries, with special emphasis on the Commonwealth Games. 2/- net.

COMMONWEALTH PARTNERSHIP. An outline of the many ways in which Commonwealth countries work together (with maps). 1/- net.

BRITAIN'S PURPOSE IN AFRICA. By Kenneth Bradley. The Director of the Commonwealth Institute explains Britain's policies in the various African dependencies (illustrated). 2/- net.

CORONA LIBRARY. Popular, well-illustrated books on the United Kingdom's dependencies. 25/- net each; HONG KONG, by Harold Ingrams, SIERRA LEONE by Roy Lewis, NYASALAND by Frank Debenham, BRITISH GUIANA by Michael Swan, JAMAICA by Peter Abrahams, UGANDA by Harold Ingrams (in preparation), NORTH BORNEO by K. G. Tregonning (in preparation).

'PIONEERS WHO SERVED' series. Short lives of David Livingstone, Mungo Park, Mary Kingsley, T. S. Raffles, J. E. K. Aggrey, F. W. Lugard, John Williams (illustrated). 6d. each net.

'WARS NOT YET WON' series. Booklets on man's struggle against scourges — The Tsetse Fly, The Locust, Leprosy, Malaria (in preparation). 6d. each net.

REFERENCE PAMPHLETS

These include: The Commonwealth in Brief (3/6 net); Constitutional Developments in the Commonwealth (2/6 net); Consultation and Co-operation in the Commonwealth (2/3 net); The Monarchy and the Commonwealth (1/- net).

MAGAZINE

COMMONWEALTH TODAY. A lively picture magazine which records the richly varied life of the Commonwealth. Each of its eight issues a year includes full colour pages. Obtainable by annual subscription only, price 10/6.

PREPARED BY THE CENTRAL OFFICE OF INFORMATION
PUBLISHED BY HER MAJESTY'S STATIONERY OFFICE
© Crown copyright 1959
Printed in England by J. & Co., Ltd., Middlesbrough & London.
WT.3600 K.400 R.O. Code No. 59-742

subtitled *A Story of the Cold War in Europe and Asia*, has Biggle's old wartime foe Erich von Stalhein now working for the Russians as a communist spy and operating behind the Iron Curtain, including in Prague. Interestingly, in the face of a sustained and concerted anti-Soviet propaganda campaign, Mass Observation found during the autumn of 1953 that although twice as many people in Britain were anti- as were pro-Russian, there existed mixed feelings towards the Americans: gratitude for their generosity but also resentment of their arrogance.[56]

While both Labour and Conservative governments during the 1950s adopted strongly pro-American, anti-communist positions, the nation chose not to integrate politically and economically with the rest of Western Europe (but more of this later). In the post-war years, as Britain rejected European economic integration, the Commonwealth and its markets and workforce assumed an increasing importance (Fig. 38). That importance is reflected in the volume and direction of the COI's overseas information policy. In its 1950 annual report the COI had set out four main aims of the overseas service: 'to spread a knowledge of the things we believe in, such as democracy, tolerance and social development'; 'to promote a favourable background to the commercial selling of exports, by showing that Britain is industrially and scientifically vigorous, and that she makes reliable and attractive goods, and that she has her share of new inventions'; 'the support of British foreign policy'; and 'the great aim of spreading knowledge of the Commonwealth'.[58]

This last aim in particular proved problematic as Britain was transitioning from Empire to Commonwealth but still insisted on seeing itself as an imperial power. As the dependencies moved towards greater independence, both the COI and the British Council were engaged in cultural propaganda that increasingly assumed political dimensions, countering communist propaganda by demonstrating to the rest of the Commonwealth that British traditions had more to offer than a communist way of life (Figs. 36a, b, c and d, and Fig. 37). In July 1952 an investigatory committee of officials concluded succinctly: '...in our view, the international situation, the Communist ideological onslaught on the free world, the need to right the balance of payments and the necessity of maintaining Commonwealth relationships, all demand an intensification of overseas information work...'.[59]

While the majority of the COI's output continued to look to the present and the future to achieve these aims, there were, however, a number of quite extraordinary publications that harked back to the colonial past. During World War II the Ministry of Information had emphasised the joint war effort of the British Empire and the Commonwealth, focusing on Britain's paternal care of its former colonies and their contribution to the British war effort. In the immediate aftermath of the war the COI

---

36. *This is the Commonwealth* (1959). This is a pull-out booklet stressing the close links between Great Britain and the Commonwealth. What is referred to as 'the Commonwealth Way' cites democracy, the rule of law, independence of the judiciary, sport ('cricket is almost a Commonwealth monopoly') and, interestingly, it also refers to the process by which Dependencies discuss ('delegates from a dependency discuss the future of their country round a table in London') and gain independence ('...and citizens rejoice as a new nation of the Commonwealth is born'). The final section focuses on the interconnectedness of the Commonwealth ('The Commonwealth Gets Together'). Teacher and student exchanges, 24 million tons of shipping, 155,000 miles of cable, and 'over 1,250,000 words are carried on the Commonwealth telecommunications system daily; it is the largest network in the world'. (PP/43/19L)

FOOTBALL IN

Whether in Bri
same enthusiasm fo
cricket, racing, tenn
Association Fo
Britain, where it ha
for over a hundred
throughout the wor
the game with grea

In recent year
have visited Britai
qualities in match
British amateur c
British sportsmen.

Stanley Matthews,
England's famous
International
outside-right and
one of the greatest
stars of football.

96

N AND AFRICA

Africa, you find the
or football, athletics,
ing.

soccer", grew up in
ed in its present form
popularity has spread
st Africa has adopted
sm and ability.

and Gold Coast teams
heir skill and sporting
some of the leading
them the acclaim of

E. C. Briandt, captain of a Gold Coast team which made a successful tour of Britain in 1951.

97

THIS CATALOGUE AND MAP DO NOT COVER THE DEPEN

2

4A

1   UNITED KINGDOM

2   CANADA

3   AUSTRALIA   3A NORFOLK ISLAND   3B PAPUA

4   NEW ZEALAND   4A WESTERN SAMOA

5   SOUTH AFRICA (UNION OF)   5A SOUTH WEST A

6   INDIA   HIGH C

7   PAKISTAN

8   CEYLON

9   SOUTHERN RHODESIA

37. *Commonwealth Sportsmen.* A large poster showing the
sporting links between Britain and the Commonwealth – in
this case Association Football, following tours made to
Britain by Nigeria (1949) and the Gold Coast (1951). The
poster shows Stanley Matthews ('one of the greatest stars
in football') and the Gold Coast captain E.G. Briandt, who
is playing in socks and no boots (as did the Nigerian team
when they played). In the centre of the poster is the 'Empire
Stadium, Wembley, where the annual Cup Final is played'.
(BL, BS/81/19)

38. *The Commonwealth of Nations* (1949). This pamphlet is a
catalogue of material about the Commonwealth available
to schools and to the public, priced threepence.
(BL, PP/113/10A)

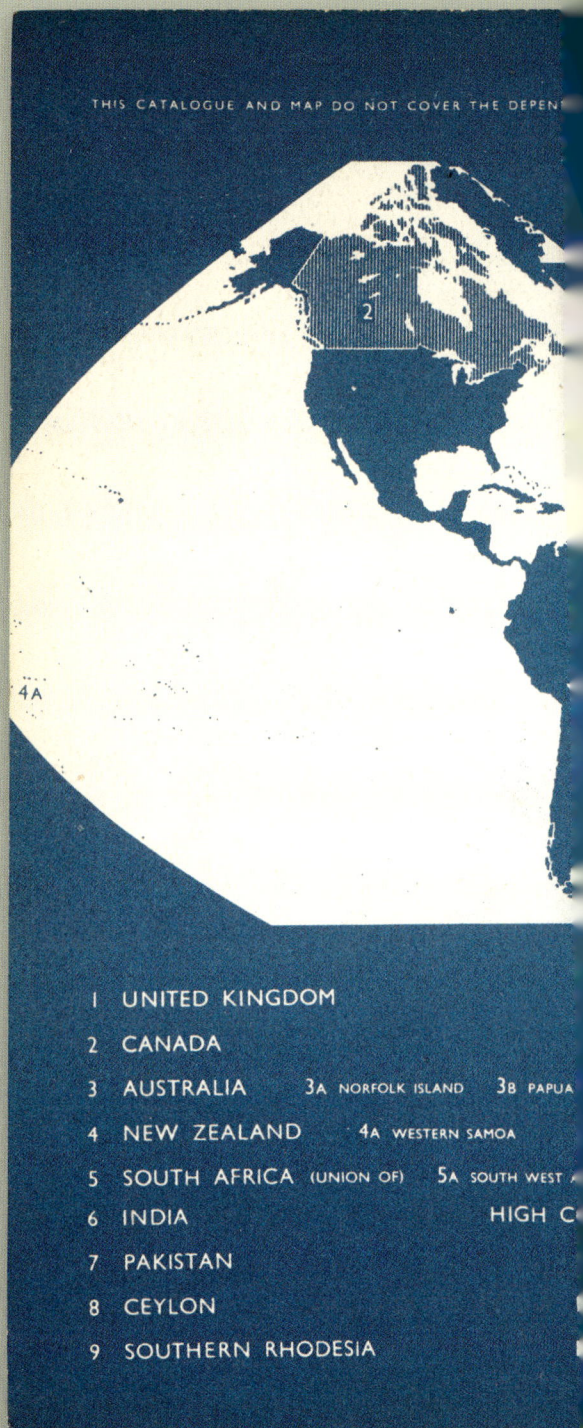

A catalogue of material about the Commonwealth
available to schools and to the public

3d
NET

7 6 7

8

3C   3D

3B

5A 11 9

3

5 12
10

3A

4

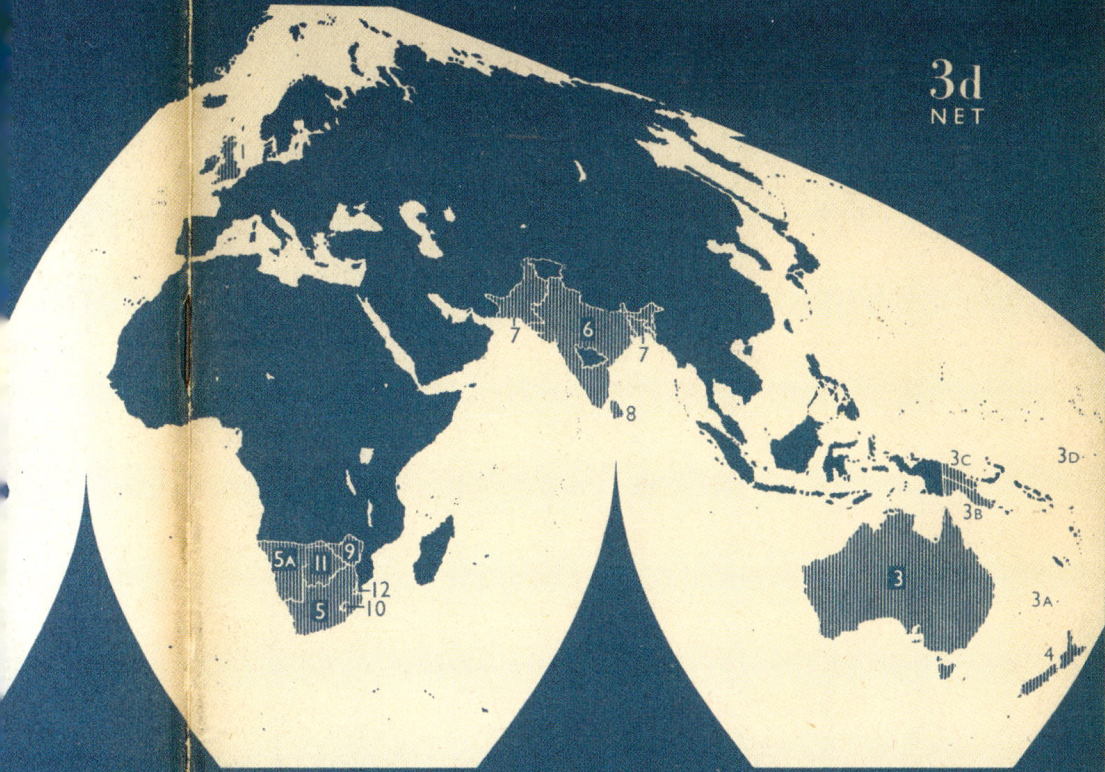

The
COMMONWEALTH
of NATIONS

HIS MAJESTY'S STATIONERY OFFICE

KINGDOM

3D NAURU

RRITORIES

PROTECTORATE

Cross Ltd., London

published a series of pocket-sized pamphlets that would now be considered to be colonialist in conception and patronising in tone. Two series in particular spring to mind and both are pocket-sized booklet formats entitled 'British Commonwealth Leaflets'.[60] The first was a series entitled 'Wars Not Yet Won' (Figs. 39a, b, c and d) and the other 'Pioneers Who Served'. These leaflets referred to the importance of international co-operation to beat diseases, but – revealingly – they concentrated most on the crucial roles played by British individuals who were among the first to research and develop a new area of knowledge or activity. In the leaflet *The Tsetse-fly*, for example, David Bruce (Figs. 40a and b) is singled out for his work in Zululand in 1894 and Uganda in 1902, investigating the outbreak of cattle disease that the natives called *nagana* – work that led some years later to his discovery of African trypanosomiasis, or 'sleeping sickness', in humans, both of which were transmitted by the tsetse fly. He was rewarded with a knighthood in 1908. The leaflet *Leprosy* ends with a call for international co-operation but it highlights the sterling work of the British Leprosy Relief Association and the Mission to Lepers in both West and East Africa as examples of best practice in the field. (The usefulness of sulphone delivered orally was a milestone in the treatment of leprosy – see Fig. 41.)

'Pioneers Who Served' (Figs. 42a, b, c, d, e and f and Fig. 43) featured an extremely interesting and eclectic mixture of largely British figures but it also included a few surprising 'pioneers' such as James Emman Kwegyir Aggrey ('Aggrey of Africa'), a black intellectual, missionary, and teacher. The focus was on the adventurous nature and daring exploits of pioneers, explorers, missionaries and mercenaries – both male and female. For example, Mary Kingsley, an English ethnographer, scientific writer and explorer whose travels throughout West Africa and the resulting work helped shape European perceptions of African cultures and British imperialism. Similarly, Mungo Park was an eighteenth-century Scottish explorer of West Africa who attempted to explore the course of the Niger River. And, of course, the series included the exploits of David Livingstone whose achievements the booklet claims 'ended slavery and opened up the continent to peaceful trade'.

At a time when former colonies and dominions were gaining independence, such literature was insensitive to say the least. However, from the British government's perspective it represents a continuation of the type of literature that it had disseminated to the Empire during the war. Implicit in these leaflets is a paternalistic assumption of the innate superiority of Great Britain as the guardian of civilisation and the belief in the notion of the 'white man's burden' that underpinned history textbooks in British schools in the 1950s and 1960s.

---

39. *The Locust, Malaria, The Tsetse-fly and Leprosy* (1961). These four pocket-sized booklets belong to the British Commonwealth Leaflets series 'Wars Not Yet Won', featuring the (disproportionate) role played by Britain in the fight against these insects and diseases responsible for extensive damage and death. (BL, PP/111/22I, 23L, 32L, 33L)

40. *The Tsetse-fly*. The illustrative narrative of the 'Wars Not Yet Won' series leaflets provide information about the roles played by individual British explorers, scientists and doctors – from a British colonial perspective. The drawing here shows Sir David Bruce and his wife (Mary Bruce) in heroic pose conducting their Tsetse-fly research in Africa. (BL, PP/111/22I, 23L)

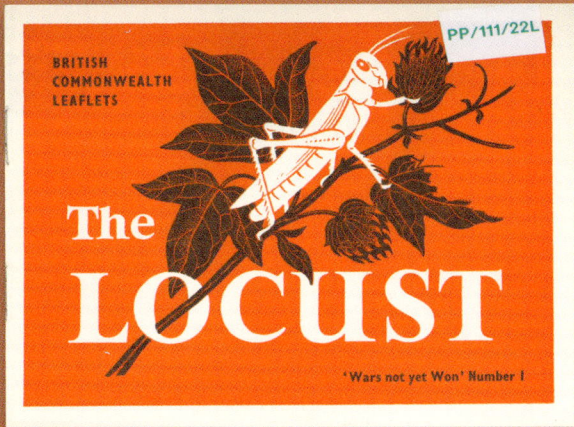

BRITISH COMMONWEALTH LEAFLETS

The **LOCUST**

'Wars not yet Won' Number 1

PP/111/22L

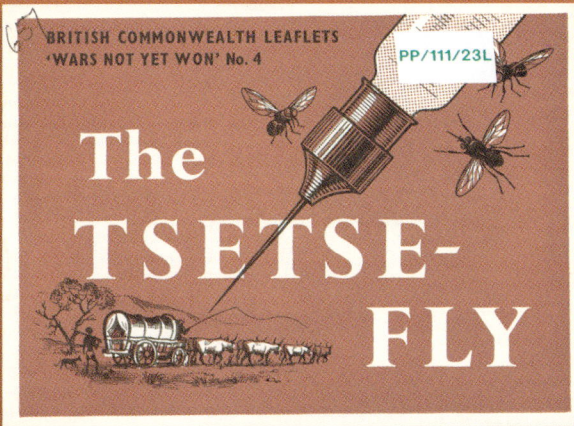

COMMONWEALTH LEAFLETS

LEPROSY

WARS NOT YET WON · NUMBER 2

PP/111/32L

BRITISH COMMONWEALTH LEAFLETS
'WARS NOT YET WON' No. 4

The **TSETSE-FLY**

PP/111/23L

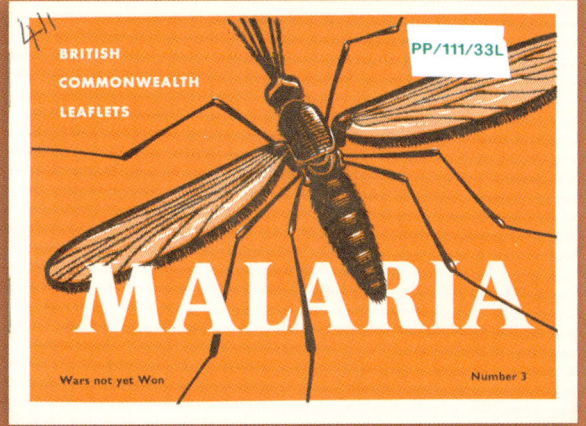

BRITISH COMMONWEALTH LEAFLETS

MALARIA

Wars not yet Won

Number 3

PP/111/33L

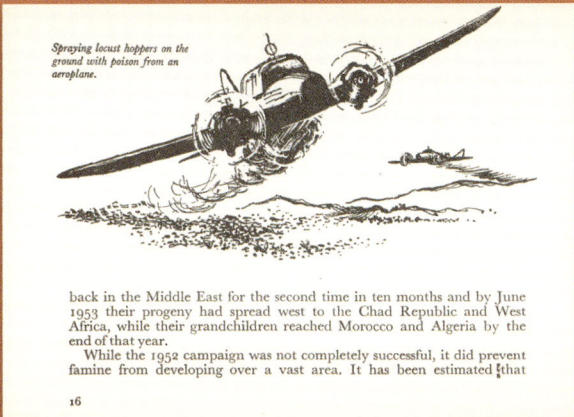

Spraying locust hoppers on the ground with poison from an aeroplane.

back in the Middle East for the second time in ten months and by June 1953 their progeny had spread west to the Chad Republic and West Africa, while their grandchildren reached Morocco and Algeria by the end of that year.

While the 1952 campaign was not completely successful, it did prevent famine from developing over a vast area. It has been estimated that

16

David Bruce and his wife set up their laboratory in a daub-and-wattle hut.

British Enterprise 1

Cured of LEPROSY

This 15-year-old boy entered the leper colony of Usuakoli, Nigeria, in October 1947. He was healed with sulphone drugs and discharged, cured, in January 1950.

British discovery brings hope to millions

BRITISH scientists have discovered a treatment for leprosy which will bring hope to the lives of millions of men, women and children who suffer from the dread disease. Experimenting with the sulphone group of drugs, they have found that D.A.D.P.S. (Diamino Diphenyl Sulphone), a compound formerly believed to be too toxic for human use, can be administered in very small doses as a treatment for leprosy. The most important aspect of this discovery is that the drug is inexpensive, reducing the cost of sulphone treatment from about £7 to 15s. a year.

Prepared by the Central Office of Information and printed in Great Britain by Peck & Cryer Ltd., London

---

41. *Cured of Leprosy: British discovery brings hope to millions* (1951). An overseas poster in the 'British Enterprise' series that tells of a British discovery that is helping in the cure of leprosy. The smiling boy had entered a leper colony in Usuakoli, Nigeria, and was later healed with the sulphone drugs discovered by British scientists. In January 1950 he was cured and discharged. The most important aspect, according to the poster, is that the drug is inexpensive, 'reducing the cost of sulphone treatment from £7 to 15s. a year'. The 'British Enterprise' series was intended to compliment the 'Wars Not Yet Won' series. (BL, BS/81/19)

42. *'Pioneers Who Served' leaflets series.* Here are editions on Mary Kingsley, J.E. Kwegyir Aggrey, David Livingstone, John Williams, Mungo Park, Thomas Stanford Raffles and Frederick Lugard. (BL, PP/111/25A, 26L, 28A, 29L, 30L, 31L)

43. *The exploits of Frederick Lugard.* This illustration shows the 1st Baron Lugard 'taking command of an expedition against Arab slave raiders ... a situation inflamed by the notorious German, Carl Peters, who followed his usual technique of persuading native chiefs to put their mark on innocent-seeming treaties which signed away their land to Germany'. (BL, PP/111/30L)

BRITISH COMMONWEALTH LEAFLETS

J.T.Raffles

(T. S. Raffles)

SERIES A 'PIONEERS WHO SERVED' No. 2

BRITISH COMMONWEALTH LEAFLETS

Mary Kingsley

SERIES A 'PIONEERS WHO SERVED' No. 1

BRITISH COMMONWEALTH LEAFLETS

Daniel Livingstone

'PIONEERS WHO SERVED'   NUMBER 5

BRITISH COMMONWEALTH LEAFLETS

J.Williams

'PIONEERS WHO SERVED'   No.6

BRITISH COMMONWEALTH LEAFLETS

F D Lugard

'PIONEERS WHO SERVED'   NUMBER 8

COMMONWEALTH LEAFLETS

Mungo Park

'PIONEERS WHO SERVED'   NUMBER 7

the task which lies before us in the future administration of this great country.'

Lugard not only portrayed the nature of the task but played a vital part in fulfilling it. After a brief interval at home he returned to Africa, this time to Uganda, as a servant of the newly formed British East Africa Company. The Company's objects were to develop legitimate trade in the vast area between the coast and the lakes and, if within the bounds of possibility, to break the slave trade. By 1888 the slavers had only just started their drive into Uganda when an internal crisis arose which threatened to play straight into their hands. A three-sided civil war seemed imminent between the converts of Catholic, Protestant and Moslem missions whose rivalries were following the old tracks of inter-tribal hatreds. The situation was further inflamed by the arrival of the notorious German, Carl Peters, who followed his usual technique of persuading native chiefs to put their mark on innocent-seeming treaties which signed away their land to Germany. Peters's action in Uganda was nullified by an Anglo-German agreement which recognised the territory as a British sphere of influence. Under the Uganda Treaty of 1890 the British East Africa Company was granted authority for the maintenance of

4

B○L

'. . . agreed to take command of an expedition against the Arab slave raiders'

5

103

WHAT OF BRITAIN'S PEOPLE

The day's work done, how do we play?

How do we live?

How do we learn?

SPORT AND LEISURE

From September to April vast crowds gather to watch professional football

The charm of England's Lake District captures many when holiday-time comes, but the seaside is the place for the family state

'In a green shade.' The long-drawn dream of cricket is an unfailing attraction to players and watchers on summer afternoons

At the pub, it looks like a fishing story. The Women's Institute believes in producing the goods, not talking about them

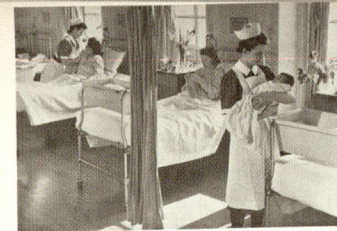

The spell of music. A typical audience at London's Royal Albert Hall during one of the Promenade Concert seasons

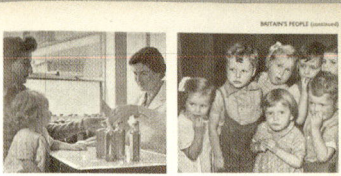

Royal Ascot. Their Majesties, staying at Windsor Castle for the Summer meeting, drive down the course before racing begins

28   29

BRITAIN'S PEOPLE (continued)

THE NEW GENERATION. In Westminster Hospital, London, recent years have seen some remarkable achievements in the welfare of mothers and children. The death rate for babies in the first year of life has been halved in the last decade. Fewer mothers—less than one in a thousand—now die in childbirth. Hospital treatment and the advice of consultants are given free under the Health Service.

ORANGE JUICE and milk are provided at natural prices for expectant mothers and for young children. Cod-liver oil and vitamin tablets are free. All are free to those who cannot afford to pay.

AT A NURSERY HOME. After a Government inquiry, Children's Departments were created by Local Councils, whose Children's Officers take charge of homeless children or those in need of care.

PEOPLE ARE CARED FOR

In 1948 a century of steady progress culminated in the coming into force of a series of Acts—the National Health Service Act, designed to give every citizen adequate medical care and attention, the National Insurance and National Insurance (Industrial Injuries) Acts, providing a greater degree of security throughout working life and in old age; and the National Assistance Act. These extensions of the social services, and others already in existence such as the welfare foods service for mothers and young children, were supported by all parties. Full employment, the newly extended social services, advances in medical knowledge and the discovery of new drugs are all playing an important part in improving the health of Britain's people.

LOCAL HEALTH AUTHORITIES provide for maternity and child welfare, health visiting and after-home nursing; welfare centres give pre-natal care to mothers and advice about their babies and young children. Here, at the clinic in Great Barr, Birmingham, a child is being examined by a visiting doctor.

Right: Eyes are tested and spectacles provided. Medical, dental and ophthalmic care are available to all under the National Health Service. The expanded social services, advances in medical knowledge, greater economic security, are all playing their part in the improvement of Britain's health.

"TWO OFF THE WHITE" A billiards lesson in a Derby and Joan Club—these are supported by voluntary contributions. The Acts of 1948 gave the people greater security while working and in old age. They swept away the remnants of the old Poor Law, which had lasted since the days of Queen Elizabeth.

32   33

THE FESTIVAL OF BRITAIN: PORTRAIT OF A PEOPLE

The reality of the situation was that Britain was in decline and no amount of propaganda could easily disguise that reality. The 'Britain Can Make It' exhibition was designed by the Labour government in 1946 to showcase British manufacturing and to demonstrate that Britain was on the road to recovery and just under a million-and-a-half people visited the Victoria & Albert Museum during the last quarter of the year. Labour recognised that post-war reconstruction of manufacturing and international trade of exported goods would require the widespread acceptance of industrial design as part of future British manufacturing. Exhibitions had an important role to play here. Britain's post-war economic position would be greatly aided by the use of propaganda. Explaining the British way of life would, so the theory ran, cause exports to increase.

This partly explains the thinking behind the Festival of Britain in 1951. It had been championed by Herbert Morrison as early as 1949 when, as Lord President of the Council, he gave the COI responsibility, under the general guidance of the Council of the Festival of Britain, for the planning and design of the buildings and for the general layout of the festival exhibition to be held on the South Bank of the Thames.[61] Morrison saw the Festival of Britain as a means of giving the British people a symbolic pat on the back for their post-war achievements and sacrifices. Gerald Barry, the director-general, claimed that the festival would prove a 'tonic to the nation'; however, not everyone was convinced – Sir Thomas Beecham described it as 'a monumental piece of imbecility'.

With the aim of promoting the feeling of recovery, the Festival of Britain opened to the public on 4 May 1951, celebrating British industry, arts and science and inspiring the vision of a better Britain. Although the main site was in London, it was a nationwide affair with exhibitions in many towns and cities throughout Britain. Celebratory events took place in 17,000 towns and villages across Britain. To accompany the festival, the COI produced for the Treasury a forty-eight-page, richly illustrated, book entitled *Britain Now* (Fig. 47). It was priced at two shillings

---

44. 'What of Britain's People?' From *Britain Now*. 'The day's work done, how do we play? How do we live? How do we learn?' No rural idyll here, the image presented is of a modern industrial society. (BL, PP/28/21A)

45. A nation enjoying itself. From *Britain Now*. A people curbed by years of total war and half-crushed by austerity and gloom, showed that they had not lost the capacity for enjoying themselves. Saturday football, the Lake District and the seaside, the Albert Hall Promenade Concert and picnics in the national parks. For him the pub ('looks like a fishing story') – and for her the Women's Institute ('producing the goods and talking about them'). And, of course, Royal Ascot. (BL, PP/28/21A)

46. The pride of the nation. From *Britain Now*. 'In 1948 a century of steady progress culminated in the National Health Service.' The Festival of Britain offered a radical vision of what Britain might be. (BL, PP/28/21A)

47. Britain Now (1951). This forty-eight-page book was designed to accompany the Festival of Britain. The cover was painted by H.S. Williamson. To point out the contrast between 'Britain Now' and the past, the Tower of London is shown more as it might have appeared in medieval times, and the picture has therefore been reconstructed from early drawings, particularly that made by Anton van den Wyngaerde (circa 1550). The cover refers to 'a new story of vigorous industrial recovery after the sacrifices of war'. (BL, PP/28/21A)

LONDON · *His Majesty's Stationery Office*

BRITAIN NOW

Britain has always been a land of freedom, of pageantry, famous for the beauty of her countryside. In this book these are the setting for a new story of vigorous industrial recovery after the sacrifices of war

H. J. WILLIAMSON

TWO SHILLINGS AND SIXPENCE net

The Coronation of Her

The Coronation Ring
The Ring, presented to the Sovereign during the ceremony, represents the Cross of St. George and is a symbol of chivalry.

The Orb of England
The golden Orb, surmounted by a Cross, is placed in the Sovereign's right hand during the ceremony.

The Royal Sceptre
The Royal Sceptre with the Cross is the symbol of sovereign power and justice.

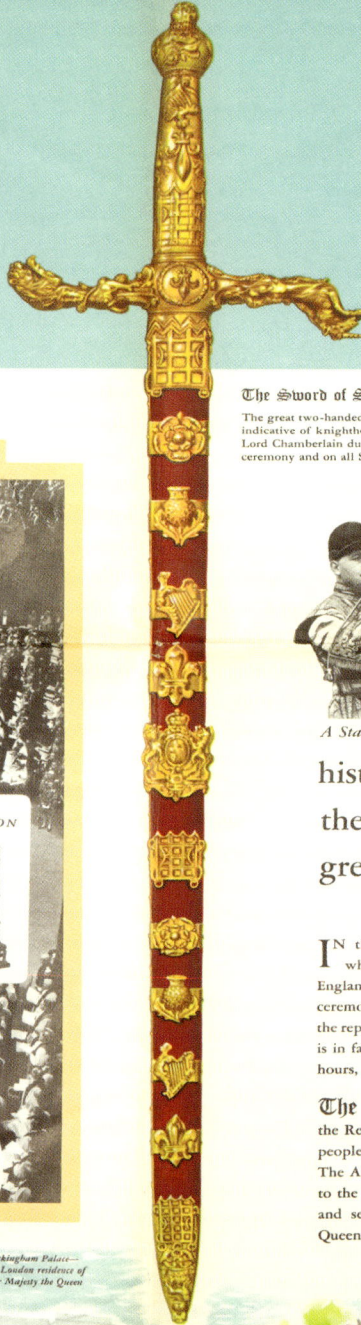

The Sword of State
The great two-handed Sword of State, indicative of knighthood, is borne by the Lord Chamberlain during the Coronation ceremony and on all State occasions.

The Scene of the Coronation

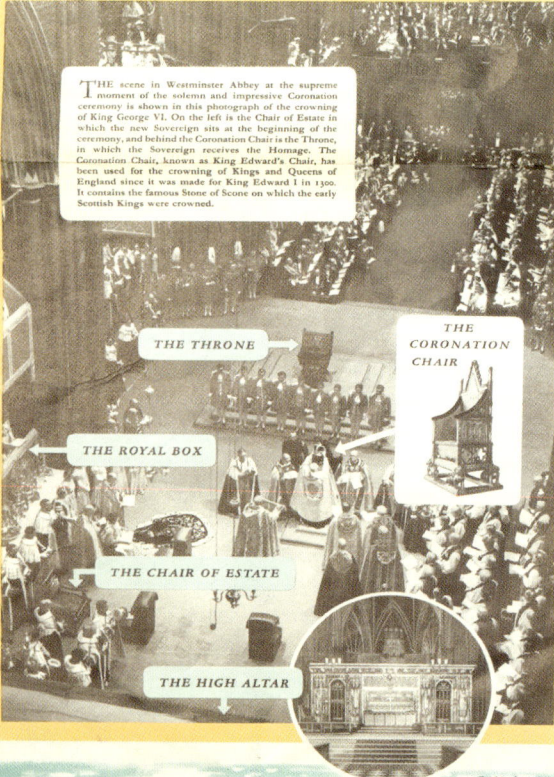

THE scene in Westminster Abbey at the supreme moment of the solemn and impressive Coronation ceremony is shown in this photograph of the crowning of King George VI. On the left is the Chair of Estate in which the new Sovereign sits at the beginning of the ceremony, and behind the Coronation Chair is the Throne, in which the Sovereign receives the Homage. The Coronation Chair, known as King Edward's Chair, has been used for the crowning of Kings and Queens of England since it was made for King Edward I in 1300. It contains the famous Stone of Scone on which the early Scottish Kings were crowned.

THE THRONE

THE CORONATION CHAIR

THE ROYAL BOX

THE CHAIR OF ESTATE

THE HIGH ALTAR

Buckingham Palace—the London residence of Her Majesty the Queen

A State Trumpeter

On June 2nd, 1953
Buckingham Palace
all the splendid pag
is rooted in the a
historic occasion Her Majesty carri
the Commonwealth and Empire, t
great family of many nations, stat

IN the magnificent setting of Westminster Abbey, where for 900 years the Kings and Queens of England have been crowned, the ancient Coronation ceremony takes place before a great gathering of all the representatives of Church and State. The Coronation is in fact a series of ceremonies, lasting for over three hours, of which the Crowning itself is the climax.

The Recognition
The ceremony begins with the Recognition, which recalls the ancient right of the people to show their acceptance of the new Sovereign. The Archbishop of Canterbury presents the Sovereign to the people, asking if they are willing to do homage and service. The whole assembly reply "God Save Queen Elizabeth" and the State trumpets are sounded.

The Coro
administers th
a solemn pro
their establish
Oath and dedi
solemnly cons
the Anointing
Royal and Pri

The Cro
moment. The
approaches the
high, in full
lowers it reve
whole congre

The Ampulla

The Ampulla, in the form of an eagle, is used in the anointing of the new Sovereign.

The Imperial State Crown

The Imperial State Crown, the Crown of Empire, is worn on all great State occasions. The central jewel is the Black Prince's ruby, worn by King Henry V at the Battle of Agincourt in 1415.

St. Edward's Crown

The great gold Crown of England, encrusted with precious stones, was made for the Coronation of Charles II in 1661. The two arches symbolize the heredity and independence of the Monarchy.

The Jewelled State Sword

This beautiful sword, which is smaller than the Sword of State (left), is used by the Sovereign during the Coronation Service.

...jesty Queen Elizabeth II goes from ...onation in Westminster Abbey, with ... solemn ritual of a ceremony which ...itions of British history. On this ... the loyal wishes of the peoples of ...e Crown is the link which unites a ...s, for a long and prosperous reign.

...Archbishop next ... Sovereign makes ...ples according to ...Having taken the ...vice, The Queen is ... the ceremony of ...n invested in the ...s the Regalia.

...ows the supreme ... by the Bishops, ...Raising the Crown ..., the Archbishop ...eign's head. The ...n their Sovereign

with "God Save the Queen". At the same moment the Peers and Officers of State put on their coronets, the drums and trumpets are sounded, and the guns at the Tower of London and elsewhere signal the great event.

The Homage

Her Majesty now proceeds to the raised Throne where she receives the homage of the Lords Spiritual and Temporal, who kneel before her in turn. When the Homage is ended, The Queen is acclaimed once more by the whole assembly. From Westminster Abbey the new Sovereign drives in State, crowned and arrayed in all the insignia of monarchy and escorted by troops from every part of the Commonwealth, through streets lined with cheering crowds to Buckingham Palace.

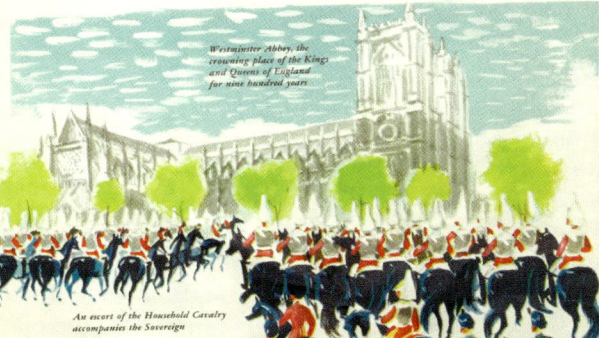

The Processional Route

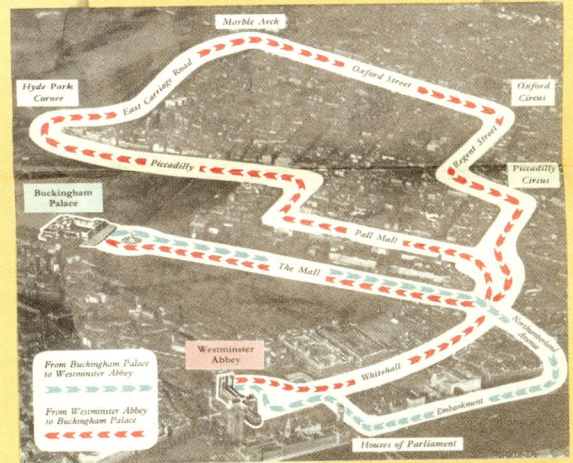

Marble Arch
Hyde Park Corner
Oxford Street
Oxford Circus
East Carriage Road
Piccadilly
Regent Street
Piccadilly Circus
Buckingham Palace
Pall Mall
The Mall
Westminster Abbey
Whitehall
Embankment
Houses of Parliament

From Buckingham Palace to Westminster Abbey
From Westminster Abbey to Buckingham Palace

Aerofilms Ltd.

Westminster Abbey, the crowning place of the Kings and Queens of England for nine hundred years

An escort of the Household Cavalry accompanies the Sovereign

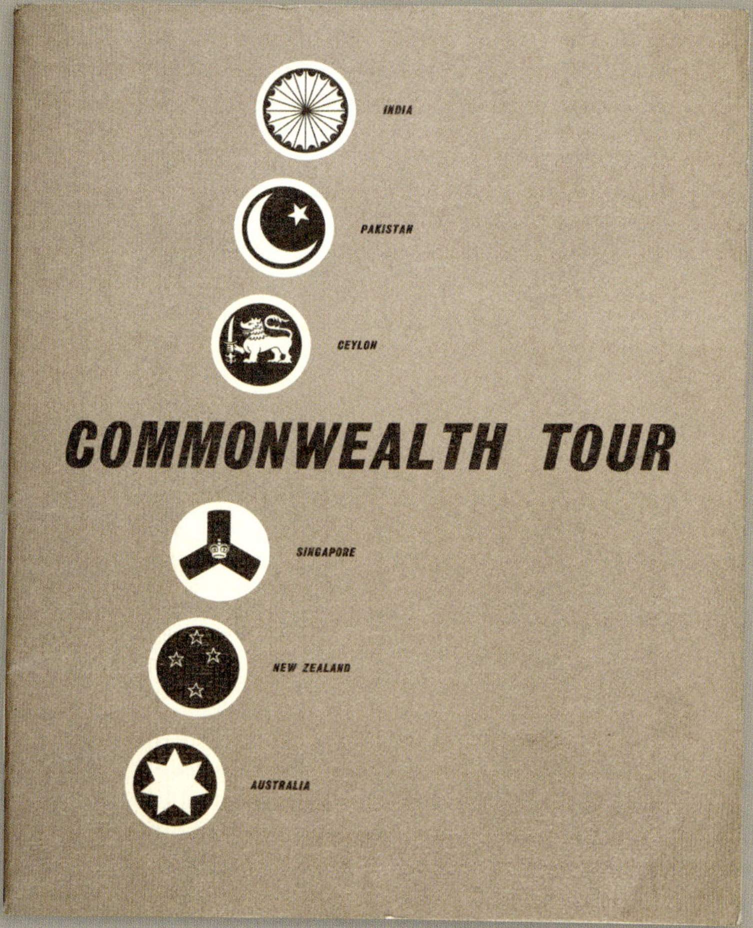
INDIA
PAKISTAN
CEYLON
COMMONWEALTH TOUR
SINGAPORE
NEW ZEALAND
AUSTRALIA

and sixpence and was targeted largely at the overseas market. The preface set out its objectives:

> This book is for those who want to know something about the everyday life of the people in Britain ... about some of the things not normally recorded in the travel guides. It shows how the British people have risen to the demands made on them in the years since the war in the fight for solvency, and how their efforts have been crowned with success. Outwardly Britain may show little change, but a glance beneath the surface will show that within the 'old' Britain there is a new, very lively country, far along the road to recovery...

As evidence of Britain's 'vigorous industrial recovery' the preface cites the suspension of Marshall Aid eighteen months earlier than expected and quotes *The New York Times*' endorsement: 'By its austerity and self-sacrifice through lean years, by hard work and by paying the *highest taxes of any democratic people in the world* [my emphasis] ...Britain deserves full credit for this remarkable recovery.' However, there is a further sting in the tail for the people who had already been taxed so heavily, which did not form part of the narrative to the festival: '...but there is now the heavy load of rearmament to be borne – and nobody doubts that such a programme calls for sacrifice.' This would have come as news to the people who flocked to the festival and the fun rides in Battersea Park. Revealingly, *Britain Now* was divided into the following chapters: 'Trade Vital to Britain', 'Industry Makes the Grade', 'Building for Today and Tomorrow', 'What of Britain's People? ' (Fig. 44) and 'Britain and the Commonwealth and Defence'. The chapter 'What of Britain's People?' drew on familiar images of the nation at work and play (Fig. 45).

The exhibits on the South Bank, together with those in the Pleasure Gardens in Battersea Park, attracted almost sixteen-and-a-half million visitors, and the historian Kenneth O. Morgan referred to it as a 'triumphant success'.[62] Yet, as Dylan Thomas noted, people liked the festival not because it was nationalistic or educational, but because it was 'magical and parochial', with whimsical touches like Emett's nonsense machine, the Dome of Discovery (which inspired, fifty years later, the Millennium Dome) and the strange-looking Skylon, with its vertical, cigar-shaped tower supported by cables, which gave the impression that it was floating above the ground (critics suggested this structure mirrored the British economy of the time by having no clear means of support!). For some, the Festival of Britain became a 'beacon for change' that proved immensely popular with thousands of elite visitors

---

48. *The Coronation of Her Majesty Queen Elizabeth II.* A large wallchart outlining, for both home and overseas consumption: [the] 'splendid pageantry and solemn ritual of a ceremony which is rooted in the ancient traditions of British history. On this historic occasion Her Majesty carries with her the loyal wishes of the peoples of the Commonwealth and Empire, to which the Crown is the link which unites a great family of many nations, states and races, for a long and prosperous reign.' The feel-good factor was soon to be punctured by the humiliation of the Suez Crisis in 1956 and the subsequent realisation that Britain's position (and Empire) in the world had diminished. (BL, BS/81/19)

49. *Commonwealth Tour.* A celebratory pamphlet detailing Prime Minister Harold Macmillan's 1958 tour of the Commonwealth. (BL, PP/113/34A)

and millions of ordinary members of the public. It helped to reshape British arts, crafts, designs and sports for a generation.[63] But was it the showpiece for the inventiveness and genius of British scientists and technologists that the Labour government had planned for? To the discerning eye Britain was quite obviously no longer the workshop of the world. Certainly, the newsreels and films depicting the design aspect of the festival reveal rather impoverished exhibits – with the exception of quality luxury goods such as pottery and glass.[64] The government had committed itself to an information policy designed to project an image abroad of confidence and economic recovery and a celebration of the achievements of a new, socialist Britain (Fig. 46) – but the gap between the image and the reality was too wide to bridge.

Always planned as a temporary exhibition, the Festival of Britain ran for five months before closing in September 1951. Nevertheless, the *Manchester Guardian* deemed it a 'moderately successful adventure' and the Archbishop of Canterbury, closing the event in the place of an ailing King George VI, declared it a 'real family party'.[65] It had been a popular success and turned over a profit. At one level the Festival of Britain was a heartwarming spectacle of obligatory pleasure taken very seriously, like National Service or a dose of cod liver oil. In the month that followed the closure, however, a new Conservative government was elected to power. Prime Minister Winston Churchill considered the festival an expensive embarrassment and a staged piece of socialist propaganda (although he did attend). David Eccles, the new Minister for Works, compared it unfavourably to Albania [sic] and said that he was 'unwilling to become the caretaker of empty and deteriorating structures'. The order was quickly made to level the South Bank site, removing almost all trace of the 1951 Festival of Britain. The only feature to remain was the Royal Festival Hall, which is now a Grade I listed building.

The Festival of Britain came out at an important transitional time for Great Britain. The acquisition of an atomic bomb and the rearmament programme – so important for the Attlee government – had, to some extent, obscured the country's declining position in world affairs. The truth of the matter was that Britain was losing an Empire and had not yet found a role. The 'afterglow' of the festival did not last for long – it was rapidly eclipsed by the Coronation of Queen Elizabeth II in 1953 (Fig. 48) – and the feel-good factor was soon to be punctured by the humiliation of the Suez Crisis and the subsequent realisation that Britain's position in the world had diminished.

In spite of the popular success of the Festival of Britain, the work of the COI, especially the overseas information services, continued to be viewed with suspicion by some and as an unnecessary expense by others. The gross Vote for the COI fell from nearly £4.5 million in 1947–48 to just over £1.6 million in 1955–56. With the exception of 1953–54, the period preceding the Suez Crisis saw the lowest level of post–war government spending on information services (about £10 million, which included spending on the British Council), paradoxically at a time when the need was for greater – not reduced –propaganda activity.

Having replaced Labour in the 1951 General Election, the Conservative Party would remain in power for the rest of the decade – indeed, until Labour returned to power in 1964. The COI continued to work assiduously for its new political masters (although initially it had few friends in Churchill's Cabinet), exhorting the people to 'Keep Britain Tidy', to observe the Highway Code when in the towns and cities and in the countryside to 'Follow the Country Code', to eat and drink more healthily, and to protect themselves against nuclear annihilation. All these campaigns will be discussed in the next chapter. Abroad, Prime Minister Harold Macmillan's 1958 tour of the Commonwealth (Figs. 49a and b) was widely covered and served to convince the nation that, in spite of hemorrhaging its Empire, Britain remained the fulcrum that held the Commonwealth together. In terms of overseas publicity, the shifting power relations within the Commonwealth led to a reduction in the output of general background material, which was directed instead to the newly independent territories. As a result, publications such as 'The British Way of Life' series of pamphlets and the magazine *Commonwealth Today* were discontinued. Instead, emphasis was placed on economic and industrial themes, and on publications addressed to specialised readerships rather than to a wide general public.

The 1960s began as very much a continuation of the 1950s – the so-called Swinging Sixties did not really emerge until the latter half of the decade and then only for some. For the COI, however, the 1960s and 1970s offered new challenges of modern information management. Public information is something of a misnomer. Although the government is placing before the people selected information – about, for example, healthy lifestyles, the need for protection in war and the importance of keeping Britain tidy – it is nonetheless doing so in order not just to inform but also to guide and shape the behaviour of ordinary people. Certainly in the 1940s and 1950s, in the aftermath of victory in war, successive governments, but particular the reforming Labour government, were appealing to the ideal of citizenship – of helping to develop an informed electorate towards the pragmatic use of information as a means of persuasion and a tool for engineering consent. When the Conservatives came to office there was a discernable shift away from such an idealistic vision. Instead of lofty ideals of recovery and building a 'New Jerusalem' for its citizens, the rest of the decade laid the framework for a more-pragmatic implementation of modern information management. It is to the public information campaigns of the 1960s and 1970s that I now wish to turn. ♔

Use the Green Cross Code

CHAPTER THREE

THE SWINGING SIXTIES

It has been said that if the 1950s were in black and white, then the 1960s were in Technicolor. Few decades have had the breadth of impact as the 1960s, from protest and war to the Space Race, The Beatles, innovative technologies, fashion and politics. The COI's services continued to expand in the 1960s, both at home and abroad, as it responded to these seismic cultural shifts. The COI provided publicity for Britain at great exhibitions like the 1967 Montreal Expo and British Weeks, which showcased the work of British companies in cities around the world. The rapid growth of television (92 per cent of households had TV sets by 1970[1]) offered a massive new platform for public communication and the COI launched a number of major campaigns alerting the public to the dangers of smoking, urging them to drive carefully and reminding them of their social responsibilities to 'Keep Britain Tidy' and to 'Watch out! There's a thief about!'

LIVING WITH CODES

Britain has a thing about codes. A code can be summarised as 'a set of rules outlining social norms, responsibilities and/or standards adhered to by a society, class, or individual'. These codes can sometimes have statutory status and be enshrined in law. A revealing aspect of British society since 1945 has been the introduction of specific codes establishing frameworks, or statutory rules, that bind individuals into agreed modes of social conduct – normally because it is believed that accepting such codes will contribute to the welfare of the individual and society as a whole ('stakeholdership' in modern parlance). A major feature of the COI's work since its inception has been codifying good and bad behaviour, and exhorting the general public to behave in a particular way. These post-1945 codes of behaviour embraced both individuals and the collective – they govern how we drive, how we consume alcohol, how pedestrians negotiate roads, how we maintain a sense of tidiness in the countryside and in the urban conurbations, how we prepare food, how we tackle crime, how we plan to have families, how we look after our children, and even how we can safely use food-slicing machines![2]

HIGHWAY CODE

One of the first codes to be introduced after the war was the one that governed the way motorists should drive once they had passed their driving test. The Highway Code is a set of information, advice, guides and mandatory rules for all road users and pedestrians to promote road safety. The first edition was published in 1931 and contained basic advice, including the arm signals to be given by drivers and police officers controlling traffic. After the war, responsibility for the Highway Code fell to the COI, whose task it was to reflect the rapidly changing nature of driving on Britain's roads, using the new technology to disseminate such messages (Figs. 50a and b). Tramway rules (which had been erased in the 1950s) returned to the Highway Code in 1994 after the first modern tram systems in Britain had been reintroduced. Motorway driving was included in the fifth edition. The sixth edition, in 1968, used photographs as well as drawings for the first time, and also updated the illustrations of road signs to take the new 'continental' designs into account (Figs. 51 and 52a and b). *The Highway Code* published in its seventy-page 1978 edition introduced the Green Cross Code (more of this later) for pedestrians and Orange Badges for less able drivers. The published format was changed to a 'taller' size in the 1990s, and the Highway Code itself caught up with developments in social media in 2011 when it joined Twitter and Facebook. A Highway Code app followed in 2012.

---

50. *The Highway Code*. The first post-war edition of *The Highway Code* was published in 1946, the year that the COI was established. It is similar, in fact, to the first edition in 1931, but with a new, ornate cover. The contents inside, however, consisted of very simple drawings in black and white. Each edition since 1946 has contained an introduction from the Minister of Transport recommending that drivers and pedestrians familiarise themselves with the contents. In the 1946 edition the Minister (Alfred Barnes) urges pedestrians and drivers to study the Code and respect its provisions: 'To do so. In fact, is a *moral* duty.' (BL, PP/37/26A)

THE

HIGHWAY

CODE

To be purchased direct from
H.M. STATIONERY OFFICE
at the following addresses:

WITH AN APPENDIX
INCLUDING DIAGRAMS
OF SIGNALS AND SIGNS

York House, Kingsway, London, W.C.2; 423 Oxford
Street, London, W.1; P.O. Box 569, London, S.E.1;
13a Castle Street, Edinburgh, 2; 1 St. Andrew's Crescent,
Cardiff; 39 King Street, Manchester, 2; Tower Lane,
Bristol, 1; 2 Edmund Street, Birmingham, 3; 80 Chichester
Street, Belfast; or from any Bookseller.
S.O. Code No. 88-80 0-46*

THE

HIGHWAY

CODE

ISSUED BY THE MINISTER OF TRANSPORT
WITH THE AUTHORITY OF PARLIAMENT
FOR THE GUIDANCE AND SAFETY OF ALL
ROAD USERS

WITH AN APPENDIX
INCLUDING DIAGRAMS
OF SIGNALS AND SIGNS

LONDON: PUBLISHED BY
HER MAJESTY'S STATIONERY OFFICE
ONE PENNY NET

APPENDIX

Signals to be given by Police
Constables and others
engaged in the regulation of traffic, as
viewed by the driver for whom they
are intended.

"Stop" signal (vehicle approaching
from the front).

"Stop" signal (vehicle
approaching from
behind).

"Stop" signal (vehicles
approaching from the front
and from behind simul-
taneously).

Drivers should note that, after they have
stopped, the Police Constable may lower
his hand or use it for giving other signals,
but they must not move on until signalled
to do so.

14

Release Signals, given according
to circumstances, are shown below.

To bring on a vehicle from
the front. (A beckoning
movement.)

To bring on a
vehicle from
behind.

To bring on vehicles
from right or left. (A
beckoning movement.)

Drivers should be specially careful to distinguish the
"Proceed" signal intended for them, from signals
intended for other traffic. This will be shown primarily
by the Constable looking in their direction.

15

THE HIGHWAY CODE

INCLUDING MOTORWAY RULES

PP/37/32A

HER MAJESTY'S STATIONERY OFFICE · PRICE 6d NET

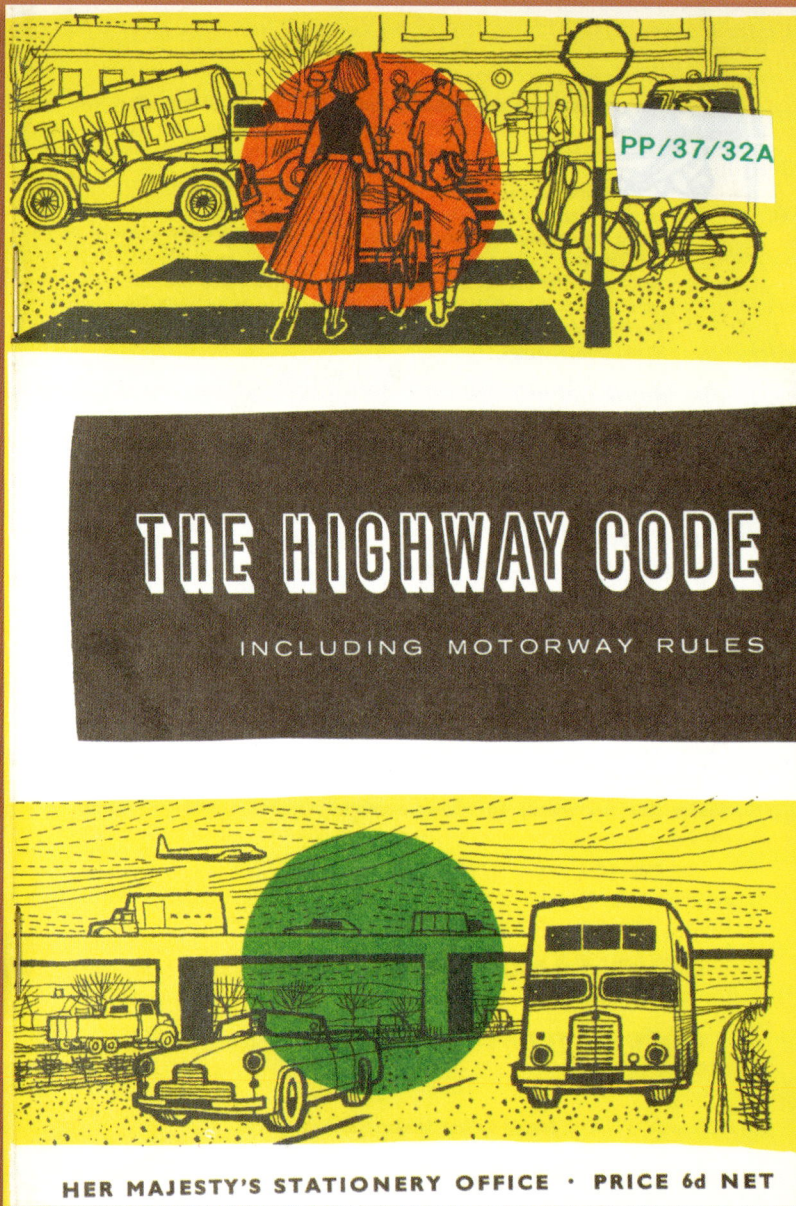

51. *The Highway Code.* The 1967 edition, priced at sixpence, included motorway rules. The sixth edition, in 1968, used photographs as well as drawings for the first time, and also updated the illustrations of road signs to take the new 'continental' designs into account. By 1970, 17 million copies had been sold (in addition to a substantial free distribution to certain categories of road users). (BL, PP/37/32A)

52. *The Highway Code.* The 1970 edition is much more glossy and reflects the proliferation of traffic and warning signs. However, it still contains the arm signals to be given by police officers in the event that they need to control traffic. (BL, PP/37/25A)

SIGNALS BY AUTHORISED PERSONS

STOP

Vehicle approaching from behind

Vehicle approaching from front

Vehicles approaching from both front and behind

COME ON

Beckoning on a vehicle from the front

Beckoning on a vehicle from the side

Beckoning on a vehicle from behind

38

TRAFFIC SIGNS
Signs giving orders – *mostly circular*

Those with red circles — mostly prohibitive

Maximum speed limit

Maximum speed limit 70 mph

Stop and Give Way

Give way to traffic on major road

No entry

School Crossing Patrol

No waiting

No stopping ('Clearway')

URBAN CLEARWAY Monday to Friday

No right turn

No left turn

No U turns

No overtaking

Give priority to vehicles from opposite direction

Except for access

All motor vehicles prohibited (plate may qualify)

Buses and coaches prohibited

Lorries prohibited

No cycling or moped-riding

Play Street 8 am to sunset except for access

All vehicles prohibited (plate gives details)

Total weight limit

Axle weight limit

Width limit

End Plate below sign at end of prohibition

No pedestrians

Blue circles with no red border — mostly compulsory

Minimum speed limit

End of minimum speed limit

Ahead only

Turn left (right if symbol reversed)

Turn left ahead (right if symbol reversed)

Keep left (right if symbol reversed)

Pass either side

Route for cyclists and moped riders (compulsory)

One way

Plate supplementing Turn signs

37

Warning signs – *mostly triangular*

STOP 100 yds

Distance to STOP sign ahead

Cross roads

Roundabout

T junction

Staggered junction

GIVE WAY 50 yds

Distance to GIVE WAY sign ahead

REDUCE SPEED NOW Plate below some signs

Side road

Sharp deviation of route to left (or right if chevrons reversed)

Bend to right (or left if symbol reversed)

Double bend first to left (may be reversed)

Series of bends

Two-way traffic straight ahead

Two-way traffic crosses one-way road

Traffic merges from left

Traffic joins from right

Road narrows on offside (nearside if symbol reversed)

Road narrows on both sides

Dual carriageway ends

Steep hill downwards

Steep hill upwards

Children

Single file traffic

Single file in each direction

Pedestrian crossing

Traffic signals

Hump bridge

Uneven road

School

Plate with CHILDREN sign at a school

Single track road

Road wide enough for only one line of traffic

Road works

Change to opposite carriageway (may be reversed)

Right-hand lane closed (symbols may be varied)

Slippery road

Patrol 200 yds

Plate with CHILDREN sign near school crossing patrol

Level crossing with automatic half-barriers ahead

Level crossing with other barrier or gate ahead

Level crossing without gate or barrier ahead

Location of level crossing without gate or barrier

'Count-down' markers approaching concealed level crossing

38

Warning Signs continued

Height limit (e.g. low bridge)

Available width of headroom indicated

Opening or swing bridge

Quayside or river bank

Headroom 16'6"

Cattle

Wild animals

Horses or ponies

Ford

Worded warning sign

Overhead electric cable; plate indicates maximum safe height for vehicles

Distance to hazard

1 mile

Falling or fallen rocks

Low-flying aircraft or sudden aircraft noise

For 2 miles Distance over which hazard extends

Dust cloud

Other danger; plate indicates nature of danger

Direction signs – *mostly rectangular*

Maidenhead A4
Gerrards Cross
Windsor A331
Datchet (B376)
Uxbridge Watford A412

Scarborough A64
Pickering A169
York A64

Bedford A6

Datchet B470
Windsor
London (A4)
Slough

Crowland B1040
Peterboro A47
Wisbech A47

Northchurch 1½
Wigginton 4
Chesham 5
Potten End 2½
Gaddesden 3½
Ashridge 4

Signs on approaches to junctions — green background on primary routes, white background on other routes. Blue bordered signs show local places. Routes in brackets are turnings off road indicated.

39

THE SWINGING SIXTIES

119

ROAD SAFETY AND THE PUBLIC

One highly effective piece of public health legislation in recent years has tackled motor-vehicle safety and the compulsory wearing of seatbelts. In 1951 there were two million cars registered on the roads of Britain, a figure that rose by 250 per cent over the next ten years. The rapid growth of car ownership in turn gave rise to government road safety campaigns.

The first post-war information film on road safety launched by the COI was *Pedestrian Crossing* in 1948. It starred Richard Massingham and it adopted a humorous approach to show both pedestrians and drivers the correct procedure at pedestrian crossings. Pedestrian crossings had been introduced in the 1930s, but research showed that in the aftermath of the war they were being ignored. Massingham played Mr A ('a perfectly straightforward type of person'), except when it came to crossing a road. The narrator points out that there are two ways of crossing a road: 'Your way – and I must say it isn't terribly attractive – and this way. You see these two rows of studs? All you have to do is walk between the studs and you won't get knocked down. You see the motorist has a legal obligation to give pedestrians right of way at crossings. Now have a shot yourself...'[3]

Following the launch of the film, the Ministry of Transport experimented with different pedestrian crossing markings to help improve visibility and by 1951 the black-and-white stripes with the Belisha beacons (named after Lord Belisha, the Minister of Transport who introduced them in the 1930s) on either side of the road were approved, and became known as 'Zebra' crossings.

TUFTY'S TIPS

Overlapping campaigns, designed to promote road safety, encouraged children to observe the short step-by-step road-crossing procedure of the Green Cross Code and to join the Tufty Club. Road safety first became a concern during World War I when blackouts led to a rise in the number of accidents between cars and pedestrians. The forerunner of the Royal Society for the Prevention of Accidents (RoSPA) was established in 1916 (the name was changed in 1941), and in 1920 a 'Think Safety' campaign was introduced to deal with the one-and-a-half million new motorists who took to the road following the end of the war. In 1931 *British Movietone News* made a film for safety week that was shown to ten million people, and the Ministry of Transport published *The Highway Code*. The RoSPA was represented on the committee responsible for compiling the code. In 1951 National Children's Safety Week was held and it was considered to be the most effective campaign in the history of accident prevention. Among those providing support were radio stars Kenneth Horne and Wilfred Pickles. Child road fatalities fell to the lowest total for twenty-five years. Extra effort was put into road safety as petrol rationing ended in May 1950 and a rapid increase in accidents was anticipated.[4]

A poster *Road Accident Deaths to Children and Teenagers* issued by the RoSPA attempted to shock with numbers, showing an astonishing 1,534 children and teenagers killed on British roads in 1960 (and then breaking down the deaths into categories, in smaller graphs).[5] The following year, the RoSPA set up the Tufty Club with the specific aim of improving road safety among children under five. Tufty Fluffytail was an iconic red squirrel who was instrumental in helping millions of children to learn about road safety from the 1950s to the 1990s. Created in 1953, Tufty and his Furryfolk friends, including Policeman Badger, Willy Weasel, Minnie Mole and Mrs Owl, helped to impart straightforward and easily understandable safety messages to children. It struck a chord, so in 1961 the Tufty Club came into being to help disseminate the message, to be targeted at pre-school children. The Tufty Club grew to 25,000 branches and an estimated two million children were members in the early 1970s. Parents were involved too, and the Tufty Club issued tens of thousands of road safety books to families.

THE GREEN CROSS MAN

The Green Cross Man is a costumed superhero created in 1970 as an aid to teaching young children the Green Cross Code and for promoting general road safety. Later, the Green Cross Code became a multi-media campaign to enable pedestrians to cross streets safely. It has undergone several changes over the years, but the basic tenets — 'Stop, Look, Listen, Think — have remained more or less the same. One exception was the film made by the COI in 1967, entitled *Kerb Drill with Batman*. It featured Adam West, the American TV Batman, who is seen in London ('Hello citizens!') urging children to: 'Be smart, be safe. Always know your Kerb Drill.'[6] The drill was also known as the Road Safety Code and it briefly forged a bridge between Tufty and the Green Cross Man (Fig. 53).

The Green Cross Man was famously played by Dave Prowse, the man who later starred as Darth Vader in the original *Star Wars* movies. A six-feet-seven-inches tall bodybuilder and former Mr Universe contestant, Prowse was chosen to bring the Green Cross Code 'to life' and he remained the road safety superhero character for fourteen years.

The 'Green Cross Code' series was part of a wider campaign to raise awareness of the Green Cross Code, and by this time Tufty Clubs were also reinforcing the lessons of the Code. Introduced in 1971, the Green Cross Code procedure and campaigns specifically targeted children, who in the early 1970s accounted for half of all casualties on the roads[7] (Figs. 54a, b and c, 55 and 56a, b and c).

Following the launch of the Green Cross Code, casualties dropped by 11 per cent. But six months later the rate was as high as before. The need to constantly relay road safety messages explains why so many public information films for pedestrians were frequent releases. In 1975, for example, the COI published a pamphlet setting out three new campaigns aimed at children, motorists and parents. Once again, the Green Cross Man was the figurehead.[8] In order to bring home the horror of child casualties on the road, the COI stepped up its campaign and produced a

The Green Cross code ✗ an

1. First find a safe place to cross, then stop. It is safer to cross at some places than others. Subways. Footbridges. Zebra and Pelican crossings. Traffic lights. Where there is a policeman, or a lollipop man, or a traffic warden.
If you can't find any good crossing places like these, choose a place where you can see clearly along the roads in all directions.
Don't try to cross between parked cars. Move to a clear space and always give drivers a chance to see you clearly.

2. Stand on th... Don't stand ... Stop a little ... away from tr... anything is ...

4. If traffic is coming, let it pass. Look all round again. If there's any traffic near, let it go past. Then look round again and listen to make sure no other traffic is coming.

5. When ther... traffic nea... straight ac... the road. W... there is no... traffic near... safe to cross. If there i... something in the distance do not cross unless you're **certain**... there's plenty of time. Remember, even if tra... is a long way off, it ma... coming very fast. Whe... it's safe, walk straigh... across the road – don'...

...w to use it.

ar the kerb.
e of the pavement.
he kerb – where you'll be
you can still see if

STAY-
BRUCE!

3. Look all round for traffic and listen.

Traffic may be coming from all directions, so take care to look along every road. And listen too, because you can sometimes hear traffic before you can see it.

LOOK ALL ROUND AND LISTEN.

NO TRAFFIC NEAR, WALK **STRAIGHT** ACROSS.

6. Keep looking and listening for traffic while you cross.

Once you're in the road, keep looking and listening in case you didn't see some traffic – or in case other traffic suddenly appears.

KEEP LOOKING AND LISTENING.

53. *The Green Cross Code and how to use it.* This illustrated poster was issued in the mid-1970s to schools and youth organisations, and it sets out the Green Cross Code in six, easy steps. Note it is the older boy, wearing the Green Cross T-shirt, who is taking the younger girl and her dog (Bruce) through the dos and don'ts of crossing a road safely in an urban environment. (BL, PP/234/41A)

54. *Take It from Green Cross Man.* Three posters from the mid-1970s, featuring Dave Prowse as the superhero, offer three different instructions on how to cross a road safely. (BL, PP/251/5A/8A/9A)

55. *Use the Green Cross Code.* In 1978 the Green Cross Man was joined by a Green Cross Woman to dispense the same advice! (BL, PP/253/16A)

Always Stop near the kerb
Use the Green Cross Code
Use the Green Cross code
PP/253/16A
COI
Printed in England for Her Majesty's Stationery Office by Leonard Ripley & Co. Ltd. London. Dd596579 Pro 11490
Issued by the Department of Transport, the Scottish Development Department and the Welsh Office.

"Always stop at the kerb. OK!"
says Joe Bugner

BE SMART
BE SAFE

the Green Cross code

"Keep yo
ears ope

"Don't cross near parked cars" says Kevin Keegan

56. *Be smart, be safe: Use the Green Cross Code.* The COI also used celebrities to enhance the importance of adhering to *all* aspects of the Green Cross Code. Here the footballer Kevin Keegan, the boxer Joe Bugner and the pop-star Alvin Stardust have donned the T-shirt to publicise a new campaign slogan and dispense different aspects of the Code. (BL, PP/235/61A/62A/63A)

Watch out for Sandra
running to the shops

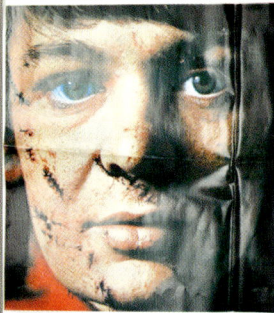

"Yes, you can go through a
windscreen at only 30mph!"

Mr. P. Flaxman of Kingham.

Clunk Click even on the <u>shortest</u> trips.

'I never wore a seat belt.
I couldn't be bothered with
the inconvenience.'

Clunk Click <u>every</u> trip.

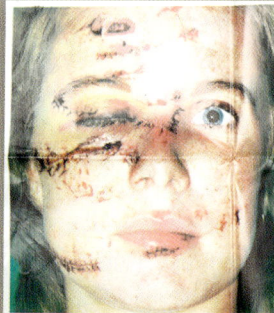

"You can get a face like mine
in <u>your</u> local high street."

Miss B. J. Clark of New Eltham.

Clunk Click even on the <u>shortest</u> trips.

PROTECTING THE PEOPLE

128

multi-media onslaught intended to shock the country. This included a number of posters and TV advertisements that showed children that were about to be hit by an oncoming vehicle because they had not followed the Green Cross Code (Fig. 57). It had an immediate impact; the number of children killed on the roads had fallen to 505 by the end of 1975, the lowest death toll since the 1950s. By 2003 the figure was as low as 171 children. However, with as many as 3,929 children also being seriously injured on the roads each year, the COI's investment in road safety campaigns continued unabated throughout the 1970s and 1980s.

Through a combination of factors, including safety campaigns, the annual death toll of children and teenagers diminished considerably. But pedestrians represented only part of the problem. Drivers of motor vehicles were the other target. For this, the COI adopted a two-pronged attack: to encourage drivers and passengers to use seatbelts; and to warn drivers of the dangers of drinking while driving.

'CLUNK, CLICK EVERY TRIP'

The introduction in Britain of seatbelt legislation in 1983 led to a 15 per cent reduction in motor accident patients being brought to hospital, a reduction by a quarter in those requiring admissions to wards, and a similar fall in bed-occupancy rates. There were fewer patients with severe injuries, and notably a reduction in face, eye, brain and lung injuries. A key task for public health authorities was the education, advocacy and lobbying required in advance of the legislation to ensure its acceptability and subsequent implementation, as a result of which 'Clunk, Click every trip' became the familiar slogan of a series of public information films and large posters (Figs. 58a, b and c). The campaign started in January 1971, featuring the now-disgraced BBC disc jockey Jimmy Savile, building on an earlier series led by television presenter Shaw Taylor. (In the United States, a similar campaign used the slogan 'Click it or Ticket'.)

In 1969–70 the COI had used Shaw Taylor (famous for *Police 5*, a long-running five-minute television programme first broadcast in 1962 that appealed to the public to help solve crimes) to gently persuade the public to use their seatbelts, which manufacturers had been legally obliged to fit in the front seats of vehicles since 1965 but were not yet compulsory to be worn. Taylor used the slogan 'Clunk Clink':

> **Shaw Taylor:** *After all, you wouldn't drive off without hearing the 'clunk' of the car door closing. Let's add another sound; the 'click' of a seatbelt being fastened. Clunk, Click. That makes sound sense, doesn't it? ... Please remember to clunk click, because your seatbelt is their security.* [Images of young children then appeared on the screen.]

---

57. *Watch out for Sandra running to the shops.* Giving names to the children in the posters was intended to bring home the human cost of road casualties. Without explicitly showing what might happen, the campaign left it to the audience's imagination. A similar poster showed 'Billy behind that parked car'. (BL, PP/253/18A)

58. *Clunk Click every trip.* Three hard-hitting posters from 1978. The quotations from the victims of road accidents together with the tragic photographs of their injuries was intended to provide powerful emotional evidence for using seatbelts 'on every trip'... even 'the shortest trips'. (BL, PP/250/64A, 63A and BL, PP/245/88A)

When Savile took over in 1971, the campaign became much more hard-hitting, and to 'Clunk Click' was now added 'every trip'. Typical is the following dialogue from a TV short from 1972:

Jimmy Savile: [sitting in his own car, seatbelt in hand] *It's very likely that 400 of you will be injured in your cars tomorrow. You will be within six miles of home and doing less than 30.*
[Cue shot of young woman driving a black soft-top Mini.]
And it's going to happen to a lot of you ladies. You'll be shopping, collecting the kids, going to the launderette…But for some of you, the face you start out with in the morning won't be the same face you end up with by the evening.
[Cue woman crashing through windscreen, then cut to woman with massive stitched wound on head and bruises under her eyes.]
Why is this happening? Clunk click. It's simple. Clunk the car door. Click the seatbelt. Even if you are just going round the corner. Clunk Click every trip.

A similarly no-holds-barred approach was employed in the accompanying poster campaign. The posters were extremely large, so that they could not be ignored, and the message (which was slightly different for each poster in the campaign) remained simple. The advertisements included graphic sequences of what could

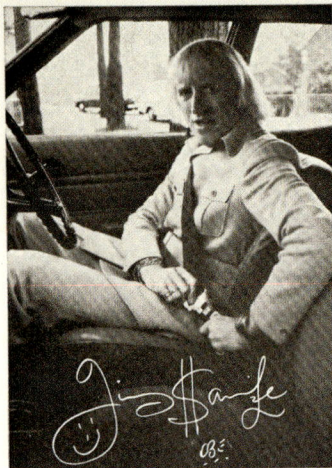

Dear Friend,
 Thanks a 1,000,000 for your Clunk Click letter. How I wish we didn't need to advertise in order to persuade people to wear seat belts, but please continue to help by spreading the message— Clunk click every trip.
 God Bless.
Jimmy Savile, O.B.E

59. *The 'Clunk Click' letters.* The COI's facsimile postcard on behalf of Jimmy Savile (who fronted the campaign), thanking the public for their support and urging them to spread the message …. 'Clunk click every trip'. Note Savile's more-in-sorrow-than-anger view: 'How I wish we didn't need to advertise in order to persuade people to wear seat belts…' (BL, PP/234/30A)

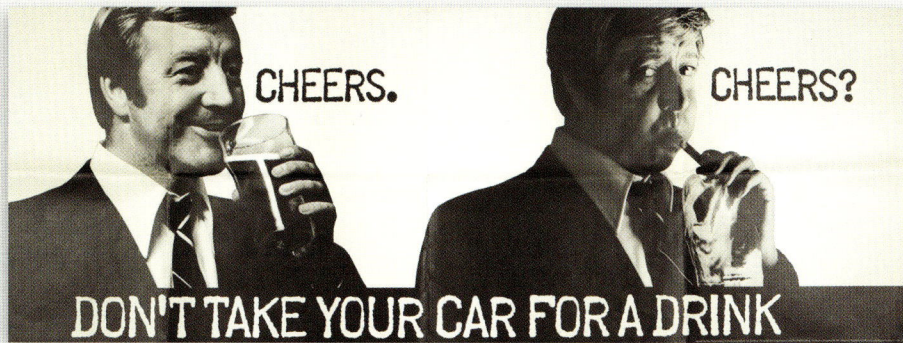

60. *Don't Take Your Car for a Drink.* A 1977 poster that emphasises not the likely horrific injuries that can be sustained from driving when drunk, but the likelihood of being caught by the breathalyser, which had been introduced the previous decade. In 1967 (when the breathalyser had been introduced) the number of road fatalities associated with drink-driving fell from just over 22 per cent to 15 per cent. But between 1969 and 1975 the proportion of crashes where alcohol was a factor climbed steadily to exceed 35 per cent. By 1979 the total number of drink-driving related deaths was 1,640, but by 2012 this figure had dropped to 290. (BL, PP/245/23A)

happen to an unbelted person in the front of a car during a crash at 30 miles per hour or faster, showing drivers being thrown through the windscreen and an image of a disfigured woman survivor. In spite of the 'Clunk Click' campaign, successive governments proposed, but failed to deliver, seatbelt legislation throughout the 1970s. Nevertheless, they helped to lay the groundwork for compulsory seatbelt use in the front seat of a vehicle, which came into force on 31 January 1983. There is no doubt that by using 'Clunk Click every trip' the COI's road safety campaign discovered a memorable 'strapline' and the slogan continued to be used until 1993.[9] Judging by the number of letters of support that Savile received, the campaign proved highly popular with the public. So much so that the COI produced a facsimile postcard for Savile, consisting of a signed message and a photograph (Fig. 59), thanking the public for their support and encouraging them to continue to support the campaign.[10]

'DON'T DRINK AND DRIVE'

Overlapping with 'Clunk Click' was the 'Don't Drink and Drive' campaign (Fig. 60). The Central Office of Information (COI) ran the government's road safety campaigns until 2000, when 'THINK!' was established as the government's designated road safety campaign. In 1964 the first-ever drink-drive campaign was launched three years before drink-drive laws were introduced. It first aired on 7 November 1964, and today's viewers will find its polite approach mildly amusing, charming even.

Worried by the rising tide of deaths, the Ministry of Transport and the COI commissioned Halas and Batchelor to create the forty-second photo-montage film. In stark contrast to the shock tactics deployed by the government's current 'THINK!' anti-drink-drive television campaign, it gently depicts an office party in full

61. *A variation on a theme.* Two posters applying anti-alcohol codes normally associated with road safety to flying and aircraft safety. *Think Before You Drink Before You Fly* and *Fly with Prudence*. A case of stating the obvious, but presumably the government felt that it had to be stated regardless. (BL, PP/154/12L and BL, PP/125/22A)

swing to a jaunty rendition of 'Jingle Bells'. Smartly dressed workers wear party hats, bat a balloon around the office – and happily quaff stiff drinks. 'Drinking and driving are dangerous', the commentator announces. 'Four single whiskies and the risk of accident can be twice as great.' A cartoon graphic superimposes a growing number of whisky tumblers against the silhouette of a partygoer's head as the commentator continues: 'Six single whiskies and the risk can be six times as great; eight, and the risk can be twenty-five times as great.' As the couple leave the party to drive home together the commentator says: 'If he's been drinking, don't let him drink and drive. Don't ask a man to drink... and drive.' The campaign slogan deliberately put the emphasis on 'the other fellow' and had the backing of 'an eminent psychologist who was consulted'.[11] From a contemporary perspective, the advertisement would be considered sexist. The wording not only reveals how, at the time, it was expected that the man in a couple would drive, but also indicates that excessive consumption of alcohol was a predominantly male problem. However, men – particularly young ones – have been the main targets of half a century of drink-driving advertising.

In 1964 it was a crime to be in charge of a car while 'unfit to drive through drink or drugs'. But there was no legal drink-driving limit and no test to determine whether or not someone was unfit to drive. Motorists suspected of having drunk too much

THINK
BEFORE YOU
DRINK
BEFORE YOU
FLY

**even a small quantity of alcohol
taken within 8 hours of flying
can affect your judgement and cause a fatal accident**

alcohol were asked to walk in a straight line. In 1966 Reginald Mount and Eileen Evans designed for the COI a very simple poster consisting of the words: *Don't Ask a Man to Drink and Drive*. The words are pink and in capitals and set against a black background. The white lines running vertically down the centre of the poster represent the walking test that police officers sometimes applied. Once again, the poster targets the man as the problem. While the early campaigns now appear dated, it should be remembered that at the time viewers would have seen little wrong in 'having one for the road'.

From 1965 to 1967 death and serious accidents continued to increase, and as a result the COI and the Ministry of Transport agreed on a sustained campaign on all aspects of road safety that would begin in 1968 and last for three years, costing approximately £3 million. A series of interlocking campaigns on separate themes such as 'overtaking', 'turning right', 'use of headlights', 'seatbelts', 'young drivers', 'safety helmets', 'pedestrian safety' and 'drinking and driving'. In addition, a new version of *The Highway Code* and new legislation on seatbelts and tyres were published. Most of the funding was spent on television, but press, cinema and poster advertising and direct mail were also used. By 1969 the Ministry of Transport's own research indicated a general improvement in road safety awareness and in particular a vastly improved recall of the campaign slogan 'You Know It Makes Sense' – now remembered spontaneously by 78 per cent of all drivers.[12]

Educating the public about certain codes of behaviour was not confined to road safety – it literally permeated the whole of human experience and endeavour in Britain from the 1960s onwards (Figs. 61a and b). On the one hand there was the need to provide health and safety advice for a particular industry, which could include quite obscure activities such as the 1968 handbook *Safety in the use of Biscuit-making Machinery* (Fig. 62). On the other hand, propaganda might attempt to shape or even govern individual behaviour – as was the case with the Race Relations Acts. Other campaigns sought to promote patriotism and a sense of duty among its citizens, such as the 'Keep Britain Tidy' campaign.

'KEEP BRITAIN TIDY'

Just as the road safety campaign had encouraged parents and children to be aware of their surroundings when driving or crossing roads, the 'Keep Britain Tidy' campaign encouraged people to take a more-proactive interest in maintaining a clean and healthy environment. Over the last fifty years the 'Keep Britain Tidy' campaign has encouraged the public to put rubbish in the bin and not litter the streets or the countryside. The problem of increasing amounts of litter was highlighted in 1954 by Lady Elizabeth Brunner, chair of the National Federation of Women's Institutes, which passed a resolution to 'Keep Britain Tidy'. Many people had a disposable income for the first time, which meant that they were able to buy more – but this also meant that they could throw more away. More and more everyday items were even being designed to be disposable, which had never been the case before. The momentum

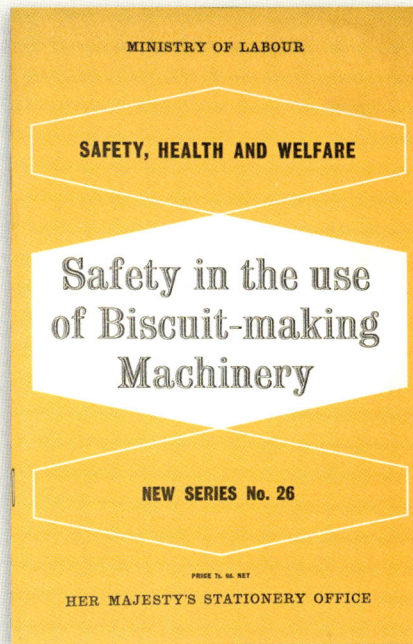

62. *Safety in the Use of Machinery*. Just what you needed to know! When it was not involved with some of the most important social and economic campaigns, a considerable amount of the everyday work of the COI involved rather mundane publications, like these two examples, setting out health and safety regulations for various industries. *Safety in the use of Biscuit-making Machinery* is a handbook published by the COI for the Ministry of Labour in 1968. The handbook provided detailed diagrams of the biscuit-making process and where the hidden danger points lay. Such handbooks covered every conceivable field of economic activity, including the safe use of food-slicing machines! (BL, PP/151/54 and BL, PP127/3A)

generated by the 'Keep Britain Tidy' campaign, in response to the 'throwaway culture' of the 1950s, directly contributed to the first piece of anti-litter legislation, the Litter Act of 1958, with fines of £10 for dropping litter. In 1961 (having registered as a charity in 1960) the campaign became an independent organisation and received government backing. This is where the COI came in. One of the earliest posters was by the designer Royston Cooper (prepared for the Ministry of Housing and Local Government by the COI in 1962), and it played on people's national pride. It consisted of a large British lion flying the Union Flag on his tail while crushing litter under his paw into a bin with the tag line: 'Keep Britain Tidy' (Fig. 63). A few years later, Cooper used the image of the pelican with a large amount of litter in its mouth, reminding people to take their litter home with them. The German-born graphic designer Hans Unger, who had fled the Nazis in the 1930s, designed one of the most threatening posters, depicting a larger-than-life admonishing finger bearing down on a litter transgressor (Fig. 64), while in 1963 Abram Games produced probably the most iconically nationalistic design, in red, white and blue, of a roadsweeper in a

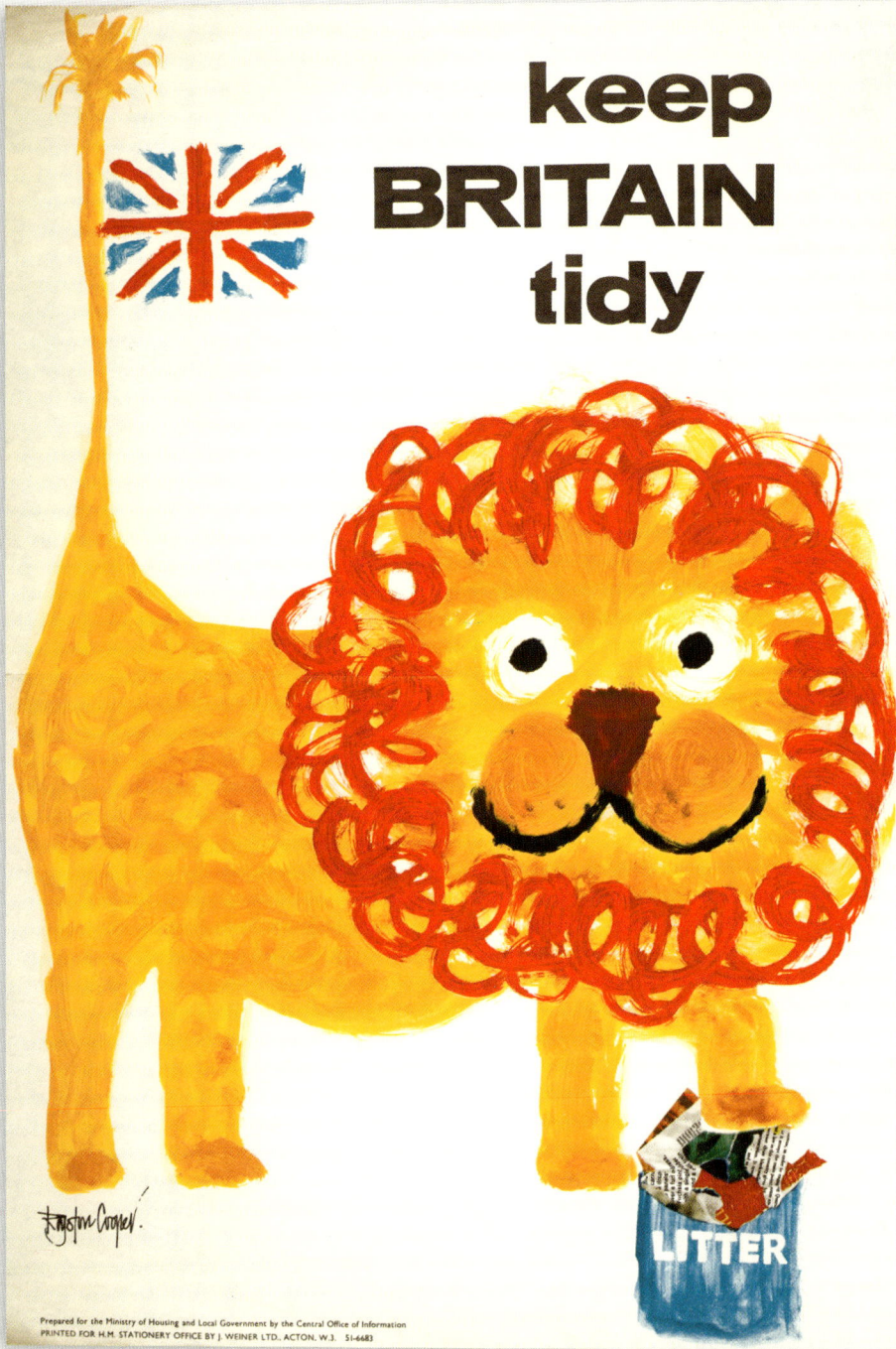

keep
BRITAIN
tidy

LITTER

Prepared for the Ministry of Housing and Local Government by the Central Office of Information
PRINTED FOR H.M. STATIONERY OFFICE BY J. WEINER LTD., ACTON, W.3.   S1-6683

63. *Keep Britain Tidy.* Royston Cooper's 1962 version of the traditional British lion, flying the flag while crushing litter under his paw. (BL, BS/ 81/19)

64. *Keep Britain Tidy.* Hans Unger's strikingly accusative finger bearing down on a litter lout. Hunger had fled the Nazis in the 1930s and after a period in South Africa during the war he moved to Britain in 1948. Delivered in a distinctively utilitarian style, the 1962 design suggests an all-seeing figure, jabbing a giant finger of scorn at someone caught in the act of wilfully dropping litter; authority is firmly rendered in heavy, brightly coloured, brush strokes. Unger was also a distinguished mosaicist, and he designed many posters for London Transport, British Rail, *The Observer* and the General Post Office. (BL, BS/ 81/19)

keep Brita TIDY

65. *Keep Britain Tidy.* Tom Eckersley's deceptively simple design of the smiling blue man in profile, bending to pick up a newspaper (which is photographed to produce a collage-like affect). His arm passes through the I in TIDY. The poster was the winner of the British Poster Design Award in 1963. The posters for the 'Keep Britain Tidy' campaign remain some of the most extraordinarily innovative (and effective) designs commissioned by the COI. (BL, BS/ 81/19)

66. *Keep Britain Tidy.* This poster for the 'Keep Britain Tidy' campaign was produced in 1963 by Abram Games, one of the twentieth century's great graphic designers. The design is a pastiche of Britannia, replaced by a smiling male dressed as a red-white-and-blue roadsweeper, with the wheel of the dustcart representing the Union Jack shield. The figure was referred to by the COI as the 'symbolic road-sweeper'.[13] (BL, BS/ 81/19)

Britannia-like pose with broom in hand and bearing the 'Keep Britain Tidy' slogan on his chest (Fig. 66).

Television also featured in the campaign, and in 1968 *Keep It to Yourself* featured a young Roy Hudd as the shadowy litterbug mischievously dropping litter. The film reveals 'Litter Defence Volunteers' (LDV) striking against 'public enemy number one' – the litter bug. The formation of LDVs was a play on the 'Local Defence Volunteers' (the Home Guard), who formed Britain's last line of defence against invasion during World War II. In 1967 there were reportedly 5,000 'Litter Defence Volunteers' pushing the 'Keep Britain Tidy' slogan. In 1969 the iconic symbol of the 'Tidyman' appeared for the first time on bins and packaging to help deliver the anti-litter message. The Tidyman, an image of a stick figure putting a piece of litter in a wire bin, now appears on most food packaging. In the 1970s and 1980s the 'Keep Britain Tidy' campaign included celebrity endorsements from Abba, Morecambe and Wise, Harry Secombe and footballers such as Michael Owen. The campaign continues to this day, and although it is over fifty years old, litter remains an important issue. In 2005 the COI launched 'Don't be a gimp, Keep Britain Tidy', which targeted 18–24-year-olds – the age group that had been identified as the worst offender, responsible for dropping millions of tons of rubbish in Britain each year.

So far, these posters and films have focused on the urban setting. But the 1958 Litter Act referred to the problem of litter for both urban and rural environments. The COI expended considerable resources on encouraging people to respect the Country Code by keeping it free of litter (Figs. 67, 68, 69 and 70). The National Parks Commission prepared with the COI a series of illustrated mini leaflets containing each aspect of the Country Code in rhyme by the cartoonist and *Punch* contributor Norman Thelwell.[14] Posters appeared in factory canteens, youth clubs, shops, libraries, hotels, schools, pubs, post offices, cafes, railway stations and Butlin's holiday camps. Acceptance of the Country Code was one of a hugely popular series of four Joe and Petunia films made by Nicolas Cartoons between 1968 and 1973. In 1971 the COI released *Joe and Petunia – Acceptance of the Country Code*. Stereotypically drawn northern cartoon characters Yorkshireman Joe (voiced by Peter Hawkins) and his rotund partner Petunia (Wendy Craig), along with the local farmer, comically

---

67. *15 Facts About Litter: A Costly, Dangerous and Dirty Nuisance.* A small pamphlet distributed to homes in Scotland in the early 1960s. The so-called facts concentrated on the cost of litter ('collection of litter in Scotland is estimated to cost over £200,000'); the dangers ('tins and broken bottles at seaside resorts result in thousands of accidents every year, many of them involving personal disability and disfigurement'); and national pride ('In many countries, notably Sweden, Norway, Denmark and Switzerland, litter is not a problem. Yet their laws do not differ greatly from our own. It is the standards of behaviour that differ.'). (BL, PP/36/1A)

68. *Leave No Litter. Take it Home* (1971). What could be nicer than a picnic in an idyllic rural setting on a glorious sunny (and colourful) day? This rather gentle approach adopts the passive persuasive image of joy and pride in the countryside. The ten rules of the Country Code are set out in this poster – 'Keep dogs under proper control', and so on – as they were in most posters for this particular campaign. (BL, PP/164/36A)

69. *Litter is Dangerous...Respect the Life of the Countryside* (1968). Reginald Mount had first used an image of an animal – the endangered (and cuddly) red squirrel – in a poster design of 1962 to suggest the fragility of the countryside and its wildlife. The message of this 1968 poster pulls no punches: 'Tins and bottles left in the countryside are *dangerous*. They may lame animals for life, or cut them so badly that they have to be destroyed. All litter is disgusting. **SO TAKE YOUR LITTER HOME**.' (BL, PP/206/46A)

PUT YOUR LITTER IN A BASKET

OR TAKE IT HOME WITH YOU

PREPARED BY THE DEPARTMENT OF HEALTH FOR SCOTLAND
AND THE CENTRAL OFFICE OF INFORMATION

Printed in Great Britain by McCorquodale & Co. Ltd.   Wt. 70634

PP/36/1A

15
facts about
LITTER

A COSTLY, DANGEROUS AND DIRTY NUISANCE

LEAVE NO LITTER
TAKE IT HOME

FOLLOW THE COUNTRY CODE

Keep dogs under proper control   Protect wild life, wild plants and trees
Keep to the paths across farmland Go carefully on country roads   Leave no litter
Guard against all risk of fire   Fasten all gates   Safeguard water supplies
Avoid damaging fences, hedges and walls   Respect the life of the countryside

Prepared by the Countryside Commission and the Central Office of Information 1971

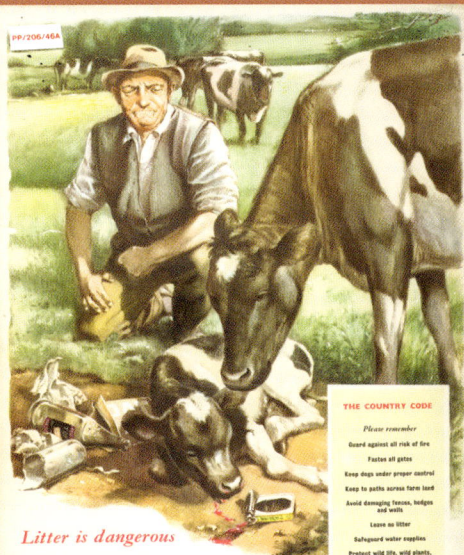

PP/206/46A

THE COUNTRY CODE

Please remember

Guard against all risk of fire
Fasten all gates
Keep dogs under proper control
Keep to paths across farm land
Avoid damaging fences, hedges
and walls
Leave no litter
Safeguard water supplies
Protect wild life, wild plants,
and trees
Go carefully on country roads
Respect the life of the
countryside

Litter is dangerous

Tins and bottles left in the countryside
are *dangerous*. They may lame animals for life,
or cut them so badly that they have to be destroyed.
All litter is disgusting. SO TAKE YOUR LITTER HOME

RESPECT THE LIFE OF THE COUNTRYSIDE

Guard against all risk of fire
Fasten all gates
Keep dogs under proper control
Keep to the paths across farm land
Avoid damaging fences, hedges and walls

OB
THE COU

PREPARED FOR THE COUNTRYSIDE COMMISSION BY THE CENT

PP/128/33L

Leave no litter
Safeguard water supplies
Protect wild life, wild plants and trees
Go carefully on country roads
Respect the life of the countryside

...VE
...Y CODE

OF INFORMATION   Printed in England for HMSO by F & H (B) Ltd

70. *Observe the Country Code.* The COI even produced bookmarkers to encourage citizens to observe the Country Code. Here are two impressive examples from the late 1960s. (BL, PP/128/33L)

Insist on....

Clean Food

CLEANLY SERVED

NEW LAWS ON MAY 1st 1959

The Clean Food Code

New laws about clean food have been made, and all handlers of food, including drink, must now follow these rules.

Clean hands and clothing at all times

Let the employer know if he has an infectious illness

Every open cut or sore must be covered with a waterproof dressing

Avoid unnecessary handling of food

No smoking or spitting when handling food

EVERY EFFORT IS MADE HERE TO OBSERVE THESE STANDARDS. Please let us know if you see anything wrong.

PREPARED BY THE DEPARTMENT OF HEALTH FOR SCOTLAND AND THE CENTRAL OFFICE OF INFORMATION. PRINTED BY GAVIN WATSON LTD., GLASGOW.

---

now wash your hands !

UNDER THE FOOD HYGIENE (SCOTLAND) REGULATIONS 1959, FOOD HANDLERS MUST WASH THEIR HANDS IMMEDIATELY AFTER VISITING THE LAVATORY.

The Clean Food Code

The Clean Food Code

NOTICE TO FOOD HANDLERS

The Food Hygiene (Scotland) Regulations, 1959, require that anyone engaged in the handling of food, including drink, must:-

✽ Protect food from contamination.

✽ Ensure by washing that his hands and finger nails are always clean.

✽ Wash his hands immediately after visiting the lavatory.

✽ Keep clean all parts of his clothing which are liable to come into contact with food.

✽ Cover any exposed cut or sore with a suitable waterproof dressing.

✽ Not smoke or chew tobacco or spit or take snuff while at work.

✽ Report to his employer immediately he knows he is suffering from, or is a carrier of, typhoid or paratyphoid fever, dysentery, or a salmonella or staphylococcal infection likely to cause food poisoning.

PREPARED BY THE DEPARTMENT OF HEALTH FOR SCOTLAND AND THE CENTRAL OFFICE OF INFORMATION.   PRINTED BY GAVIN WATSON LTD., GLASGOW.

play out the historic conflict of interests between town-bred recreationalists and the farmers and landowners who have resented relinquishing their land for leisure use . The script reads:

> **Petunia:** *Oh, Joe! I have enjoyed our country walk.*
> **Joe:** *Yes, we've come a long way, Petunia. Look! You can see our tracks right across that yellow cornfield.*
> **Petunia:** *Oh yes! It's ever so nice in this field. I'm glad those cows have gone.*
> **Joe:** *Aye! They've taken themselves off for a walk down't road – look – through that gate I opened; the one marked 'Private'.*
> **Petunia:** *Oh yes!*
> [sound of enthusiastic barking and baa-ing of terrified sheep]
> **Petunia:** *Our little Bingo is having a lovely time playing with those sheep. The exercise will do him good.*
> [Joe throws a stone. A bottle smashes.]
> **Joe:** *He, he! I've hit that bottle, Petunia! It smashed up a treat.*
> **Petunia:** *Oh. Very clever.*
> [Enraged-looking farmer.]
> **Joe:** *You know, there's a farmer down there with a purple face.*
> **Petunia:** *I expect it's all that sun and the open-air life, Joe.*
> [Angry farmer hopping with anger.]
> **Joe:** *Now he's doing one of those country dances.*
> **Petunia:** *I don't think he looks very friendly.*
> **Joe:** *Ah, mebbe you're right, tho' it can't be anything we've done.*
> **Petunia:** *No! But I won't stay where I'm not wanted. Come on, Joe!*
> **Farmer:** *When folk come out to the country, why oh why won't they follow the Country Code?*

Public health continued to be a preoccupation in the 1960s and 1970s. As we have seen, warnings regarding the dangers of contagion ('Cough and Sneezes Spread Diseases') extended after the war into the 1950s. A related concern in the 1960s was to persuade the public and all catering establishments to follow the Clean Food Code. New regulations were introduced following the Food Hygiene Act (1959). The public was encouraged by means of a concerted propaganda campaign that included pamphlets, fliers, posters and TV advertisements to 'Insist on Clean Food Cleanly Served' (Figs. 71a, b, c and d). Part of the Notice to Food Handlers warned they must: 'Not smoke or chew tobacco or spit or take snuff while at work.'

---

71. ***The Clean Food Code*** (1960). *The Clean Food Code* pack was available to all those involved in the handling of food, including drinks, who under the 1959 Food Hygiene Act were now charged with the responsibility of 'protecting food from contamination'. Food establishments were encouraged to display a copy of the Clean Food Code with a declaration at the bottom of the poster: 'Every effort is made here to observe these standards. Please let us know if you see anything wrong.' (BL, PP/30/20A, 22L)

ANTI-SMOKING CAMPAIGN

By the 1960s there was also a growing awareness of the harmful consequences of smoking, triggering a series of posters to discourage the habit, particularly among young people (Figs. 72 and 73). In fact, the epidemiologists Richard Doll and Bradford Hill had determined the link between smoking and lung cancer as early as 1950. By the late 1940s approximately 80 per cent of men and 40 per cent of women were smokers. The initial response in the United Kingdom to the discovery of the connection between smoking and lung cancer was 'cautious' and the Conservative government's anti-smoking campaign did not really begin until the 1960s. As Iain Macleod, Minister of Health, admitted privately in 1954, 'we all know that the Welfare State and much else is based on [taxes raised from] tobacco smoking'. By 1956 tobacco duty was bringing the Exchequer £670 million a year.[15]

But political procrastination was not solely about revenue, there was also a cultural factor to consider. The notion of long-term 'risk' was not part of the public health debate in the 1950s. Cigarette advertising often featured happy, healthy-looking film stars or sports figures advocating a particular brand (Stanley Matthews, for example, declared 'Craven A is the cigarette for me'). Smoking, according to the Ministry of Health, was not a 'disease' in the same way as cancer – it might lead to disease, but only in the long term, if at all. The publicity approach would involve asking people to curtail a habit that was then deeply embedded in everyday culture. There was also the issue that a cancer phobia might generate a demand for services at a time when National Health Service costs were becoming a political issue (again).

The Royal College of Physicians (RCP) 1962 report *Smoking and Health* provided further evidence of the link between smoking and lung cancer, as well as heart disease, and it called on the government to be more proactive in reducing cigarette smoking. The report was widely covered in the media (including a BBC *Panorama* programme) and 33,000 copies had been sold by the autumn of 1963. It galvanised the Ministry of Health into a more-committed approach and in 1963 the first official anti-smoking film, *Smoking and You*, was commissioned and aimed at teenagers. One of the recommendations of the RCP report had been that there should be a ban on television commercials for cigarettes and this was implemented in 1965. Following the publication of the 1964 Cohen Report, which emphasised the role of the mass media in health education and called for a greater degree of central publicity, the COI changed its stance from information-giving publicity to a habit-changing approach – just knowing the risks of cigarette smoking was no longer enough. In spite of the storm of publicity that these reports generated, the government's anti-smoking campaign throughout the 1960s continued to adopt a somewhat gentle approach. In the early 1960s, Reginald Mount had designed an anti-smoking poster showing a man – a hacking relative of the man he had drawn for *Don't Brag About Your Job* (Fig. 119) – holding a lighted cigarette and coughing profusely. Pointing to the cigarette, the poster warns 'Cut it out or cut it down. Cigarettes harm your health'. Mount also designed a very different type of poster that showed a vacant-

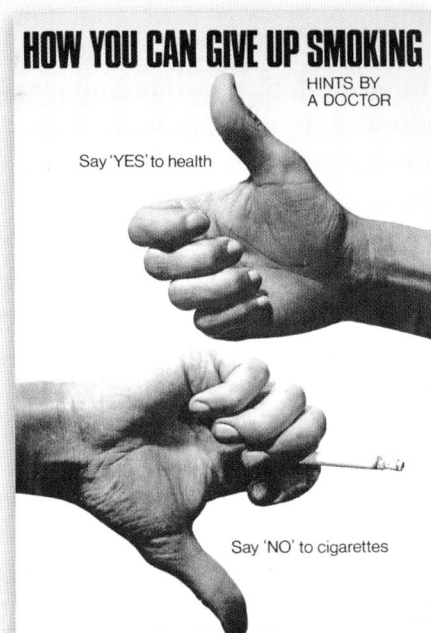

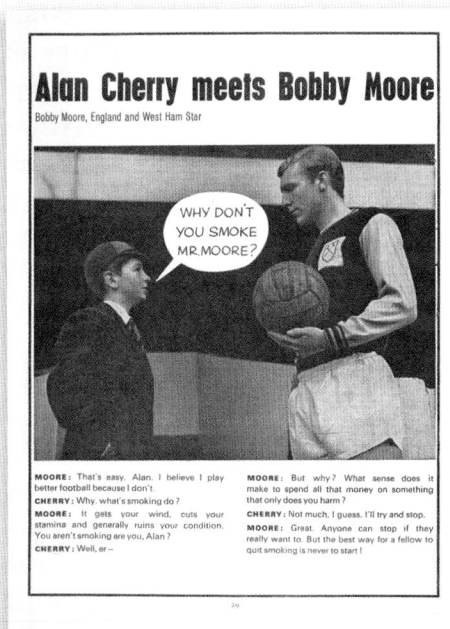

72. *How You Can Give Up Smoking.* A poster and leaflet from the early 1960s gently persuading individuals to give up – or at least cut down on – smoking. The message would become far more hard-hitting as the decade progressed, when the harmful effects of nicotine on health would be highlighted more forcefully. (BL, PP/ BS/17/31)

73. *Alan Cherry Meets Bobby Moore* (1964). The start of a cultural shift. In the 1950s, footballers such as Sir Stanley Matthews had endorsed smoking certain brands of cigarettes ('Craven A is the cigarette for me'). By 1964 Bobby Moore, the England captain, was now discouraging young Alan Cherry from taking up smoking – both for health and financial reasons. (Welch collection)

looking sheep with a cigarette in its mouth: 'Yes I smoke! But then I'm just another sheep.... What about you?'

Although cigarette advertising on television had been banned in 1965, the printed media still promoted an image of smoking associated with glamour and style that continued to appeal to young people. However, the social revolution that was taking place in the Swinging Sixties was very much a youth phenomenon, much of it centred on aspects of youth culture like music and fashion. In 1966 the COI tapped into this and attempted to change the perception of smoking as a fashionable habit by suggesting that there was more money and fun to be had 'if you don't smoke!' The designers Marsden and Willson produced a series of posters aimed at both sexes showing young people wearing T-shirts with the slogan 'I DON'T SMOKE', surrounded by fashion accessories associated at the time with cool youth culture (Fig. 74).

In 1967 Halas and Batchelor produced for the COI a jolting, anti-smoking animation short called *Dying for a Smoke* that reinforced both the health and

74. *More Money, More Fun, If You Don't Smoke.* Two posters disseminating the same message. A young man or a young woman, depending on the version of the poster, is shown surrounded by Swinging Sixties–style consumer goods to emphasise the social and economic benefits of not smoking. (TNA, INF 13/254/9 and INF 13/255/25)

economic arguments against smoking. Full of their signature humour, it consisted of a villainous cartoon character ('Old Nick O'Teen') who attempts to lure unsuspecting teenager ('Sam Sucker') into the cigarette habit.[16] Initially, Sam associates smoking with manliness, pleasure, popularity and self-esteem, but following expert advice from a doctor (who replaces these traits with ill-health, bronchitis, heart disease and lung cancer) and straight talk from a friendly lorry driver ('At the rate you are carrying on, that's a small fortune going up in smoke. Why waste money when you can buy something you really want'), Sam renounces the habit. Revealingly, it is the lifestyle argument to which he aspires that trumps the health argument: 'I hadn't thought of it that way.' Lorry driver: 'Now you are thinking...It's *your* money and *your* life!'

Redefining smoking was also part of a broader move within public health that stressed individual responsibility for healthy 'lifestyles' and behaviours. In 1968 an officially funded Health Education Council (HEC) replaced its neglected predecessor, the Council for Health Education, which had been judged ineffective by the Cohen Report. Far-better resourced and more media-savvy than its predecessor, the HEC was able to give tobacco advertising a run for its money. New, modern, advertising agencies, like Saatchi & Saatchi (as opposed to individual designers like Reginald Mount, who had been working for the COI since the war), were increasingly engaged to deliver this new agenda. Health warnings started to be printed on cigarette packets in 1971 and a few years later tar/nicotine tables were published. For the first time, the anti-smoking campaign was extended to television. One of the first TV advertisements made by Saatchi & Saatchi in 1971 showed smokers crossing London's Waterloo Bridge intercut with footage of lemmings throwing themselves off a cliff. A voiceover states: 'There's a strange arctic rodent called a lemming which every year throws itself off a cliff. It's as though it wanted to die. Every year in Britain thousands of men and women smoke cigarettes. It's as though they want to die.' Another important shift was that the anti-smoking campaign began to target women, pregnant women especially.

In 1965 Reginald Mount designed a lithograph poster of a glum, young woman smoking, with silver coins replacing the cigarette smoke – thus representing the expense of buying cigarettes. She is thinking of a friend who has recently managed to give up smoking: 'So she said she was giving up smoking as she could save money and I said don't be daft you won't save a penny and my Norman agrees with me. But the next thing you know she's got herself one of these cut out dresses and a trouser suit and [a] pair of those white boots on top of which she's got rid of that cough and what's more my Norman's dating her up. Honestly you can't trust some people can you!'[17] Women, unlike men, had shown no reduction in smoking prevalence between 1946 and the early 1970s. Perhaps the most-shocking image from a campaign run in 1973 was one of a naked, pregnant, smoking woman. *Is it fair to force your baby to smoke cigarettes?* the poster asked (Fig. 75). The message along the side of the pregnant woman pulls no punches: smoking can 'restrict your baby's normal growth inside the womb. It can make him underdeveloped and underweight at birth. Which, in turn, can make him vulnerable to illness in the first delicate weeks of his life. It can even kill him.' Unashamedly intended to elicit a sense of shame, guilt and fear, the admonitory message crucially offers a positive resolution: 'If you give up smoking when you're pregnant your baby will be as healthy as if you'd never smoked.'

The anti-smoking campaign slowly had the desired effect. Increasingly, from the late 1960s onwards, health education placed its faith in the sense of citizenship and responsibility of its recipients. Often this would involve a combination of enlightenment, admonishment and guilt. The health agenda that grew out of this redefinition involved particular stress on modern techniques of mass persuasion. The anti-smoking campaigns since the 1960s have consistently employed an impressive combination of visual and verbal imagery to disseminate an increasingly hard-hitting message. In 2013 the Department of Health launched a hard-hitting £8 million campaign. It looked to capitalise, by way of images designed to shock smokers into quitting, on the British penchant for making health-related New Year resolutions. The campaign, embracing television, posters and billboards, and the Internet, showed a cigarette mutating into tumours while being smoked. The voiceover message was brief and to the point: 'When you smoke, the chemicals you inhale cause mutations in your body ... and mutations are how cancer starts. Every fifteen cigarettes you smoke will cause a mutation. If you could see the damage you'd stop.' Additional laws have

Is it fair to force your baby to smoke cigarettes?

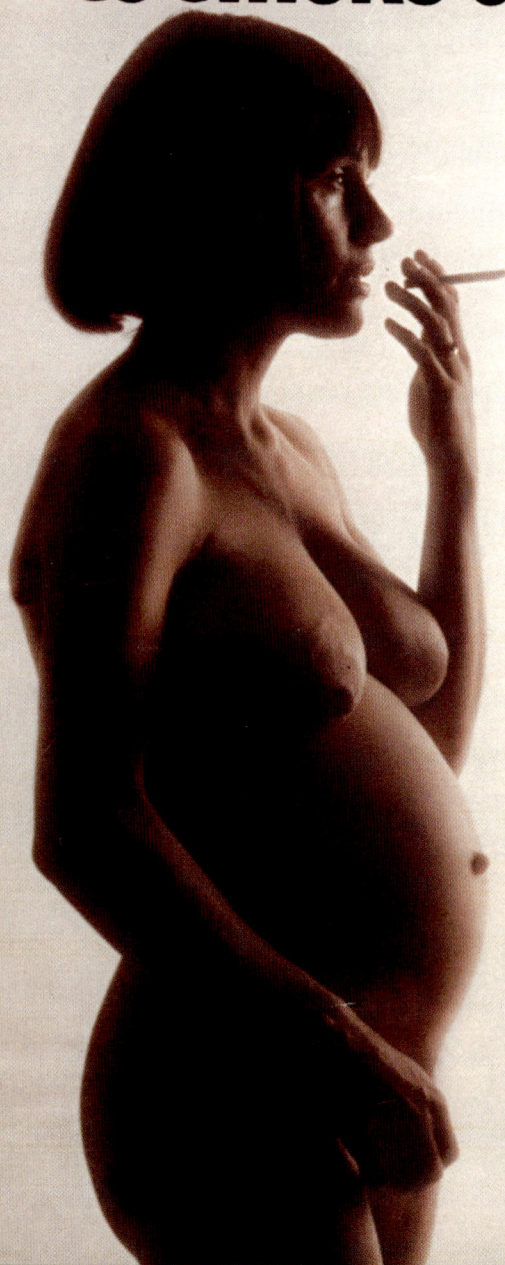

This is what happens if you smoke when you're pregnant.

Every time you inhale you fill your lungs with nicotine and carbon monoxide.

Your blood carries these impurities through the umbilical cord into your baby's bloodstream.

Smoking can restrict your baby's normal growth inside the womb.

It can make him underdeveloped and underweight at birth.

Which, in turn, can make him vulnerable to illness in the first delicate weeks of his life.

It can even kill him.

Last year, in Britain alone, over 1,500 babies might not have died if their mothers had given up smoking when they were pregnant.

If you give up smoking when you're pregnant your baby will be as healthy as if you'd never smoked.

The Health Education Council

further marginalised smoking, and by implication those who smoke. Research from the 1980s onwards raised concerns about passive smoking and this has been a key factor in the various bans introduced in subsequent years. Beginning with voluntary workplace bans, these measures have progressed through compulsory public transport bans to the 2007 legislation that outlawed smoking in enclosed public places. That smoking rates have more than halved since 1974 reflects a sea change in both public and private attitudes to cigarette smoking that has made an accepted, indeed glamorous, habit of the twentieth century socially unacceptable in twenty-first century Britain.[18] Virginia Berridge reminds us that in the 1940s the government offered tobacco tokens as an economic supplement to old age pensions: in the late 1990s, nicotine replacement therapy was free to those in deprived areas as a remedy for inequality. 'The contrast in state responses shows the change which had taken place over the half-century.'[19] ♛

75. *Is it Fair to Force Your Baby to Smoke Cigarettes?* A compelling new anti-smoking argument: the impact of passive smoking on an unborn child. The shocking image, from 1973, of a naked pregnant women smoking, represented a new emphasis on adults (particularly women) taking more responsibility for their lifestyles. In the 1980s children were targeted following statistical evidence that suggested smokers usually started before the age of ten, and in the 2000s the campaign refocused on the effects of passive smoking on children after it was shown that they were more prone to lung cancer or even Sudden Infant Death Syndrome if their parents smoked. (Advertising Archives)

CHAPTER FOUR

THE STRESSFUL SEVENTIES: A NEW DIRECTION

This was a decade of exceptional social strain. Oil shortages, rampant inflation, power cuts, industrial unrest, a three-day week, a miner's strike and high unemployment all put intense strains on the country and its economy. The COI helped to prepare the country for decimalisation before Britain eventually joined the European Economic Community (EEC) in 1973, only for a referendum to be called two years later. It was also a decade marked by the introduction of progressive legal protection in the fields of race relations, sex discrimination, equal pay for women and employment protection, improved pension provision, new housing allowances and home-improvement grants.

While the 1960s was a decade of rapid cultural change that remains inexorably associated with the Swinging Sixties, it was also not without its economic challenges. However, towards the end of the decade there was a brief period of optimism (Fig. 76). By 1967 the British economy was in meltdown, with the manufacturing sector flagging. The budget for that year set the greatest deficit in post-war history and later in the year the government abandoned three years of attempting to maintain the exchange rate and devalued the pound sterling. Although this represented political and economic failure on the part of the Labour government, devaluation did offer an opportunity for British exports, as long as government and industry seized that opportunity – something that the COI was eager to focus on.

I'M BACKING BRITAIN... BUY BRITISH

In the early weeks of January 1968, a post-devaluation Britain was enlivened by the advent of a campaign to haul the country out of the economic doldrums. John Boyd-Carpenter (Conservative MP for Kingston-upon-Thames) wrote to *The Times* suggesting that if a number of people sacrificed the first Saturday of every month by working on that morning without extra pay, 'it would show the world that we were in earnest'.[1]

The idea was seized upon by Fred Price, marketing director of Colt Ventilation and Heating in Surbiton, Surrey, who wrote to his employees: 'If everyone in the country worked an extra half day every week Britain will soon be the wealthiest nation in the world.' The memo was taken up by five secretaries working at the company's head office who agreed to work an extra half an hour a day without extra pay. They urged others to do the same with the slogan 'I'm Backing Britain' (Fig. 77). A wave of patriotism quickly swept the UK and the campaign became a frenzied nationwide movement within a week.[2] Britain was flooded with hastily made 'I'm Backing Britain' badges, mugs, car stickers and T-shirts – most of which turned out to have been made in Portugal!

Even Harold Wilson, the Prime Minister, offered his support. 'There is too much knocking of Britain', he said. 'What we want is "Back Britain" not back-biting.' A franking mark was produced by the Post Office and used on 84 million letters, while the newly appointed Poet Laureate, Cecil Day-Lewis, took to verse to support the initiative, which was now being run by the Industrial Society. The poem, entitled 'Now and Then', was commissioned by the *Daily Mail* and appeared on its front page on 5 January. The poem compared Britain's current economic situation with the Blitz and concluded:

---

76. Research and British Industry. The front cover of a 1966 pamphlet extolling the virtues of British research and industry. The Royston Cooper-designed lion was first used in 1962 in the 'Keep Britain Tidy' campaign. In 1966 it coincided with England winning the World Cup, for which the team mascot was Willie the Lion. Inside, the introduction states: 'To buy the food and raw materials they need to feed 54 million British people sell things that no one else can make so well or so cheaply, even things that no one else can make at all. So British industry must have new products, new ideas, new techniques in abundance.' The illustrations within the pamphlet were drawn by Topolski, another remarkable artist who worked for the COI. (BL/PP/119/20A)

RESEARCH AND BRITISH INDUSTRY

UPSWING

No. 6 1968
PREPARED BY THE
DEPARTMENT OF
ECONOMIC AFFAIRS

The five girls from Colt's who began "Backing Britain". Congratulating them the Prime Minister said any agreed step to increase Britain's competitiveness is of immense value.

1968 CHALLENGE!

NO EASY PATH

For five years we have been spending abroad more than we have been earning. Devaluation gives us an opportunity to square our accounts because:

● It will make our exports cheaper to the customer abroad, or more profitable to the British exporter—or a combination of the two.

● Foreign goods will be more expensive in Britain and not such an attractive buy.

But we have first to produce the extra goods to sell and this puts a big extra load on industry. In 1968 we shall not be able to do all the things we want to do at once—to increase exports and to raise the standard of living and to increase Government spending on social and welfare services as much as we would wish. Exports must come first.

Pay rises this year must be strictly limited. To make devaluation work we shall have to avoid, like the plague, the spiral of rising prices, rising wages and rising costs.

If the opportunity is taken, by the end of this year devaluation will be helping Britain to get out of the red and to start repaying our debts.

The £ has been devalued. The purpose is to get Britain out of the red on our balance sheet with other countries. But what does devaluation mean to the ordinary man and woman? What can they expect and what are they expected to do to help Britain pull out of the economic crisis?

Devaluation means that foreigners can buy more pounds with their own currency. It means that British export prices can be quite a lot lower, and that we have to pay more for goods from abroad. Because we have to import so much, these higher import prices will certainly mean higher prices in the shops both for goods which are imported and goods made in Britain which contain rubber, copper, aluminium or hundreds of other materials we have to buy abroad from countries which have not devalued.

Because we shall be able to sell British goods abroad at a lower price (or in some cases because it will be more profitable to sell British goods abroad) the devaluation of the £ gives Britain a real chance to boost exports. This should help us to get a big switch round from being well in the red to being well in the black in our trading accounts with other countries.

How does it affect me?

PRICES

Some prices will go up because imports cost more. And in addition to higher prices caused by devaluation, prices may change with justification for other reasons (seasonal changes for example). The Government are redoubling their efforts to make sure that prices are not put up without good reason.

As the countries which supply us with much of our eggs, butter and bacon have devalued with us, devaluation should make little difference to the price of these items. Some food which depends on imports—bread for instance—will cost more. In the case of imported furniture, cars and clothes, you can always buy British goods whose price should not rise so much. Food prices are already going up. Other price increases will take longer to reach the shops.

WAGES

Before devaluation no one was automatically entitled to more pay. But increases could be allowed in certain cases—particularly where a real productivity pact was agreed or for very low paid workers. This is still the case. But people are asked not to seek rises in pay to make up for increases in prices which are caused by devaluation. If this happened, it could increase the cost of our goods abroad and cancel out the advantages to our exports.

In the week after devaluation the General Council of the T.U.C. said that they would not regard increases in prices arising from the reduced external purchasing power of the £ as constituting in themselves justification for increases in wages. They also said that they would not regard as compatible with incomes policy claims for improvements in wages due to take effect within twelve months of the previous settlement.

What must I do?

The message to British businessmen is to switch into exports in a big way. Sell—sell and sell again wherever there is an opportunity abroad.

The message to people working in factories and offices is to put up with rising prices for a short time to give Britain a chance to break through. These rises should not be happening without good cause and the Government will not hesitate to refer cases to the National Board for Prices and Incomes, and if necessary, to use its powers of delay. The Government will also be watching dividends, and the need to restrain them from hardship these sections of the community which are most likely to suffer from the effects of rising prices.

BIG EARNER

"Big Spender" was one of her hit records in 1967. But Shirley Bassey is also one of the most successful British entertainers helping our balance of payments with their big earnings overseas....

Britain stars appearing abroad, and rights to British films, records, books and TV programmes help to swell our "invisible" earnings of foreign money. In 1968 our total "invisible" earnings—they include payments for shipping, airlines, insurance and business services and interest on investments—came to nearly £3,000 million. For every £5 earned from ordinary export sales, some £3 is "invisible". British services—from shipping to shipping—should become even more popular throughout the world as a result of devaluation.

BRITISH EXPORTS— A BRIGHTER OUTLOOK IN 1968

SOME EXPORT-BOOSTING COMPANIES

Textile machinery under construction at a Yorkshire factory. The company, Wilson and Longbottom Ltd., winner of a Queen's Award to Industry for export achievement, exported 70 per cent of production in 1967. Overseas markets include North America, Europe, Pakistan, Australia and Japan.

Prepared by the Department of Economic Affairs and the Central Office of Information

---

77. *Upswing: 1968 Challenge!* A COI broadsheet publication (no 6) prepared for the Department of Economic Affairs to encourage industry and entrepreneurs to take advantage of the recent devaluation of the pound sterling. At the top of the front cover, to the right of centre, are the five secretaries from Colt Ventilation and Heating who began the 'I'm Backing Britain' campaign. 'Congratulating them, the Prime Minister said any agreed step to increase Britain's competitiveness is of immense value.' Also mentioned is 'Big Earner' Shirley Bassey: '"Big Spender" was one of her hits. But Shirley Bassey is also one of the most successful British entertainers helping our balance of payments with their big earnings overseas'.... Such successes swelled the country's 'invisible' earnings of foreign currency. (BL, PP/128/54A).

78. *Britain Expo67.* The COI programme for the events taking place in and around the British pavilion (shown on the front cover), designed by Sir Basil Spence, at Montreal's Expo 67. Sir Laurence Olivier performed with the National Theatre, and visitors could experience the hovercraft ('a British invention') on the St Lawrence River, call in at The Bulldog Pub, travel on a London 'Routemaster' manned by London Transport drivers and conductors, and visit British boutiques. (BL, PP/123/50L)

To work then, islanders, as men and women
Members one of another, looking beyond
Mean rules and rivalries towards the dream you could
Make real, of glory, common wealth, and home.

The Union Flag logo could be seen throughout the country on shopping bags as the British people became caught up in a wave of patriotic fervour. On 8 January 1968, Pye Records issued a single titled 'I'm Backing Britain' in support of the campaign. Written by the husband and wife hit-making songwriters Tony Hatch and Jackie

Sir Laurence Olivier heads the National Theatre Company in its visit to Montreal.

English Opera Group

11–16 September	EGLISE ST. JACQUES
11, 13, 15	"The Burning Fiery Furnace": Britten
12, 14, 16	"Curlew River": Britten
18–23 September	THEATRE MAISONNEUVE
18, 22	"A Midsummer Night's Dream": Britten
19, 20	"The Beggar's Opera": Gay/Britten
21, 23	"Acis and Galatea": Handel
	"The Bear": Walton

The English Opera Group, which is closely associated with Benjamin Britten, stages chamber operas mainly by British composers.

Northern Sinfonia Orchestra

15 October	THEATRE PORT ROYAL.
	Conductor: Boris Brott
	(Works by Handel, Bartok, Damase and Schubert)

The National Theatre of Great Britain

18–28 October	THEATRE MAISONNEUVE
18, 20, 24, 26	Othello: Shakespeare
19, 22 (mat. & eve.)	Love for Love: Congreve
25, 28 (mat. & eve.)	
21 (mat. & eve.)	A Flea in her Ear: Feydeau, translated by
27 (mat. & eve.)	John Mortimer

The National Theatre season will close the World Festival, which opens with the Théâtre de France. The Company's visit to Montreal will follow a two weeks' Centennial tour in Western Canada.

British Day, 1 June 1967

A large-scale modern pageant presentation on Britain's National Day, 1 June, has been arranged to take place in the Place des Nations, an open air arena seating 10,000 people.

The telephone number of the British Pavilion at Expo is 871–1141/2/3

Prepared for British Information Services by the Central Office of Information 1967
Printed in England for Her Majesty's Stationery Office by M.M.P. Ltd.
Dd. 160854. S.67. 1194.

When visiting Expo, make sure to—

take a trip by Hovercraft
A new experience in transport. The Westland SRN 6 will ferry passengers on the St. Lawrence River, to and from the exhibition site and the mainland. The Hovercraft, a British invention, which rides on a cushion of air over land and water, is coming into use in many parts of the world.

call in at "The Bulldog" pub
and enjoy the hospitable atmosphere of an English inn. Well stocked with English beers, Scotch whiskies and London gin. In the La Ronde area, "The Bulldog" is sponsored by the Distillers Company Ltd., the largest exporters of Scotch whisky, and Whitbread and Co. Ltd., brewers since 1742.

travel in a London bus
The latest type of 72-seater "Routemaster" manned by London Transport drivers and conductors, will carry passengers to and from Expo. Regular daytime service from Dominion Square to La Ronde and evening service between Place des Arts and La Ronde.

visit the British boutiques
At the British Bookshop over 50 British publishers are displaying and selling a wide selection of their books. Sponsored by the Book Development Council of Britain and operated by The Classic Bookshop, Montreal. At another boutique confectionery by leading British manufacturers will be available.

Other events in Canada

In addition to the part being played at Expo 67, Britain is making an important contribution in the Centennial Year to extend our mutual trade. There will be major participations in the National Industrial Production Show, Toronto, 1–5 May, and at the British Columbia International Trade Fair, Vancouver, 17–22 May, and store promotions in various cities, all culminating in a great commercial and cultural event, The British Week in Toronto, 12–21 October—the first British promotion of this magnitude to be held in the North American continent.

BRITAIN
expo67
Canadian World Exhibition, Montreal
28 April to 27 October

PP/123/50L

The British Pavilion at
expo67

The theme of the British Pavilion is "The Challenge of Change". It shows how the British people are meeting this challenge in the modern world, as they have done many times in the past. Organised by the Central Office of Information, the Pavilion was designed by Sir Basil Spence, O.M. It has five exhibition areas and a cinema showing films related to the theme.

Shaping the Nation,
the first section, provides an exciting introduction. Sean Kenny's imaginative design, which breaks away from normal exhibition techniques, takes the visitor through 3,000 years of history, evoked by dramatic use of shapes, sounds, colour and projected images.

The Genius of Britain,
in the upper part of the 200-ft. tower, was designed by Beverley Pick and recalls the achievements of many famous British men and women. Among them are writers, musicians, artists, scientists, explorers, statesmen and reformers who have made outstanding contributions to human progress.

Britain Today,
designed by James Gardner, the third section presents the British at home, at work and at play. Interesting, entertaining and often humorous, in a warm and friendly atmosphere, it shows many aspects of British day-to-day life, British institutions and the British character.

Industrial Britain,
the fourth section, shows how Britain in the sixties is moving into a new industrial era in which automation and new techniques are changing man's relation to the machine. Designed by Theo Crosby, it is an "Aladdin's Cave" of industry, presenting fascinating examples of British invention and technical skill.

Britain in the World,
the final section, dominated by giant sculptured figures symbolising Man and his world, contains a series of displays showing Britain's role in world trade, as a member of the Commonwealth, as a good neighbour providing assistance to the developing countries and as a contributor to world culture and understanding. It ends by showing how Britain is playing a major part in international affairs and working for a better future for mankind.

Right, above: a model of the British Pavilion.
Below: an artist's impression of "The Genius of Britain" section

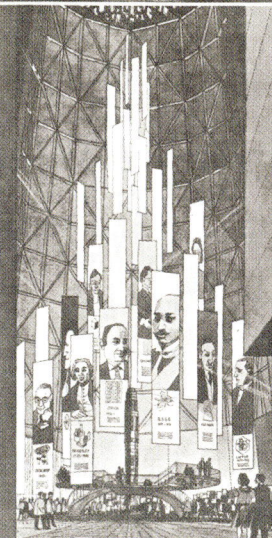

British events in the World Festival

Britain is making a major contribution to the World Festival at Expo 67. Important events in the theatre, music, ballet, opera and the visual arts have been organised by the British Council.

The British programme comprises:

Bristol Old Vic Company

22–27 May	EXPO THEATRE
	Three Shakespearian productions:
22, 27 (mat. & eve.)	Measure for Measure
23, 24 (mat. & eve.)	Hamlet
25, 26	Romeo and Juliet

The Bristol Old Vic Company, formed in 1946, is one of Britain's most distinguished repertory companies. Hamlet and Romeo and Juliet are directed by Val May and Measure for Measure by Sir Tyrone Guthrie.

Royal Ballet

7–10 June	SALLE WILFRID PELLETIER
7 (eve.)	Cinderella
8 (eve.)	Triple bill: Brandenburg Nos 2 and 4
	Paradise Lost ; The Dream
9 (mat. & eve.)	Cinderella
10 (mat. & eve.)	Triple bill, as above

The Company, led by Dame Margot Fonteyn and Rudolf Nureyev, is making its seventh visit to Montreal, during an extended tour of North America from mid-April to mid-July.

Yehudi Menuhin and the Bath Festival Orchestra

	Leader: Robert Masters
	Soloists: Yehudi Menuhin, violin
	Hephzibah Menuhin, piano
	George Malcolm, harpsichord
	Jacqueline du Pré, cello
22–27 June	THEATRE PORT ROYAL
22	Bath Festival Orchestra: Conductor: Menuhin (Works by Bach, Mozart, Weinzweig, and Britten)
23	Yehudi Menuhin and the Bath Festival Ensemble (Works by Beethoven, Mozart and Schubert)
25	Bath Festival Orchestra: Conductor: Menuhin (Handel, Mozart, Goehr, C.P.E. Bach and Haydn)
26	Yehudi Menuhin and the Bath Festival Ensemble (Works by Brahms)
27	Bath Festival Orchestra Conductors: Yehudi Menuhin, George Malcolm (Works by Mozart, Tippett and Haydn)

The orchestra was formed in 1958 by Yehudi Menuhin from leading quartet and chamber music players.

Britain / expo67

The British Pavilion has as its theme 'The Challenge of Change'. It shows how the British people are meeting this challenge in the modern world, as they have done many times in the past. The story is told in five chapters —

SHAPING THE NATION, the opening section, tells how an island people were moulded by successive invasions, by the coming of Christianity and the influence of the Church, by the authority of kings and the disputes between throne and people, into a society based

on law and order. It shows how Britain then became a great outward-looking democracy whose influence spread throughout the world. Some living links with 3,000 years of Britain's history, preserved in the present, are illustrated on the next page.

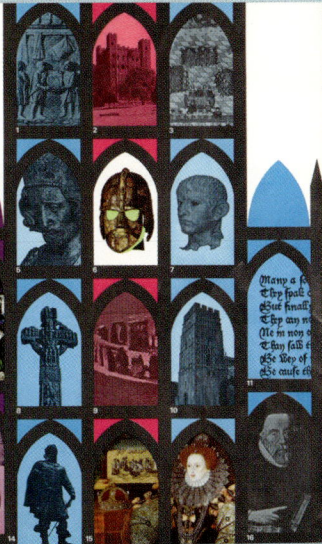

79. *'Shaping the Nation' and 'The Genius of Britain'.* These were two of the five 'chapters' providing the historical theme that made up the British pavilion. 'Shaping the Nation' was a theatrical presentation by Sean Kenny to summarise 3,000 years of British History, while 'The Genius of Britain,' devised by Beverley Pick, was a reminder for visitors of the achievements of outstanding Britons. A three-dimensional mural, with a mirrored feature of the Concorde engine in the centre, depicted literature, music and arts and the works of British scientists, inventors and constructors alongside the contributions of famous parliamentarians, reformers, explorers and economists. (BL, PP/123/47A)

BRITAIN EXPO'70

80. *Britain Expo'70.* The front and back covers of the British brochure juxtapose a modernist abstract design with the rural splendour of an ancient cathedral-adorned landscape. (BL, PP/174/34A)

英国　EXPO'70

Trent, and sung by one of Britain's favourite TV entertainers Bruce Forsyth, the song seemed destined for chart success. The chorus included: 'The feeling is growing, so let's keep it going, the good times are blowing our way.'

By the end of March, the campaign had dissipated into general patriotic exhortations to 'buy British' and was clearly past its peak. The Surbiton typists seemed like a refreshing response to the stereotypical image of the British worker. But dissenting voices came from the trades unions, which were, understandably, not keen on a campaign that involved unpaid overtime. The Bruce Forsyth song 'I'm Backing Britain' had sold only a few thousand copies, and by August the campaign was virtually over.

While the campaign was short-lived, and although it did not involve the COI, the patriotic sentiments that it generated did chime with much of the work undertaken by the latter during this period. An overlooked aspect of the COI's portfolio was the work undertaken abroad by the Overseas Film and Television Division to promote British trade and the British way of life – especially at trade fairs. The COI was responsible for the design and production of the British pavilions at all three World Expositions held since the end of World War II – at Brussels in 1958, Montreal in 1967 (Figs. 78a and b) and Osaka in 1970.

For the British pavilion at Expo 67, the COI decided to tell the history of the British (in their continuously developing environment) from early times to 1967. This consisted of five chapters in separate halls: 'Shaping the Nation', 'The Genius of Britain', 'Britain Today', 'Industrial Britain' and 'Britain in the World' (Figs. 79a, b and c). A major theme of the exhibition was 'the Challenge of Change' and the COI's stated objective was to 'show how the British people were meeting this challenge in the modern world'.

The main theme of Expo 70 was 'The Progress and Harmony of Mankind'. The COI devised a floating pavilion of four exhibition halls suspended from steel masks, which featured a kaleidoscopic montage presentation of Britain's historic contribution to culture and the arts and to world progress in industry and architecture (Figs. 80a and b). By 1970 two-thirds of the COI's budget for overseas was directed towards direct or indirect support of the export effort. The aim had been to tell the story of industrial Britain in specific terms to generate confidence in British industry and technology, and to support manufacturers' efforts to sell their goods overseas. It also attempted to encourage foreign investment into the country. The propaganda for Expo 70 projected Britain as a modern energetic state that was open to business and tourism (Fig. 81), and that really was the case – the country was about to embark upon two seismic acts of modernisation, economically and politically, and the COI would play a major role in both.

81. *You Have 50 Million British Friends: Isn't it About Time you Visited Some of Them?* This was part of the COI's propaganda drive to encourage tourism to Britain and to meet 'The Friendly British Islanders', who are described thus: 'They can be quiet and gracious if you like but they're also wildly exciting....Whatever happened to the old "British reserve?" Try standing, looking lost on a street corner. Before you can open your "How to find it" book you'll find a friend to help. That's Britain. Give us a call. Our number is: Britain 1970.' (BL, PP/174/34A)

YOU HAVE 50 MILLION BRITISH FRIENDS

isn't it about time you visited some of them?

That makes quite a welcome because British friends are the best of friends.

They're helpful. Fun. Kind. Pleased to show you round.

They can be quiet and gracious if you like but they're also wildly exciting. You'll find them in London clubs, Cornish pubs, discotheques and bars from Scotland to Wales. Whatever happened to the old 'British reserve' bit you will wonder. Try standing, looking lost on a street corner. Before you can open your "How to Find it" book you'll find a friend to help.

That's Britain. Give us a call. Our number is: Britain 1970.

British Travel Association,
Rm. 246, Tokyo Club Building,
2-6, 3-chome, Kasumigaseki,
Chiyoda-Ku, Tokyo 100.
Tel : 581—3603

The friendly British Islanders

DECIMAL CURRENCY BOARD

**Decimal Currency:
Three years to go

Facts and forecasts**

HMSO Price 1/- net

The system

1 The Decimal Currency Act, which was passed on 14 July 1967, finally decided which decimal currency system we are to have. Our decimal system, like our present money system, will be based on the pound sterling. **But from 1971 the pound will be divided into 100 new pence** instead of 20 shillings each of 12 pence. There will be a new halfpenny as the lowest value coin.

2 At present we use three units to measure money values: the pound, the shilling and the penny. Under the decimal system we shall use only two: the pound and the new penny. We can call the decimal system a 'pound-new penny' system as against the present 'pounds, shillings and pence' system.

3 The symbol for pound will remain £ and the abbreviation for new penny or new pence will be p. Neither should be followed by a full stop unless it ends a sentence. The new halfpenny should be expressed as a vulgar fraction—½p. A decimal point should be used to separate pounds from new pence and amounts should be written either like this: or like this:

this:	or like this:
£275	£275·00
£6	£6·00
97p	£0·97
6p	£0·06
3½p	£0·03½

Mixed amounts of pounds and new pence should be written like this: **£29·27   £1·05**
(This is explained more fully in the Decimal Currency Board's publication *Decimal Currency: Expression of Amounts in printing, writing and in speech*).

The coinage

4 Seven £sd coins are in general use now. There will be six decimal coins.

5 There will be three bronze ('copper') coins:
½p—current value 1·2d
1p—current value 2·4d
2p—current value 4·8d
The new penny (1p) will be much smaller than the present penny, about the size of the old farthing. It will be half the weight of the 2p and twice the weight of the ½p, so weight will be proportional to value. Mixed bronze coins can be weighed, rather than counted, to get their value.

6 **There will be cupro-nickel ('silver') 5p and 10p coins of the same value, size, weight and metal content as the shilling and florin and completely interchangeable with them.** These two coins constitute a strong link between the old coinage and the new. Because the new coins are so similar to the old ones, the Government have decided to issue 5 and 10 new penny pieces during 1968 to maintain supplies of shillings and florins, which will no longer be minted. The 5 and 10 new penny pieces can be used as shillings and florins before Decimal Day, and afterwards the many shillings and florins still in circulation can be used as 5 and 10 new penny pieces. There will be no need to withdraw shillings and florins from circulation.

7 **The sixth decimal coin will be the 50p, which replaces the 10 shilling note.** The general specifications of the other five coins were defined in the Decimal Currency Act 1967. The specification of the 50p was announced in early May 1968. It will be a seven-sided coin of constant breadth—an 'equilateral curve heptagon'. It will be of cupro-nickel and rather less than half-crown size.

8 The Government decided on a 50p coin rather than a note for economic reasons. The 10 shilling note has a life of only four to five months and the costs of distribution and withdrawal are high. A coin, though more expensive to produce, has a life of half a century.

DECIMAL CURRENCY BOARD

New Coins

All the new coins carry on the obverse the portrait (by Mr Arnold Machin, OBE, RA) of the Queen wearing a diamond tiara, a wedding present from Queen Mary. The reverse designs of the coins are by Mr Christopher Ironside

The Royal Crown

A portcullis with chains royally crowned, originally a badge of King Henry VII, and for long closely associated with the Palace of Westminster

The badge of the Prince of Wales. Three ostrich feathers enfiling a coronet of crosses pattée and fleurs-de-lys, with the motto 'Ich Dien'

The badge of Scotland. A thistle royally crowned

Part of the crest of England. A lion passant guardant royally crowned

Britannia seated beside a lion

DECIMAL CURRENCY BOARD

Decimal Facts

1 The United Kingdom will start to change to decimal currency on Monday 15 February 1971—Decimal Day or D Day.

2 The pound (£) will not be changed.

3 There will be 100 new pence (100p) to each pound; so each new penny will be worth 2·4 of our present penny.

4 The symbol for pound will remain £ and the abbreviation for the new penny will be p; the new halfpenny will be expressed as ½p.

5 Our £sd coins and the 10s note are being replaced by six decimal coins; the changes will not all take place at once so that we can get used to them gradually.

6 The cupro-nickel ('silver') 5p and 10p coins came into circulation as legal tender on 23 April 1968. Except for the designs, these coins are identical in value, size, weight and metal content with the shilling and two-shilling piece and completely interchangeable with them.

7 Ten shilling notes are being replaced by a 50p coin. This coin is made of cupro-nickel ('silver'), it has a seven sided shape and is somewhat larger than a 10p (2s) coin. Banks are not re-issuing 10s notes because they are being replaced by the coin. The 50p coin is worth exactly 10s in £sd and is used as a high value coin. Meanwhile 10s notes remain legal tender and may be used for shopping etc. They can always be cashed in banks and therefore will never become worthless.

8 There will be three bronze ('copper') coins: ½p (1·2d), 1p (2·4d) and 2p (4·8d). The new penny (1p) will be about the size of the old farthing. It will be half the weight of the 2p and twice the weight of the ½p, so weight will be proportional to value.

9 The bronze coins will not be legal tender until D Day, but souvenir sets of coins, including the 5p and 10p 'silver' coins, are now available from banks. Later, coins will be available for training purposes.

10 The halfpenny ceased to be legal tender on 1 August 1969, and the halfcrown on 1 January 1970; so both coins will have disappeared before D Day. The penny, threepenny bit and sixpence will cease to be legal tender at the end of the changeover period, not later than August 1972.

**Decimal Currency Board, Standard House
27 Northumberland Avenue, LONDON WC2**

Prepared by the Decimal Currency Board and the Central Office of Information, 1968.
Printed for Her Majesty's Stationery Office at The Baynard Press.
November 1969.   Dd. 715759

DECIMAL DAY

The first seismic shift took place on 15 February 1971 and was known as Decimal Day. It was a day that many had been dreading, the decimalisation of the United Kingdom's currency. Out went the shilling, the half-crown and the sixpence, with all their historic associations. In came a new, unfamiliar European-style currency. For many people such a radical change represented almost a betrayal of the past and was resented, especially by elderly people who had more difficulty accepting the decision and then adapting to it. Such a major break with the past necessitated a sustained public information campaign. Nearly four years in advance of Decimal Day, the Decimal Currency Board (Fig. 82a and b) was set up and it called on the COI to carry out a number of preparatory campaigns.

These preparatory changes had to be carefully explained. The COI had carried out a continuous survey (through a market research company) among the general public at two-monthly intervals to gauge their attitude towards decimalisation. Surveys were also undertaken with industry and retailers to discover what preparations they were making and what information they required to make the transition as smooth as possible. The first campaign took place in the second half of 1968 to announce the introduction of the 5p and 10p coins. The cost of the campaign was £72,000 and in the national press the advertising produced the highest reading and noting figures from the public in the entire history of the Gallup surveys.[3] The second and third campaigns started in the latter part of 1969 and dealt with the introduction of the 50p coin and the withdrawal of the old half-crown (Fig. 83a and b). There was a final, substantive publicity push in the weeks prior to Decimal Day, including a song, by the popular entertainer Max Bygraves, called 'Decimalisation'. The BBC broadcast a series of five-minute programmes, *Decimal Five* and a special *Merry-go-Round* programme for school; and ITV produced a patronising short drama called *Granny Gets the Point*, where an elderly woman (played by Doris Hart from *On the Buses*), who does not understand the new system is taught to use it by her grandson.

On 14 February 1971, there were twelve pennies to the shilling and twenty shillings to the pound. The following day all that was history and the pound was made up of 100 new pence. Decimalisation – a currency based on simple multiples of ten and 100 – had been a long time coming to Britain.[4] The old currency had been deeply embedded in our national life and seemed a proud symbol of our island identity, that had set us apart from the rest of Europe. The adoption of the metric system proved less successful for similar reasons (Fig. 84). Meanwhile, as Britain was preparing

82. *Decimal Currency: Three Years to Go* (1968). The newly established Decimal Currency Board's booklet (priced one shilling) to explain the dramatic changes that were going to take place with the UK currency on 15 February 1971. (BL, PP/128/36A)

83. *New Coins and Decimal Facts* (1969). Strange new coins. A double-sided, pocket-sized reminder of the new coins (and their design) together with some helpful tips on how to calculate the new currency. (BL, PP/128/1A)

reluctantly for decimalisation, its government had also been attempting to negotiate an even closer union with Europe by joining the Economic European Community (EEC). In a few short years towards the end of the 1960s, the COI went from supporting the 'I'm Backing Britain' campaign to making the case for Britain to join the EEC.

BRITAIN, EUROPE AND THE 1975 REFERENDUM

Although Britain only joined in 1973, the EEC's antecedents go back much further. The Organisation for European Economic Co-operation (OEEC) established in 1948 had agreed to work co-operatively for economic recovery on a regional rather than on a strictly national basis. In 1951 the European Coal and Steel Community (ECSC) was set up between the three Benelux countries and France, Italy and West Germany, and in 1957 the so-called 'Six' signed the Rome Treaty, which established the European Economic Community. The ideological division of Cold War Europe between East and West was compounded by the growing division between the Six and the rest. In November 1959 seven of the eleven remaining states within the OEEC, preferring looser economic and political integration, formed the European Free Trade Association (EFTA) as a counterweight to the EEC. EFTA comprised Austria, Denmark, Norway, Portugal, Sweden, Switzerland and the United Kingdom. However, it soon became clear that EFTA could not match the growth of the EEC, and the two blocs attempted to reconcile their differences. Continuing economic problems in Britain evidenced by low growth, adverse trade balances and recurring sterling crises contrasted with the strong economic performance of the EEC countries. In October 1961 Britain had a change of mind and opened negotiations for entry into the EEC (Figs. 85 and 86a, b, c and d). However, moves towards expansion of the EEC were forestalled by General de Gaulle, who famously vetoed British entry in 1963 and again in 1967.

Harold Macmillan, the Prime Minister, informed Parliament on 2 August 1961 that he would start negotiations to join the EEC. He spoke of the struggle for freedom, and said it was both our duty and in our interest to add to Europe's strength in that struggle. He insisted that we should not take the final step unless our Commonwealth and other obligations could be reconciled, for otherwise the 'loss would be greater than the gain'. Macmillan concluded: 'We have much to gain from membership of the Community and we have also much to contribute.'[5] Following Macmillan's

---

84. *Going Metric in the Engineering Industry* (1969). A poster by the recently established Metrication Board encouraging the engineering industry to plan for full metrication by 1975. In 1965 the then Federation of British Industry informed the British government that its members favoured the adoption of the metric system and the Board of Trade agreed to support a ten-year metrication programme. However, progress was slow and resistance stubborn. By 1980, when the Metrication Board was abolished, the government had virtually abolished compulsory metrication. British people continued to buy petrol by the gallon and not the litre, cheese by the ounce and not the gramme, and if asked the distance from Dover to Calais they would invariably answer 21 miles and not 34 kilometres! In 2007 the European Commission announced it was dropping its attempts to bring the UK into line with the rest of the EU. (BL, PP/151/15A)

FACTS ON
EUROPE

Six countries are setting up a Common Market—
the European Economic Community. They are removing
trade barriers between themselves and working
towards a common tariff on goods from outside. Britain
and other countries are negotiating for membership
or association. This map shows the countries involved.

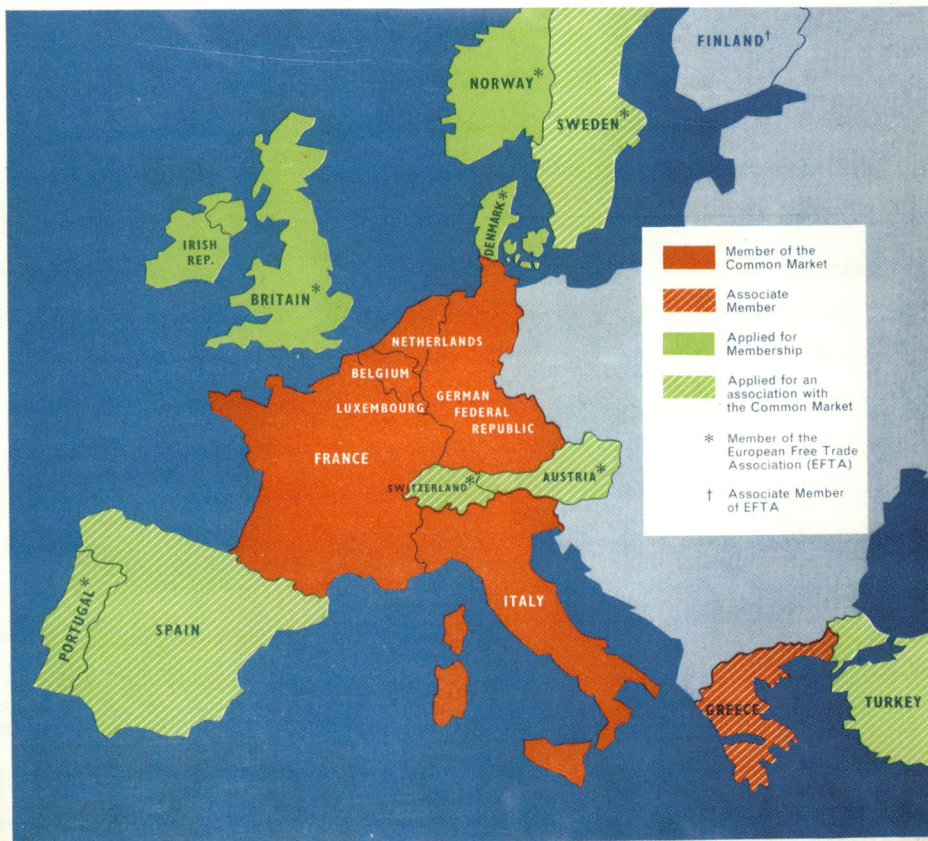

FINLAND†

NORWAY*

SWEDEN*

DENMARK*

IRISH
REP.

BRITAIN*

NETHERLANDS

BELGIUM

LUXEMBOURG

GERMAN
FEDERAL
REPUBLIC

FRANCE

SWITZERLAND*

AUSTRIA*

PORTUGAL*

SPAIN

ITALY

GREECE

TURKEY

Member of the
Common Market

Associate
Member

Applied for
Membership

Applied for an
association with
the Common Market

* Member of the
European Free Trade
Association (EFTA)

† Associate Member
of EFTA

This poster is the first of a series. Copies are available from Circulation Section (H), COI, Hercules Rd., London, S.E.1.
See also the new series of Common Market booklets. From Government Bookshops or any bookseller. Price 6d net.

No. 1. November 1962. Prepared by the Information Division of the Treasury and the Central Office of Information.   Printed in England for H.M. Stationery Office by M.M.P.Ltd.Wt.29977-2090

* Common Market Series

BROADSHEETS ON BRITAIN AND EUROPE No. 3

The first two Broadsheets in this series described the Common Market—the European Economic Community—and how it works. This Broadsheet is about two other European Communities—Britain has applied to join both—one for coal and steel and one for atomic energy.

Coal, Steel and Atoms

The European Coal and Steel Community is older than the European Economic Community but more limited in scope. Its object was to create a common market in coal and steel, and we have to go back to the years just after 1945 to understand how it came about. At that time, there were several organisations of European countries doing various jobs. The habit of working together was beginning to grow and people were coming to think that problems were more easily solved in this way.

In May 1950, Robert Schuman, who was then Foreign Minister of France, proposed that France and Western Germany should set up a community to pool their coal and steel resources. Other European countries would also be able to join.

The idea was taken up by six countries in all—France, Germany, Italy, Belgium, the Netherlands and Luxembourg—the same six who now form the European Economic Community. They all agreed to set up the European Coal and Steel Community (the ECSC) by the Treaty of Paris in April 1951 and the Community came into being in July 1952. Since 1954, Britain has had an association with ECSC to exchange information, to consult and to co-ordinate action where this was appropriate.

---

* Common Market Series

BROADSHEETS ON BRITAIN AND EUROPE No. 5

The last Broadsheet was about industry in the Six and in Britain. This one turns to agriculture and discusses some differences and similarities and the aims and methods of agricultural policy.

Agriculture in Europe

Agriculture (including horticulture) employs more people than any other single industry. This is true both of Britain and of the six countries of the Common Market. Agriculture is a complicated business, and so are Government policies for agriculture. Simple descriptions can be misleading and what follows is no more than a general indication.

Agriculture in the economy

In Britain about one person in twenty earns his living on the land. In the Six (taken together) the figure is nearly three in twenty, but it varies from country to country (see diagram). There are about three times as many people in the Common Market as in this country, and more than ten times as many people get their living from the land. In Britain agriculture provides about one-twentieth of our total national production. In the Six (taken together) its share of total production is about one-ninth.

Facts about agriculture

The Common Market countries produce the same sorts of agricultural products as we do. Italy, where the climate generally does not favour grass production, relies much

---

* Common Market Series

BROADSHEETS ON BRITAIN AND EUROPE No. 6

This Broadsheet is about the foreign trade of Common Market countries and of Britain. It shows the value of trade, what goods are traded, who buys them and how trade has grown in recent years.

Trade and the Common Market

Britain's prosperity has been built on foreign trade. We buy overseas about half our food and most of the raw materials we use in our factories. We pay for these imports mainly with exports—that is, selling abroad some of the goods we make. (We earn more than we pay out on other things such as overseas insurance and interest on investment; but these are not described in this Broadsheet.) The six Common Market countries are also large traders.

The value of trade

In 1961 the Six imported £11,500 million worth of goods and exported goods worth £11,550 million. (These figures include the trade of the Six with each other *and* with the rest of the world.) Britain's imports cost £4,400 million, and total exports earned £3,840 million.

Per head of the population, our imports are more important—about a quarter more—than the imports of the Six. Sales to other countries, per head, are roughly the same from both Britain and countries of the Six. The Six together are, of course, much larger traders than Britain.

---

* Common Market Series

BROADSHEETS ON BRITAIN AND EUROPE No. 7

This Broadsheet deals with social security in Britain and the Six. It shows how it is paid for and describes some of the services. It considers how the Rome Treaty affects social security.

Social Security in the Six

Social security is an important part of life in Britain. Apart from what we get from our national insurance system in return for our contributions, we benefit from other social services financed mainly from taxation. Nearly everyone, whether employed or not, is covered by our social services: the system is run by the nation for the whole community.

In the six countries of the Common Market, the main emphasis is on social insurance for people employed. However, this social insurance covers the great majority of their people. And the coverage is increasing.

How much is spent?

Exact comparisons between life in Britain and the Six are difficult to make. This is inevitably true of social security—the more so as it differs widely within the six Common Market countries themselves. So we can give only a broad picture in comparing such things as health, old age pensions, industrial injury and unemployment benefits, and family allowances. (This Broadsheet does not deal with education or housing.)

One comparison of spending on social security has been made by the International Labour Organisation. (The ILO is a body run by representatives of governments, employers and workers.) This study shows the proportion of national income spent on social security by each country. The results for Britain and the Six are shown in the

---

85. *Facts on Europe* (1962). A large poster setting out in very simple terms the geographical structure of Western Europe in 1962. At the bottom it states that this is the first in a series of publications and directs readers to forthcoming Common Market booklets. (BL, PP/39/41A)

86. *'Common Market Series'* (1962–1963). A collection of booklets providing detailed information on different aspects of the Common Market. The booklets were detailed, but all firmly in favour of the overall benefits to be gained by joining the EEC. They are priced at twopence and were published in 1962 and 1963, just before de Gaulle's first veto. (BL, PP/39/45A, 47A, 48A, 49A)

Background to the Negotiations

BRITAIN and the European Communities

HER MAJESTY'S STATIONERY OFFICE · PRICE 3s. 6d. net.

MAY 1950 M. Robert Schuman proposes the Coal and Steel Pool.

APRIL 1951 Six countries (Belgium, France, W. Germany, Italy, Luxembourg and the Netherlands) sign the Treaty of Paris setting up the European Coal and Steel Community.

JULY 1952 The ECSC comes into being.

JUNE 1955 The Foreign Ministers of the six countries meet in Messina and declare their intention to set up a common agency to develop atomic energy and to move towards a general common market.

APRIL 1956 Report of a group headed by M. Spaak, Belgian Foreign Minister, on the possibilities of setting up a common market.

MARCH 1957 Two Treaties signed in Rome by the six countries. These arrange for the setting up of :
1. The general Common Market — the European Economic Community.
2. The European Atomic Energy Community—Euratom.

JANUARY 1958 EEC and Euratom come into being.

NOVEMBER 1958 Negotiations are suspended after failure to reach agreement on a free trade area to include the Six, Britain and other European countries.

JULY 1960 The European Free Trade Association comes into being. Britain, Austria, Denmark, Norway, Portugal, Sweden and Switzerland agree to secure the benefits of a free trade area among themselves and to try to work to the removal of trade barriers between European countries.

AUGUST 1961 Parliament approves of the decision to begin negotiations to see if suitable terms can be arranged for Britain's joining EEC.

OCTOBER 1961 Britain's opening statement in the EEC negotiations is made to the Six.

JULY 1962 Britain's opening statements in the Euratom and ECSC negotiations are made to the Six.

SEPTEMBER 1962 Commonwealth Prime Ministers' Conference held in London.

© Crown Copyright 1962

Published by
HER MAJESTY'S STATIONERY OFFICE
To be purchased from York House, Kingsway, London, W.C.2; 423 Oxford St., London, W1; 13a Castle Street, Edinburgh, 2; 39 King Street, Manchester, 2; 35 Smallbrook, Ringway, Birmingham, 5; 109 St. Mary St., Cardiff; 50 Fairfax Street, Bristol, 1; 80 Chichester Street, Belfast, 1; or through any bookseller.

*Printed in England under the authority of Her Majesty's Stationery Office by Fox Printing Press Ltd., Marshall Road, E.20. S.O. Code No. 63-193-1 · B*² 3161 3.9/C .

PP./39/50A :

The COMMON MARKET in action

A SERVICE OF INFORMATION ABOUT BRITAIN AND THE EUROPEAN COMMUNITIES

Her Majesty's Stationery Office   Price 6d net

THE COMMON MARKET —and what it could mean to you

Factsheets on Britain and Europe
ISSUED BY HM GOVERNMENT

The purpose of this series is to present the facts about the Common Market, the considerations which have led the Government to apply for membership, the problems which have to be overcome and the progress so far made in the negotiations.

LEAFLETS AVAILABLE HERE

THE COMMON MARKET GET THE FACTS

Factsheets on Britain and Europe
NO. 1
ISSUED BY HM GOVERNMENT

The purpose of this series is to present the facts about the Common Market, the considerations which have led the Government to apply for membership, the problems which have

What is the

simple and informative
FREE AT YOUR LOCAL POST OFFICE

ISSUED BY HER MAJESTY'S GOVERNMENT

YOUR FREE FACTSHEETS ON BRITAIN AND EUROPE

87. *Britain and the European Communities* (1962). A forty-eight-page booklet setting out in considerable detail the background to the negotiations. This was extraordinarily expensive at three shillings. (BL, PP/164/24A)

88. *The Common Market in Action* (1962). A fifteen-page leaflet setting out the history of the EEC and how it operates. It was priced at sixpence. Speaking to Parliament on 2 August, Prime Minister Harold Macmillan had commended Britain's entry to the EEC as follows: 'The underlying issues, European unity, the future of the Commonwealth, the strength of the free world, are all of capital importance, and it is because we firmly believe that the United Kingdom has a positive part to play in their development – or they are all related – that we ask the House to approve what we are doing.' (BL, PP/39/50A)

89. *The Common Market: Get the Facts.* After Charles de Gaulle's resignation in 1969, the public information campaign continued unabated until Edward Heath eventually led Britain into the EEC in 1973. Here is a sample of posters and (free) fact sheets intended to be used as display sets in Post Offices throughout the country. (BL, PP/178/21L/28A/23A)

90. *The Common Market Display Set.* These are the information sheets that the COI sent to Post Offices to illustrate how the display sets should be arranged on the display towers: 'It is intended for use on Post Office display "towers" to draw the attention of the public to the Factsheets and other official literature on the Common Market. Each tower is an 8-foot high drum consisting of three identical, interlocking, sections' ... 'For maximum effect, the posters and stickers on each section should be arranged in identical style and when completed should look like this: ...'. (BL, PP/178/18A)

91. *The European Community.* A poster proudly showing the new, enlarged European Community, following the admission of the United Kingdom, the Irish Republic and Denmark in 1973. (BL, PP/253/8A)

92. *Shotgun Wedding* (1971). This cartoon by Arthur Horner appeared in *New Statesman* on 14 May 1971. Prime Minister Ted Heath is portrayed as a rotund John Bull, forcing a reluctant Britannia into marriage. In the background is a smirking President Pompidou (depicted in stereotypical louche Gallic stance, with a cigarette dangling from his mouth). (AH0327, British Cartoon Archive, University of Kent, Canterbury)

SHOTGUN WEDDING

decision, and for the rest of the decade and into the 1970s, the COI produced a veritable barrage of dense propaganda, intended to prepare the British people for entry and to persuade them of the overwhelming merits of membership (Figs. 87, 88, 89a, b and c, and 90a and b).

After de Gaulle's resignation in 1969, the diplomatic climate improved and his successor, Georges Pompidou, was more-favourably disposed to enlarging EEC membership. The changing circumstances provided the basis for Britain, under the leadership of Edward Heath, to negotiate entry into the EEC on 1 January 1973. A cartoon by Arthur Horner explored the ambiguous British attitudes to Europe during the period of admission, characterising Britain's admission into the EEC as a 'shotgun wedding' (Fig. 92). In order to depict Britain's ambivalent attitude to Europe, the cartoonist employed stereotypes from the nineteenth century. Prime Minister Heath, who negotiated with obstinate determination to achieve British admission, is portrayed as a rotund John Bull, forcing a reluctant Britannia into marriage with the Community. Behind Heath stands an accommodating 'groom' in the form of President Pompidou (depicted in stereotypical Gallic stance, with a cigarette dangling from his mouth). The cartoon reminds us, albeit indirectly, that after 1945 moves towards European integration were accompanied by a painful process of decolonisation and eventual loss of empires on the part of many Western European states. Nevertheless, in 1973 Britain (together with the Irish Republic and Denmark) became a full member (Fig. 91).

Two years later, the new Labour government under Harold Wilson's leadership implemented its General Election manifesto promise to renegotiate the country's terms of EEC membership and then put it to a referendum – a piece of political engineering designed largely to resolve tensions within the Labour Party. This was the first national referendum ever to be held throughout the entire United

Kingdom and it posed a difficult challenge for Wilson's government: how could it ensure an informed debate without being seen to prejudice the result?

In the 1975 referendum the government distributed three pamphlets to voters in the weeks prior to the referendum. The Keep Britain in Europe group produced a pamphlet *why you should vote YES*, the National Referendum Campaign *why you should vote NO* and the government produced its own pamphlet *Britain's New Deal in Europe* that outlined the government's rationale for recommending a yes vote. It was distributed by the Post Office to 21.6 million households in a package that included the official pamphlets from the remain and leave campaigns.

Britain's New Deal in Europe was not officially credited to the COI; the document referred simply to HM Government. In fact, Jim Callaghan (then Foreign Secretary) had set up a temporary Cabinet Office Referendum Information Unit to centralise all official information disseminated to the public. Nevertheless, the content and style of the pamphlet suggest that the COI was involved in all but name. The fifteen-page document was (literally) a red-white-and-blue official government 'guide' bearing the national arms on the front (Fig. 93), with plenty of statistics and a reassuring foreword by Harold Wilson that is addressed, in the form of a personal letter (Fig. 94), to 'Dear Voter':

> ... *We explain why the Government, after long, hard negotiations, are recommending to the British people that we should remain a member of the European Community.*
>
> *We do not pretend, and never have pretended, that we got everything we wanted in those negotiations. But we did get big and significant improvements on the previous terms.*
>
> *We confidently believe that these better terms can give Britain a New Deal in Europe. A Deal that will help us, help the Commonwealth, and help our partners in Europe.*

The government's case consisted of a mixture of negative and positive arguments. Focusing on the inherent risks of being outside the Community, the pamphlet argued that by voting no, 'there would be a risk of making unemployment and inflation worse' and that the UK would be relegated to the status of 'outsiders looking in' (Figs. 95a, b, c and d). On the other hand, the pamphlet made much of the substantial achievements renegotiated by the Labour government since coming to office (something that David Cameron was unable to demonstrate prior to the 2016 referendum).[6] The reassurance about our future relations with the Commonwealth was important; many people felt that by joining the EEC, Britain was cutting its historic ties. The pamphlet dispels such fears by demonstrating that the new terms 'include a better deal for our Commonwealth partners' and actually that 'Commonwealth Governments want Britain to stay in the Community'. According

BRITAIN'S NEW DEAL IN EUROPE

'Her Majesty's Government have decided to recommend to the British people to vote for staying in the Community'

HAROLD WILSON, PRIME MINISTER

DEAR VOTER

This pamphlet is being sent by the Government to every household in Britain. We hope that it will help you to decide how to cast your vote in the coming Referendum on the European Community (Common Market).

Please read it. Please discuss it with your family and your friends.

We have tried here to answer some of the important questions you may be asking, with natural anxiety, about the historic choice that now faces all of us.

We explain why the Government, after long, hard negotiations, are recommending to the British people that we should remain a member of the European Community.

We do not pretend, and have never pretended, that we got everything we wanted in those negotiations. But we did get big and significant improvements on the previous terms.

We confidently believe that these better terms can give Britain a New Deal in Europe. A Deal that will help us, help the Commonwealth, and help our partners in Europe.

That is why we are asking you to vote in favour of remaining in the Community.

I ask you again to read and discuss this pamphlet.

Above all, I urge all of you to use your vote.

For it is *your* vote that will now decide. The Government will accept *your* verdict.

Harold Wilson

YOUR RIGHT TO CHOOSE

The coming Referendum fulfils a pledge made to the British electorate in the general election of February 1974.

The Labour Party manifesto in the election made it clear that Labour rejected the terms under which Britain's entry into the Common Market had been negotiated, and promised that, if returned to power, they would set out to get better terms.

The British people were promised the right to decide through the ballot box whether or not we should stay in the Common Market on the new terms.

And that the Government would abide by the result.

That is why the Referendum is to be held. Everyone who has a vote for a Parliamentary election — that is, everyone on the Parliamentary election register which came into force in February 1975 — will be entitled to vote.

The European Community and its world-wide links

THE NEW DEAL

WILL PARLIAMENT LOSE ITS POWER? (cont)

IF WE SAY 'NO'

IF WE SAY 'YES'

AND NOW—THE TIME FOR YOU TO DECIDE

93. *Britain's New Deal in Europe.* The Labour government's 'advisory' pamphlet recommending that the people vote to remain in the European Community. (BL, PP/209/5A)

94. *Your Right to Choose.* Prime Minister Harold Wilson's 'personal' letter explaining the basis of his government's 'New Deal in Europe'. The letter concluded: 'For it is *your* vote that will now decide. The Government will accept *your* verdict.' (BL, PP/209/5A)

95. *The New Deal.* In this pamphlet, explaining the government's 'New Deal in Europe', Prime Minister Harold Wilson is quoted: 'I believe that our renegotiation objectives have been substantially though not completely achieved.' Such restrained political rhetoric added to the widespread belief that the government's 'advisory' pamphlet represented a balanced assessment of the pros and cons of Britain's membership of the EEC. Moreover, it chimed with the views of 'moderate' politicians whom the British public appeared to respect. (BL, PP/209/5A)

to the pamphlet, the most important issues (particularly during the renegotiations of the year before) were 'FOOD', 'MONEY' and 'JOBS'. Perhaps most interestingly (in the light of the 2016 Referendum), the issue of immigration did not feature at all; at a time when Britain was seen as 'the sick man of Europe', nobody thought that European workers were anxious to come and work in Britain. Throughout the referendum, *The Sun* (which supported remain) ran a front-page caption 'Crisis Britain'. Following the oil crisis of 1973, inflation was running at close to 25 per cent; a balance of payments crisis was placing intense strain on the currency, while labour relations were deteriorating rapidly. 'Anti-marketeers' were more worried about *outward* migration, with young Britons forced to seek work on the continent.

The fear that the UK was no longer in control of its destiny was one of the strongest cards played by the 'Out' campaign. Their posters warned *Brussels – The New Capital of Britain*. The concern over 'sovereignty' was something that the government pamphlet addressed, citing four 'Facts' that ensured that Parliament would not lose its supremacy: 'Remember: All the other countries in the Market enjoy, like us, democratically elected Governments answerable to their own Parliaments and their own voters. They do not want to weaken their Parliaments any more than we would.' The 'Keep Britain in Europe' campaign went even further and employed emotive historical lessons. One stark, black-and-white poster proclaimed: 'Forty million people died in two European wars this century. Better lose a little national sovereignty than a son or daughter. Vote Yes to keep the peace.'

In 1975, all the press, apart from the communist *Morning Star*, backed staying in the EEC. Almost the whole of finance and business were behind the pro-Europe campaign. Harold Wilson agreed to let his Cabinet ministers campaign on opposite sides of the debate, the so-called 'agreement to differ', as the price of Labour unity. The most concerted opposition came from the left of the party, led by Tony Benn and Michael Foot. In the 1970s the Conservatives backed British membership although there was some opposition on the far right, notably from Enoch Powell. As a result, Tony Benn, Barbara Castle, Michael Foot and Peter Shore found themselves campaigning on the same side as Enoch Powell. Margaret Thatcher, the new leader of the Conservatives, bought into the prevailing orthodoxy and Ted Heath's enthusiasm for membership of the EEC. Thatcher campaigned actively to remain in Europe and famously posed wearing a pullover adorned with European flags (it was later said that it was the last time she was to be seen sporting a tricolour next to her heart!).

Not only could the 'In' campaign call on almost all the leading figures across the political spectrum, but it also assembled a galaxy of actors, sports stars and celebrities who attended meetings, sent messages of support and generally boosted the political and economic arguments for remaining tied to the EEC ('Don't Knock Britain Out. Keep Britain in Europe', says Henry Cooper'). The 'Out' campaign simply could not match this; a disadvantage further compounded by the finances of the two campaigns. The government gave each side a grant of £125,000, on top of which they could raise whatever money they pleased. The 'Out' campaign raised £8,000 plus contributions in kind from some of the unions. The 'In' campaign raised more than £2 million. Thus, when membership was put to a referendum in 1975, it had the support of Britain's three main parties and all its national newspapers. The eventual referendum on 5 June 1975 asked the voters: 'Do you think the United Kingdom should stay in the European Community (the Common Market)?' British membership of the EEC was endorsed by 67.2 per cent of those voting (32.7 per cent opposed), with a turnout of 64.5 per cent. This represented a major defeat for the anti-marketeers at the time, with only two of the sixty-eight counting areas returning 'No' majority votes. The European project had been put before the British people and they supported it overwhelmingly.

There is certainly some truth in the notion that the Yes campaign was a project masterminded by the political elite. Remember also that Britain had only been a member of the EEC for two years and had been particularly badly weakened by the oil price spike of 1973–74. Some voters were dissatisfied with aspects of Britain's EEC membership but willing to endorse it for fear that exit would leave the UK internationally isolated. Pro-Europeans had not sought the referendum in the first place, but they were content with how things went. After the results were declared, Harold Wilson told journalists that 'fourteen years of national debate' had come to an end. But the 1975 Referendum did not end the debate, far from it. There was no immediate economic stimulus – in fact, strikes and power cuts continued, and rising oil prices caused double-digit inflation. Europe has remained a toxic issue in British politics.

RACE RELATIONS

Further toxic issues confronting the country in the 1970s were those of immigration and race relations. In 1967 Conservative Member of Parliament Enoch Powell spoke of his opposition to the immigration of Kenyan Asians to the United Kingdom after the African country's leader Jomo Kenyatta's discriminatory policies led to the flight of Asians from that country. On 20 April 1968, Powell gave his infamous 'Rivers of Blood' speech in Birmingham in which he warned his audience of what he believed would be the consequences of continued unchecked mass immigration from the Commonwealth to the UK. Powell was voicing his concerns about the Labour government's Race Relations Act, which was going through Parliament at the time. The Act would make it illegal to refuse housing, employment or public services to a person in Great Britain on the grounds of colour, race, ethnic or national origins. Powell was sacked from Ted Heath's Shadow Cabinet the following day and the Act became law in October 1968. The Act extended the powers of the Race Relations Board (RRB) to deal with complaints of discrimination; and it set up a new body, the Community Relations Commission, to promote 'harmonious community relations'. Presenting the Bill to Parliament, the Home Secretary, Jim Callaghan, said: 'The House has rarely faced an issue of greater social significance for our country and our children.'

The shortcoming of the existing legislation, and particularly the powers available to the Race Relations Board and the Community Relations Commission, were

'DISGUSTED', BINCHESTER

A seven-minute cartoon film, 'Disgusted', Binchester, which has been made for the Race Relations Board by Nicholas Cartoon Films and the Central Office of Information, is now available from the Central Film Library.

Through the character of 'Disgusted', the film sets out to show that, through the ages, legislation bringing about social advance has always been resisted.

It was 'Disgusted' who led the opposition to the Elizabethan Poor Law; who protested against the abolition of slavery and saw no reason to prohibit small children from working in coalmines. When universal compulsory education was introduced he expected revolution to follow. Needless to say he did not have a good word for the Race Relations Act 1968.

The odd thing is that all the reforms 'Disgusted' automatically opposes have at least one common feature. They become part of

the accepted landscape of society so quickly that if anybody subsequently attempts to interfere with them, 'Disgusted' will be among the first to protest about that too.

Central Film Library, Government Building, Bromyard Avenue, Acton, London W3 7JB

Scottish Central Film Library, 16–17 Woodside Terrace, Charing Cross, Glasgow G3 7XN.

Welsh Office Film Library, 42 Park Place, Cardiff CF1 3PY.

Don't know what the country is coming to!

England will never be the same again!

Mollycoddling

The country just cannot afford it

Dear Sir, We the British...

96. *'Disgusted', Binchester* (1973). A poster and a feature promoting the film in the Race Relations Board's journal *Race Relations*. Disgusted is shown opposing the introduction of the royal courts in the reign of Henry II, opposing the Elizabethan Poor Law, protesting against the abolition of slavery and small children from working down coalmines, and fearing revolution following the introduction of universal compulsory education. 'Needless to say he did not have a good word for the Race Relations Act 1968'. 'Disgusted will always be with us, but the Race Relations Board believe that if he can be seen in the perspective of history, so can the Race Relations Act 1968.' (BL, PP/162/19A and 14A).

becoming increasingly evident by the early 1970s. The COI, in liaison with the RRB, embraced a number of initiatives to foster 'harmonious community relations'. In 1973 it undertook a two-pronged approach. The first consisted of an information pack for schools and educational establishments entitled *A Project on Race Relations*. This consisted of bite-sized features on the 'Role of the Law', 'Migration to and from Britain', 'Laws about Discrimination', 'Colour and Prejudice', etc. Information was provided on why the 1968 Act was necessary and it generally challenged stereotypes about immigrants living in the country.[7] The second approach used humour to expose existing bigotry and prejudices. A seven-minute cartoon film was commissioned to look at episodes of the life and times of 'Disgusted', the man who is always writing to the newspapers and protesting about some new law or other. To promote the films the RRB caricatured 'Disgusted' in its own journal *Race Relations* (Figs. 96a and b).

A more-serious poster campaign was launched the following year in 1974. The poster featured an ethnically diverse group of smiling, happy children headlined *It's Their Future: Treat Them on Their Merits* (Figs. 97a and b). It's not particularly a hard-hitting slogan, but it is revealing that six years after it had been introduced, the government still felt it had to justify the fairness of the 1968 Act. The Labour government that came to power in 1974 therefore proposed reform, in parallel

Disgusted, Binchester

The Race Relations Board have commissioned a seven-minute cartoon film which may be hired from the Central Film Library.* Made by Nicholas Cartoon Films Ltd. for the Central Office of Information, the film takes a look at some of the lives and times of Disgusted, the man who is always writing to the newspapers and protesting about some new law or other.

If there had been newspapers in the reign of Henry II, Disgusted would have been the first to protest about the introduction of the royal courts, which first gave Englishmen an alternative to the rough justice of barons and bishops.

It was Disgusted who led the opposition to the Elizabethan Poor Law; who protested against the abolition of slavery and saw no reason to prohibit small children from working in coalmines. When universal compulsory education was introduced he expected revolution to follow. Needless to say he did not have a good word for the Race Relations Act 1968.

The odd thing is, that all the reforms Disgusted can be counted on to protest about have at least one common feature. They become part of the accepted landscape of society so quickly that if anybody subsequently attempts to interfere with them, Disgusted will be among the first to protest about that too.

Disgusted will always be with us, but the Race Relations Board believe that if he can be seen in the perspective of history, so can the Race Relations Act 1968.

*Central Film Library, Government Building, Bromyard Avenue, Acton, London W3 7JB.

Scottish Central Film Library, 16-17 Woodside Terrace, Charing Cross, Glasgow C3

Central Film Library of Wales, 42 Park Place, Cardiff CF1 3PY.

Prepared by the Race Relations Board and the Central Office of Information 1973
Printed in England for Her Majesty's Stationery Office by Eden Fisher & Co. Ltd., London EC3M 5JE   Dd. 9.73

97. *It's Their Future: Treat Them on Their Merits* (1974). The poster campaign was published in a number of languages. 'Everybody wants to be treated on their merits. But what will happen to these youngsters? For some of them the future will depend simply on their abilities. For others it may depend on the colour of their skin. <u>That is unfair</u>. The 1968 Race Relations Act exists to give everyone an equal opportunity regardless of race or colour, in jobs, in housing and in services. There is no question of privilege in that. It is simply a matter of fair play.' (BL, PP/162/40A, 42A)

इनका भविष्य

सभी चाहते हें कि उनेक साथ उनकी योग्यता के अनुसार व्यवहार किया जाय । मगर इन नई उम्रवालों का क्या होगा ?

कुछ का भविष्य केवल उनकी क्षमताओं पर निर्भर होगा । लेकिन संभव है कि कुछ औरों का भविष्य उनकी चमड़ी के रंग पर निर्भर हो ।

यह अन्याय है ।

रेस रिलेशंस ऐक्ट 1968 इसीलिये है कि जाति या रंग के मेदभाव के बिना सभी को नौकरिभी, नौकरियों आवास और सेवा आदि के क्षेत्र में समान अवसर प्राप्त हों ।

इसमें विशेषाधिकार जैसी कोई बात नहीं है । यह तो केवल न्याय मिलने की बात है ।

अगर आपको लगे कि इनमें से किसी क्षेत्र में आप जातिगत मेदभाव के शिकार हुए हें या आप किसी व्यक्ति को जानते हें जो इस प्रकार के मेदभाव का शिकार हुआ है या अगर आप केवल यह जानना चाहते हें कि इस कानून का आशय क्या है, तो रेस रिलेशंस बो ड़ से संपर्क कीजिये ।

BIRMINGHAM
Daimler House
(4th Floor)
33 Paradise Circus
Queensway, Birmingham
B1 2BJ
Tel : 021-643 7525

GLASGOW
24 Drury Street
Glasgow G2 5AA
Tel : 041-221 4470

LEEDS
Yorkshire Insurance
Building
4 South Parade
Leeds LS1 5QX
Tel : Leeds 34413

LONDON
5 Lower Belgrave Street
London SW1W 0NR
Tel : 01-730 6291

MANCHESTER
Scottish Life House
(3rd Floor)
Bridge Street
Manchester M33DH
Tel : 061-834 7543

NOTTINGHAM
Birbeck House
Trinity Square
Nottingham NG1 4AX
Tel : Nottingham 44873

इनके साथ इनकी योग्यता के अनुसार व्यवहार करो ।

Prepared by the Race Relations Board and the Central Office of Information 1974 Printed in England for Her Majesty's Stationery Office by Balding & Mansell Ltd, Wisbech. Dd. 223859-3/74

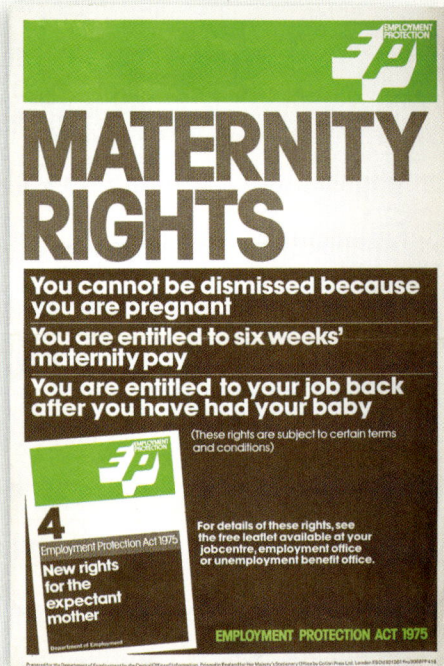

98. *Will you be Entitled to Maternity Allowance?* A poster designed in 1974 by the Mount/Evans studio for the COI. The trendy looking mother pushing the pram is encouraged to seek out further information about her entitlements to maternity allowance and whether or not she is paying sufficient contributions ('Check NOW that you are paying the right stamp'). (BL, PP/182/19A)

99. *Maternity Rights* (1976). A poster and leaflet from the Employment Protection Agency. The UK introduced its first maternity leave legislation through the Employment Protection Act 1975. For the first time, female employees were protected from being dismissed from their job due to pregnancy. In addition, women were granted maternity leave with reinstatement rights at their place of work prior to confinement over a period of 29 weeks, beginning in the week of confinement. The terms and conditions for an employee taking leave could not be less favourable than those which would have been applicable if she had not been absent (for example, with regard to seniority, pension rights). (BL, PP/227/61A)

100. *Equal Pay for Women* (1977). A poster urging women to collect a COI leaflet outlining their rights under the Equal Pay Act 1971 and the Sex Discrimination Act 1975. (BL, PP/240/48A)

equal pay for women

What does it do for you?

free
leaflets
available
here

Retirement Pension increase

Most retirement pensioners will not lose any supplementary pension they may have when their retirement pensions go up from 22 July

And any retirement pensioner getting a rent or rate rebate or rent allowance before 22 July will not lose this on account of the pension increase

RETIREMENT PENSION INCREASE

with legislation on Sex Discrimination (Figs. 98 and 99). It is argued that this factor was of crucial importance. The Sex Discrimination Act of 1975 served as a model for the legislation on racial discrimination, and both Acts were built upon the same principles. The extent of racial discrimination and disadvantage was increasingly being demonstrated, and in 1976 a new Race Relations Act superseded the 1968 Act. The new legislation significantly strengthened the law and for the first time it defined direct and indirect discrimination, and also established the Commission for Racial Equality (CRE).

YOU'RE ENTITLED TO IT!

At the same time as the secretaries in Surbiton were 'Backing Britain' by preparing to work extra hours for no pay to help haul the country out of the economic doldrums, other women were taking very different industrial action. In 1970 the Equal Pay Act was passed, prohibiting unequal pay and working conditions between men and women (Fig. 100). The Act did not come into force until 1975. Its foundations had been laid by women's industrial action at the Ford car-manufacturing plants in 1968 and the resulting legislation introduced in 1970 by the MP Barbara Castle. The 1970s saw workers fighting for their rights regardless of gender, ethnicity and class. Women in particular fought for trade union recognition in the Grunwick strike and the Nigh Cleaners dispute. This radical shift in attitudes towards women workers would bring, it was hoped, equal pay and conditions along with it. The equality legislation, the Sex Discrimination Act, passed in 1975, was intended to ensure this. As well as equal pay and an end to sex discrimination, workers also fought for better pensions (Fig. 101), which led to the passing of the Pensions (Increase) Act in 1971 and the Social Security Pension Act, 1975. The underlying purpose of the legislation was to maintain the purchasing power of state retirement and public service pensions. In 1978 the State Earnings Related Scheme and Guaranteed Minimum Pensions came in to being. ♔

101. *Retirement Pension Increase* (1974). A rather patronising poster from the Mount/Evans studio, which uses stereotypical images of two pensioners reading about their new pension increases under the 1971 Pensions (Increase) Act. By 1967 more than eight million employees working for private companies enjoyed a final salary pension, along with four million state workers. In 1978 the Labour government introduced a fully fledged 'earnings-related' state top-up system (SERPS) for those without access to a company scheme. (BL, PP/182/23A)

102. *Don't Just Sit There – Get a House Renovation Grant.* Two posters, both from 1978, that use humour to get across the message that grants were available to improve the home. These grants were to provide inside lavatories. Not only is it surprising that this was still an issue in the late 1970s, but it is also revealing that the COI chose to front the campaign with a saucy seaside-type postcard design that was synonymous with the work of Donald McGill. The posters were complemented by a TV advertisement entitled *Outside Loo*, featuring the actor Roy Kinnear. (BL, PP/277/46A, 45A)

CHAPTER FIVE

LIVING WITH THE BOMB IN THE ENTERPRISING 1980s

The 1980s was arguably the most controversial decade in modern British history; it was the era of Thatcherism and a time of extraordinary change at home and abroad. Britain went to war over the Falkland Islands and by the end of the decade the Berlin Wall had crumbled, and the Cold War had ended. Microsoft, IBM, Intel and Apple began to have an impact on all our lives as small computers became cheaper and more accessible. The 1980s also marked an important turning point for the COI, as market forces began to have a profound impact. It became a trading fund and executive agency. Government departments no longer had to use COI, so it had to charge for its services and financially break-even. As major industries were taken out of public ownership and sold on the stock market, COI advertising supported major privatisations for BT, British Gas ('Tell Sid'), Rolls-Royce, BAA and the water industries. Between 1981 and 1996, the COI handled 25 privatisation campaigns. As the European enlargement movement grew, the COI helped the Department of Trade and Industry with one of the first fully 'integrated' campaigns involving publications, radio, presentations for business and the COI's regional services. The COI also introduced government departments to the latest technologies. An electronic news distribution service (NDS) allowed them to send press releases instantly to every national newspaper and broadcaster. Sophisticated databases and telephone response systems were introduced for the RAF and Royal Navy recruitment campaigns. The COI's Direct Marketing team now had more experience of telephone response handling than any other publicity agency.

The role and nature of the COI's propaganda was changing dramatically. It no longer had exclusive responsibility for shaping government policy objectives. Rather, it was competing for work as a glorified advertising and marketing agency. For this chapter I have chosen a theme that is not confined to the 1980s – its roots can actually be traced back to the late 1940s and the threat of nuclear war.

'PROTECT AND SURVIVE': LIVING WITH THE BOMB

World War II ended in 1945 with the devastation of the Japanese cities of Hiroshima and Nagasaki, as the United States demonstrated its powerful atomic bombs. The Soviet Union did not lag far behind, successfully testing its first atomic weapon in 1949. As the arms race between the world's superpowers accelerated, the threat of a deadly global war became increasingly real, held back only by the threat of 'mutually assured destruction' and, especially in the Western world, an increasingly war-weary public. The term Cold War is itself a metaphor, using an indication of temperature to describe a state of politics short of an actual 'hot' war. One of the consequences of developing weapons of mass destruction was the difficulty of coming to terms with imagining a nuclear war.

George Orwell, writing two months after the atomic attack on Japan, complained: 'Considering how likely we are to be blown to pieces by it within the next five years, the atomic bomb has not roused so much discussion as might have been expected'.[1] Given the suffering and deprivation that people had experienced since 1939, it is perhaps not surprising that the immediate public reaction in Britain to events in Japan was somewhat muted. After all, they had experienced an election, the dropping of an atomic bomb and the end of the war – all within a matter of weeks. It was a moment for a war-weary people to take stock. The response of the new Labour government, as we have seen in Chapter Two, was less muted. Britain's leaders viewed the possession of nuclear weapons not only as a necessary military deterrent but also as a symbol of prestige, guaranteeing Britain's power status. Ernest Bevin had famously proclaimed at a Cabinet committee discussing the acquisition of such a weapon, 'We've got to have the bloody Union Jack on top of it'.[2]

The Cold War nuclear arms race focused much of the propaganda on national security and fear – two incendiary factors, which led to the most-extreme forms of xenophobia and to claims and counter-claims that gained momentum. In such a climate it frequently became impossible for individuals to challenge prevailing assertions for fear of being labelled 'unpatriotic' or, worse, a communist or capitalist spy. In the United States, fear of communist infiltration (whipped up by the accusations of Senator Joseph McCarthy and his Senate investigating committee), spy mania and the knowledge that the Soviet Union now possessed a nuclear capability led to increased spending on nuclear armaments and intense and prolonged propaganda campaigns to inform the American public of what precautions could be taken in the event of a Soviet nuclear attack. The Federal Civil Defense Administration (FCDA) produced posters, pamphlets and a number of short films for television and movie theatres. The new medium of television proved particularly receptive. The most famous example in this genre was the cartoon series *Duck and Cover*, which featured Bert the Turtle, who informed television and cinema audiences how they should react during an atomic explosion. In the early 1960s the FCDA produced a number of television and film series (that actually started in 1954 with *The House in the Middle*)[3] intended to reassure the American public that the Defense Department was continuing research in the area of Civil Defence, and to encourage citizens to educate themselves.

On 3 October 1952, Britain detonated its own atom bomb, thus becoming the world's third nuclear power. This symbolic act not only reaffirmed the country's status as a great power but in so doing Britain avoided complete dependence on the United States, which was refusing to share atomic information. However, one of the consequences of acquiring weapons of mass destruction was that the British government had to think about how it would protect its own citizens in the event of a nuclear attack. The threat of nuclear annihilation persuaded the Attlee government to imagine a type of war that had not occurred. With the end of World War II, Civil Defence measures were rapidly run down. The advent of the Cold War, however, put Civil Defence back on the agenda and in 1948 the Civil Defence Act established the Civil Defence Corps (CDC) – a civilian volunteer organisation that came into effect in 1949 to mobilise and take local control in the aftermath of a major national emergency, principally envisaged as a Cold War nuclear attack. Attlee's Labour government launched a major recruitment campaign, to be co-ordinated by the COI by means of a national publicity campaign bearing the slogan: 'You can't be certain. You can be prepared.' Posters and films were used in the campaign, including the Crown Film Unit production entitled *The Waking Point* (1951), which targeted the citizen's social conscience and attempted to expose the global communist threat to democratic life. By March 1956 the CDC had 330,000 personnel. By 1960 the government was claiming that it was the fourth arm of the country's services with over half a million recruits.[4]

Civil Defence encouraged civilian populations to anticipate the terror of a nuclear attack and also to assure them that it was possible to survive such a war. The antecedents of Civil Defence can be traced to a British government leaflet issued in 1938 entitled *The Protection of Your Home Against Air Raids*. Two years later in June 1940, the wartime government published a sixty-four-page booklet *Air Raids – What You Must Know, What You Must Do*. During the 1950s it was assumed, initially at least, that after an exchange of nuclear weapons there would be a period of conventional warfare ('broken-backed' warfare), which would need industrial support. Civil Defence would therefore still play a part in protecting the civil population, transport capabilities and industrial capacity. The advent of the hydrogen bomb in the mid-1950s changed all that.

In 1954 the British government convened a secret committee of Civil Servants to explore the implications for Britain of the hydrogen bomb in a nuclear war. Headed by William Strath, a small group of experts assessed the country's ability to survive a thermonuclear attack. The conclusions of the Strath Report in 1955 (which were kept secret from the British public until 2002) were profoundly pessimistic. Its portrayal of widespread devastation and the likely collapse of civil society shocked politicians and government officials, and led not only to massive revisions in the UK's plans for war but to official attempts to suppress public discussion of thermonuclear weapons and Civil Defence.

Having made the decision in 1954 to develop the hydrogen bomb, Britain exploded its first hydrogen bomb in 1957 as part of a series of tests. The development of the hydrogen bomb meant that nuclear war became increasingly associated in the public's mind with the Apocalypse. Moreover, the tests raised a major debate about the dangers of nuclear weapons and led to the founding in 1958 of the Campaign for Nuclear Disarmament (CND), which pressed for British, and ultimately international, abandonment of nuclear weapons. The Cold War and the arms race between the superpowers had reached a peak by the 1960s.

The advent of the hydrogen bomb in the mid-1950s and the worsening economic situation only made Civil Defence measures harder to achieve. The explosive power of the hydrogen bomb and the resulting public disquiet once again caused the government to consider Civil Defence measures. The 1957 Defence White Paper (in the wake of the Suez debacle) not only ended conscription but also emphasised two, arguably contradictory, approaches: a reliance on nuclear deterrence as the only means of confronting the Soviet Union in the Cold War and the need to save money. It also acknowledged (probably in the light of the secret Strath Report) that there was no means of providing adequate protection for the people in the face of a nuclear attack. It is therefore all the more surprising that in the same year the COI launched a new recruitment campaign for the CDC and sought to reassure the public that it was possible to survive a thermonuclear attack. Nevertheless, recruitment campaigns to the CDC continued, together with the issuing of information that sought to reassure the public that it was possible to live with the bomb.

Objectively, the government faced a significant manpower problem. The Home Secretary reported in both 1952 and 1953 that despite (or because of) the voluntary nature of the Civil Defence organisation, it was seriously below the authorised peacetime strengths. In fact, the impact of the Korean War led to a rise in recruitment, demonstrating that a sense of real or perceived danger was a far more persuasive incentive to signing up than publicity campaigns. Nevertheless, the desire not to alarm the public was clearly more important than facing up to reality. Civil Defence, so the publicity claimed, would protect the country.[5] The slogan chosen was 'Civil Defence is Common Sense'. In 1957 the COI produced a poster, *Civil Defence Today* (Fig. 103), illustrated with a cartoon by Leslie Illingworth (cartoonist for the *Daily Mail*) that had been specially commissioned. The cartoon shows three

---

103. *Civil Defence Today.* This 1957 poster features a government-commissioned cartoon by Leslie Illingworth, 'If You Think it's Hopeless, You're Wrong'. A full-page advertisement of the poster was placed in all the 'important' national and provincial newspapers by the COI. (TNA, INF 2/12211)

H BOMB THREAT

IT'LL NEVER HAPPEN...

WHAT'S THE USE...

THERE ISN'T ANY...

CIVIL DEFENCE

IF YOU THINK IT'S HOPELESS, YOU'RE WRONG

Specially drawn for H.M. Government by Illingworth

FOUR STRAIGHTFORWARD SIMPLE FACTS ABOUT
Civil Defence Today

The basic minimum of information for every responsible man and woman

1 **The H-Bomb: we hear too much of the horrors, not enough about our chances of survival.** Some people will tell you that if this country were attacked with H-Bombs, every man jack of the population would be wiped out. *That just isn't true: it isn't anything LIKE the truth.*

There would be terrible devastation, but for millions and millions of people, chances of survival would be very good. It depends very much on our Civil Defence. The more people we have in it, the better.

2 **Civil Defence is well on with the job already.** Some people think of Civil Defence equipment as a long-handled shovel, a rather odd tin hat, and so on.

Well, it's not like that at all. Civil Defence today is a modern, country-wide Service, which offers you training with first-class equipment—radio and radiation-testing instruments, fire-fighting apparatus and rescue gear, and the latest four-wheel-drive vehicles. There are thousands of qualified Instructors, three full-time Instructors' Schools, and a Staff College for advanced courses and studies.

The more you get to know about Civil Defence, the more impressed you become.

There is a Civil Defence organisation in every town in the Kingdom, and there are units in thousands of industrial firms. There are *half a million* people in the Civil Defence Services today. But half a million is not enough: not nearly.

3 **Civil Defence is useful to you now, in peace.** In Civil Defence today, you *learn.* That is the whole aim and object of joining.

You learn, first and foremost, how to live with your eyes open in the same world as the H-Bomb. You begin to learn what this new, nuclear-age world is really like. You acquire a fuller, deeper understanding of many important events that we are all involved in, whether we like it or not.

Besides this, there is a practical, everyday value in the things you learn. Take just one part of it—First Aid. In Great Britain in 1956 there were over a *quarter of a million* casualties from motor accidents, and probably at least another *million* casualties from accidents in the home. What you know—or don't know—about First Aid could make all the difference to somebody.

Do you know how to put out a fire? Do you know how to operate a radio transmitter? These are two more of the useful, interesting things that Civil Defence could teach you, now.

Do you remember the East Coast floods, the Lynmouth disaster, the Harrow rail smash? These are three of the emergencies where trained volunteers from Civil Defence were ready and able to help. They were needed.

4 **Civil Defence wants more volunteers, NOW.** It's no good saying "I'll be there on the day." That's too late. There wouldn't be time to train you and organise you.

It's no good leaving Civil Defence to other people. For everybody else, *The Other Fellow is YOU.*

You live in this world, you are part of the nuclear-age—there is no opting-out for anybody. Civil Defence *matters*—and matters to YOU.

Go along to your Council Offices today, and ask about Civil Defence. There's no commitment, no 'bull', no length-of-service engagements.

Your training takes only about *one hour a week.* The classes are free, and are near your own home. The knowledge you gain could be useful to you at any time, and would be VITAL to you if we were at War.

Civil Defence is sound common sense. It's high time you were in it.

The FOURTH Arm

Traditionally, we have three Services in this country: the Royal Navy, the Army, and the Royal Air Force. Now, we have a fourth service of the Crown—unarmed, volunteer, part-time—but not less vital than the others: Civil Defence. We have peacetime Civil Defence for just the same reasons that we have a peacetime Navy, Army and Air Force: it is an essential part of our ordinary peacetime national preparedness. *That is all there is to it.*

WHAT YOU CAN DO IN CIVIL DEFENCE

Five Sections: *which will you join?*

WARDEN. This is a job for a man or woman with a quick, cool head and the power of leadership—and something of a flair for getting on with people. The Warden takes control of the area in an emergency and directs the other services where they are required.

Warden Section

HEADQUARTERS. This is the nerve-centre, where the reports come in and the orders go out. If you are an office or scientific worker, a radio 'ham', motor-cyclist or driver—here is interesting, important work that you could train for now.

Headquarters Section

RESCUE. Members of Rescue Squads are highly skilled. Each man carries a pack containing saw, wrecking-bar, lashings, wire-cutters and First Aid kit—and he is trained in the use of all of them. Backing up the Rescue Squad is a special Rescue Vehicle, with scaffold-poles, cables, winches, stretchers and heavy rescue gear. A rescue man needs intelligence as well as strength.

The AMBULANCE AND CASUALTY COLLECTING Section want two sorts of people—casualty collectors, to give First Aid and see that the injured get back safely to the ambulances—and drivers to take the ambulances back to hospital. This is work for both men and women—and if you drive a car already, so much the better.

Ambulance and Casualty Collecting Section

The **WELFARE** Section would be called on first to help in bringing care and comfort to some millions of evacuees. But that is only the beginning of their job. After an attack, there would be more millions of people, to be housed, clothed, fed and kept healthy. Our very survival could depend on what the Welfare Section did then. The Welfare Section needs dependable, intelligent, capable men and women; and it needs them now.

AND THE AUXILIARY FIRE SERVICE, which also has really worth-while, practical training to offer. The work is important; a nuclear explosion sends out an intense heat-wave, and fires would be numerous and quick to spread. The A.F.S. has special nuclear-war fire-fighting apparatus: you would do your training with it.

IN EVERY SECTION

YOU GET

FIRST AID TRAINING

Welfare Section

Rescue Section

Auxiliary Fire Service

Civil Defence Recruiting Drives are going on now, all over the country.

Their object is to tell you all about Civil Defence — what it can do,

what it IS doing and what there is in it for you.

CIVIL DEFENCE *is common sense*

Go to your Council Offices and ask, today. They will be glad to see you.

ISSUED FOR H.M. GOVERNMENT BY THE CENTRAL OFFICE OF INFORMATION

citizens – representing a cross-section of class and gender – with their heads in sand buckets. In the background, a huge black cloud envelopes a village church with 'H Bomb Threat'. A Civil Defence volunteer is looking on from his jeep in disbelief at the ostrich-like denial of the 'headless' civilians, who are muttering: 'It'll never happen', 'What's the use…' and 'There isn't any…'. The inference to draw being that the public was ignorant of the facts and that its concern was misplaced. Below the cartoon, and to counter such defeatism, the headline claims 'Four Straightforward Simple FACTS about Civil Defence Today', The first 'fact' is worth quoting in full:

> **The H-Bomb: we hear too much of the horrors, not enough about our chances of survival.** *Some people will tell you that if this country were attacked with H-Bombs, every man jack of the population would be wiped out.* **That just isn't true: it isn't anything LIKE the truth.**
>
> *There would be terrible devastation, but for millions and millions of people, chances of survival would be very good. It depends very much on our Civil Defence. The more people we have in it, the better.*

That such 'official' assertions were disseminated by the COI on behalf of the government flew in the face of the classified information that the Cabinet had received from the Strath Report. It beggars belief that the reality of a thermonuclear attack could be distorted in such a manner in order to offset the public's genuine fears. The assertion that chances of survival depended on Civil Defence volunteers is frankly derisible. But it did not stop there. A year later, in 1958, the COI launched a much-grander campaign strategy of recruitment to the CDC. In an undated open letter at the front of the campaign booklet, R.A. Butler, the Home Secretary, referred to the 'public's indifference to civil defence' and talked about the need to break down apathy and 'create a better climate for recruitment'. The sixteen-page campaign guide (Fig. 104) once again referred to 'What you can do about the H-Bomb' and once again it asserted that, with the help of the Civil Defence, for 'millions and millions of people, the chances of survival *could* [my emphasis] be very good'.

Perpetuating a false sense of security that it *was* possible to survive the H-Bomb, the government and the COI decided to repeat the exercise in 1960 (1959 was a General Election year) with a similar publicity guide, but this time with an even more dramatic front cover. The 1960 campaign guide was larger and was intended to 'set forth the war-time and peace-time arguments for Civil Defence' (Figs. 105 and 106). Apparently the previous guide had been the most-effective printed recruiting aid ('demand had outrun supply') and so it was decided to reissue the 1960 version in larger numbers for general distribution and to embark upon an enhanced recruitment publicity campaign that featured, for the first time, individuals and their reasons for joining the CDC (Fig. 107). The 1960 booklet also included a section on how films could be used both for recruiting purposes and as instructional manuals.

Due to the imaginary character of nuclear war, nuclear strategy and its

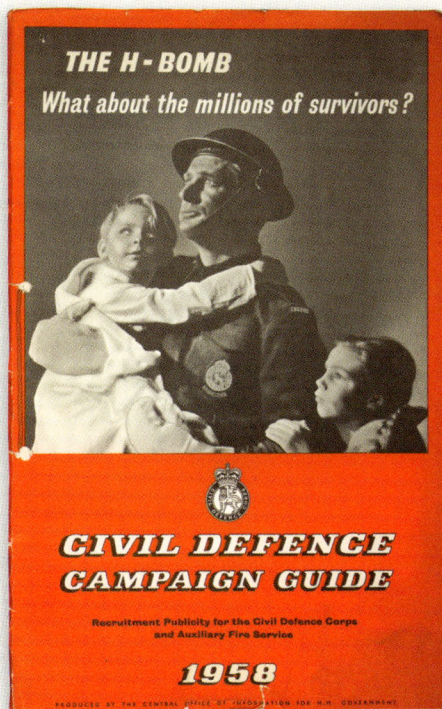

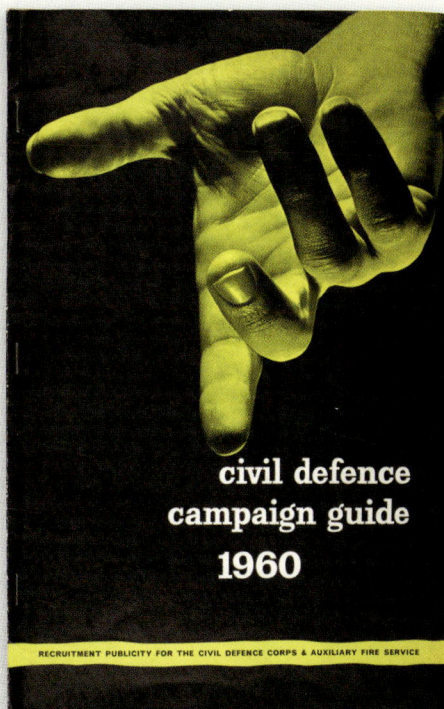

104. *Civil Defence Campaign Guide.* This 1958 publication bears echoes of the images employed by the Ministry of Information in World War II, but instead of air raids the emphasis was now on surviving the H-Bomb. On the back page a 'warrior' figure bearing a medieval shield continued to symbolise civil defence 'defiance' in the face of thermonuclear attack. (BL, PP/30/17A)

105. *Civil Defence Campaign Guide.* The cover for the 1960 guide was used as a poster that came in two sizes. The campaign guide referred to it as 'printed in black with the hand in a powerful contrasting shade of yellow, and a magenta colour for the words "Give a Hand in Civil Defence"' (which featured on the poster but not the campaign guide). (BL, PP/30/16A)

communications were no longer a prerogative of the military. The role of COI propaganda was to help imagine the unimaginable, in a way that did not inevitably lead to hopelessness, panic and fear. Following on from the recruitment campaigns for the CDC, further advice on how to survive a nuclear war was issued in 1963, after the Cuban Missile Crisis brought the threat of nuclear war closer than ever before. This advice came in the form of a detailed handbook prepared by the Home Office and the COI entitled *Advising the Householder on Protection against Nuclear Attack* (Fig. 108). It was referred to as a 'training publication' and consisted of twenty-three carefully illustrated pages of instructions on what to do in a nuclear winter. Civil Defence plans had written off the chances of those living in the immediate vicinity of an attack. Instead, the advice focused on improving the chances of those who lived

NATIONAL ADVERTISING CAMPAIGN SCHEDULE

	Week commencing Sept. 18th	Week commencing Sept. 25th	Week commencing Oct. 2nd	Week commencing Oct. 9th
DAILY EXPRESS 4,130,069				
DAILY HERALD 1,467,214				
DAILY MAIL 2,084,378				
DAILY MIRROR 4,545,036				
DAILY SKETCH 1,152,449				
NEWS CHRONICLE 1,206,309				
THE TIMES 254,684				
DAILY TELEGRAPH 1,154,768				
THE GUARDIAN 190,134				

☐ 11" x 3 cols. wide   ☐ 13½" x 5 cols. wide

☐ ½ page horizontal   ■ Whole page

☐ ½ page vertical

<u>Schedule of National Press Advertising</u>
This chart shows where and when the various National Press advertisements will appear. Altogether, the newspapers listed in the schedule sell well over 16 million copies, and it is estimated that their readership covers approximately 84 per cent of the adult population in England and Wales.

—5—

NATIONAL PRESS CAMPAIGN

Why Dorothy F. joined Civil Defence...

Dorothy F. is a 49-year-old housewife, married to a busy West Riding doctor and with three daughters, all of them grown up, two of them married. She is pretty definite in most of her opinions but only argues when she knows her subject. Her natural sympathy for young people stems from her belief that today's teenagers are no worse—and no better—than teenagers ever were. She serves on the local hospital committee and is an expert gardener. She had not seen any point in civil defence training until she heard this argument.

The purpose of civil defence is to train a nucleus of responsible people who would know what to do themselves and how to assist others in an emergency. To prepare for a war emergency—should it ever come—is the main job of civil defence but, with their training, civil defenders have been able to help in many peacetime disasters, too—and are ready to help again.

This is why—on June 2nd, 1958—Dorothy F. joined the West Riding Civil Defence Corps.
There were her reasons for joining—and there are other good ones, too. Think about it, and ask for all the civil defence information you want at your local Council Offices.

Give a hand in Civil Defence—It's common sense

—6—

---

106. *Civil Defence Campaign Guide* (1960). This page shows the advertising schedule in the national press covering a four-week period in September and October 1960. The chart demonstrates where the various national press advertisements were to appear. Altogether, the newspapers listed here sold well over 16 million copies, and it was estimated that their readership covered 84 per cent of the adult population in England and Wales. (BL, PP/30/16A)

107. '*Why Dorothy F. joined Civil Defence...*' 'Dorothy F. is a 49-year-old housewife, married to a busy West Riding doctor and with three daughters, all of them grown up, two of them married. She is pretty definite in most of her opinions but only argues when she knows her subject. Her natural sympathy for young people stems from her belief that today's teenagers are no worse—and no better—than teenagers ever were.' The advert goes on to say that she had not seen any point in civil defence training until she heard the argument that the purpose is to train a nucleus of responsible people who would know what to do and how to assist others in an emergency – 'This is why … Dorothy F. joined the West Riding Civil Defence Corps'. The advertisement ends with the CDC slogan: 'Give a hand in Civil Defence – It's common sense.' (BL, PP/30/16A)

108. *Civil Defence Handbook No 10: Advising the Householder on Protection against Nuclear Attack.* This 1963 booklet tells you what you can do to protect yourself, your family and your home. Not surprisingly, there are no images of death or of treating radiation sickness. Instead, the back page reassuringly recommends that in the event of a nuclear winter the first aid kit includes: adhesive plaster, safety pins and scissors, a half-pound of household salt, a four-ounce pack of baking powder, paper handkerchiefs, a reel of cotton and talcum powder. (BL, PP/30/23A)

109. *Civil Defence Handbook No 10.* The handbook was published shortly after the Cuban Missile Crisis (1962), which narrowly missed turning the Cold War into a 'hot' war by drawing the two superpowers into a nuclear confrontation. It is in this context that the introduction to the handbook states: 'The primary purpose of the Government's defence policy is to prevent war, but until general disarmament has been achieved and nuclear weapons brought under international control, there still remains some risk of nuclear attack.' The first section of the handbook sets out the 'basic facts' of what would happen when an H-bomb explodes and identifies three long-term dangers following such an attack: 'heat', 'blast' and 'fall-out'. (BL, PP/30/23A)

110. *Civil Defence Handbook No 10.* All quiet on the thermonuclear front! The handbook show extraordinarily eerie scenes of normality following a nuclear war. The impression given is that everyday life would not be disrupted for long and the urban landscape would remain the same. (BL, PP/30/23A)

CIVIL DEFENCE HANDBOOK No. 10

Advising the Householder on Protection against Nuclear Attack

LONDON: HER MAJESTY'S STATIONERY OFFICE
NINEPENCE NET

Introduction

The primary purpose of the Government's defence policy is to prevent war; but until general disarmament has been achieved and nuclear weapons brought under international control there still remains some risk of nuclear attack.

If such weapons were used in war they would cause casualties and damage on a vast scale. In areas close to the explosions most people would be killed instantly and nearly all buildings would be completely destroyed. Outside these areas the destructive effects of nuclear weapons diminish and there are precautions which could be taken to mitigate them further. Survival during and immediately after an attack would depend largely upon the actions taken by individual men and women.

This booklet tells you what you could do to protect yourself, your family and your home.

1 BASIC FACTS

What happens when an H-bomb explodes

The explosion of an H-bomb would cause total destruction for several miles around; the size of the area would depend on the size of the bomb and the height at which it was exploded. Outside this area survival would be possible but there would be three dangers:

HEAT BLAST FALL-OUT

HEAT An H-bomb explosion creates a huge white-hot fireball which lasts for about 20 seconds and gives off tremendous heat. The heat is so intense that it can kill people in the open up to several miles away. It could also burn exposed skin very much further away. Striking through unprotected windows it could set houses alight many miles away.

BLAST Blast would follow the heat waves like a hurricane. Buildings would be destroyed or severely damaged for several miles from the explosion, and there would be lighter damage for many miles beyond. There would be a further large area where, although houses suffered no structural damage, windows would be broken and there would be danger from flying glass.

FALL-OUT Fall-out is the dust that is sucked up from the ground by the explosion and made radio-active in the rising fireball. It rises high in the air and is carried down-wind, falling slowly to earth over an area which may be hundreds of miles long and tens of miles wide. Within this

6 WHAT TO DO IMMEDIATELY AFTER ATTACK

FIRES

As soon as the blast wave has passed, go round the house and *put out any fires before they take hold*. Turn off the gas and any fuel oil supply, if that has not been done already. Try to make sure that you are safe from any fires which have started nearby.

WATER

If the mains supply is still functioning, you could use the water for fire-fighting. But as soon as possible turn off the water supply at the stopcock to prevent the possibility of fall-out contaminated water entering the system.

Remember that when the stopcock has been turned off, water heaters and boilers should also be turned off, or put out. To leave them going might be dangerous.

Tie up the ball-cock in the W.C. cistern, so that clean water is not used for flushing.

STOPCOCK

WATER HEATER

BOILER

These jobs are so important that they should be done despite the unknown risk from fall-out, but if you have to go outside put on gumboots or stout shoes, a hat or headscarf, coat done up to the neck, and gloves. When you return, take these clothes off and leave them outside the fall-out room in case there is fall-out dust on them.

When you have seen to your own household, help any neighbour in need.

LISTEN FOR WARNING SIGNALS OF APPROACHING FALL-OUT

20

7 LIFE UNDER FALL-OUT CONDITIONS

THE FIRST DAYS

Once you know that there is danger from fall-out, **TAKE COVER AND DO NOT GO OUTSIDE AGAIN UNTIL YOU ARE TOLD BY WARDENS OR THE POLICE THAT IT IS SAFE TO DO SO.**

Listen for announcements on your radio. It will probably be safe to leave the fall-out room for short periods if visits to other parts of the house are necessary, for example, to obtain further supplies of food or water. *But do not go outside the house.*

This is only a general guide. The amount of fall-out would vary. It would be worst in the middle of the fall-out area, and would grow less and less towards the fringes. Everywhere, the danger from fall-out would grow less with time (see page 6).

You could not tell for yourself how bad fall-out was. This could be done only by people with special instruments, such as members of the civil defence, police and fire services. They would tell you when it was safe for you to come out in the open.

21

further away from the initial blasts. While much of the advice would not provide a great deal of protection from a hydrogen-bomb attack, it offered a sense of comfort, that even nuclear war could be managed and prepared for. The handbook told people what to do to protect themselves, their family and their home: from how to build internal and external fall-out shelters and put together a survival pack to what to do if a warning sounds. On the one hand this document represents a terrifying glimpse of life under the threat of nuclear attack, and on the other hand it exposes how the government wished to sanitise the threat of nuclear warfare (Figs. 109 and 110). There is, for example, no mention of radiation sickness and less than a page on 'how to manage later' with no timescale for when 'later' would be.

The precautions for leaving the house after an H-Bomb attack have more to do with making people feel they could do something to protect themselves should nuclear war happen, rather than coping with the onset of a nuclear winter. People are reminded to take a 'travelling rug' with them if they have to flee their homes – and drivers are asked to offer a lift to their neighbours. Readers are advised: 'If you have to go outside put on gumboots or stout shoes, a hat or headscarf, coat done up to the neck, and gloves.' Under the heading 'Protective Measures', householders are informed on how they could make their own homes safer, such as building an internal 'fall-out room' (a cupboard under the stairs is suggested), sealed against radioactive dust. Whitewashing the windows 'would greatly reduce the fire risk by reflecting away much of the heat' and 'clear away newspapers and magazines' (echoes here of the American version, *The House in the Middle*). There are no images of death and destruction anywhere in the document; instead, reassuringly, a Civil Defence warden measures fall-out before giving the all-clear, streets remain undamaged and there is even an illustration of a man in a shirt, tie and cardigan cradling a cat and the message 'do not forget your pets'. While householders were encouraged to adopt a business-as-usual approach, government officials were making preparations for house demolition and maintaining the water supply, homelessness and disposal of the dead.

Half a million copies of *Advising the Householder on Protection against Nuclear Attack* were printed, priced at ninepence. The handbook was accompanied by a series of public information films produced in 1964 for television and cinemas called *Civil Defence Information Bulletins*. These broadcasts were only intended to be shown in a state of emergency. They lasted for approximately four minutes and consisted of a senior police official speaking to camera and reconstructing the defence manual for film purposes.[6] According to Matthew Grant, Civil Defence measures were a 'façade' – a propaganda tool for the government's deterrence policy, grown out of the state's own difficulty in imagining nuclear war.[7] The House of Commons was equally bemused by the advice, calling for its withdrawal. In a debate on the publication of the pamphlet on 2 December 1963, the Labour MP Emrys Hughes wondered why, if the handbook was so important, it was not distributed free to the public. He then drew the House's attention to the damning report of the Estimates Committee:

Your Committee do not feel that this pamphlet achieves any useful purpose ...Your Committee do not feel that many householders will purchase the pamphlet from the Stationery Office, nor do they feel that those who do will be convinced of the effectiveness of the measures proposed therein. In the opinion of Your Committee the average householder who reads what to do in the event of imminent nuclear attack, and is told, if driving a vehicle, that he should 'Park off the road if possible; otherwise alongside the kerb', will not form the impression that the civil defence measures taken by the Government are of any value whatsoever. Your Committee are anxious that the public should be aware of the steps that are being taken to protect them, and they feel that this pamphlet creates entirely the wrong impression. They therefore recommend that Civil Defence Handbook No. 10 should be withdrawn.

Hughes continued with his own criticisms: 'What are the main features of the pamphlet advising the householder on protection against nuclear attack? It contains some remarkable understatements. On almost the first page we are told: "The explosion of an H-bomb would cause total destruction for several miles around; the size of the area would depend on the size of the bomb and the height at which it was exploded. Outside this area survival would be possible but there would be three dangers...". When the authors of this pamphlet say that there will be total destruction for several miles around, are not they understating the whole problem that would arise?' He concluded: 'The recommendations of the Estimates Committee can be summarised thus, "This thing is phoney; this thing is rubbish; put it in the waste paper basket".'

Responding to Hughes's claims of 'illusion' and 'deception', C.M. Woodhouse, the Joint Under-Secretary of State for the Home Office, rejected the criticisms of the Estimates Committee on the grounds that the committee 'had called for the handbook to be withdrawn without proposing that anything should take its place'. Woodhouse retorted that the House should be clear about the purpose of the book 'because it is clearly set out inside the cover': 'It is a training publication for the civil defence, the police and the fire services with the aim of indicating to their members the sort of advice which should be given in a period of alert by all available means to the general public about what they might do in their homes or out of doors.... That advice is concerned with the sort of precautions which the ordinary man in his home: could take on a "do it yourself" basis'. Woodhouse defiantly proclaimed that the government was right to 'make available simple and straightforward advice that could be transmitted to the public in an emergency' and therefore had no intention of withdrawing the handbook.[8]

Advice similar to that prepared for the 1963 handbook appeared briefly in Peter Watkins's controversial 1965 BBC dramatised documentary, *The War Game*. Filmed in black and white and lasting 50 minutes, *The War Game* depicts the prelude to, and the immediate aftermath of, a Soviet nuclear attack against Britain. Its frightening realism caused dismay within the BBC and also within government, and it was subsequently withdrawn before its television schedule date of 7 October 1965.

Unlike the blandness of the COI Civil Defence handbooks, *The War Game* pulled no punches and depicted a society in a state of collapse due to overwhelming radiation sickness and the depletion of food and medical supplies. There is widespread psychological damage and consequently a rising occurrence of suicide. The country's infrastructure is destroyed; the army burns corpses, while police shoot looters during food riots. The provisional government becomes increasingly disliked due to its rationing of resources and use of lethal force, and anti-authority uprisings begin. Civil disturbance and the obstruction of government officers become capital offences; two men are shown being executed by firing squad for such acts. Several shell-shocked and bewildered orphan boys are interviewed about what they want to be when they grow up. 'I don't want to be nothing,' says the first tiny, barely audible voice. 'Neither do I want to be nothing,' says the next. The film ends bleakly on the first Christmas Day four months after the nuclear war, held in a refugee compound in Dover with a vicar who futilely attempts to provide hope to his traumatised congregation, by playing 'Silent Night' on a portable gramophone.

The BBC withdrew the film and issued a statement that 'the effect of the film has been judged by the BBC to be too horrifying for the medium of broadcasting. It will, however, be shown to invited audiences...'[9] The BBC insisted that it had come under no pressure from the government in arriving at its decision. However, previously classified Cabinet Office papers released in 2015 show that the role of Whitehall in the film's original TV banning was much more extensive than anything publicly acknowledged by either the government or the BBC at the time. Watkins resigned from the BBC in protest shortly after the ban, claiming its much-vaunted charter of independence from government had been violated. *The War Game* became one of the iconic films of the 1960s, especially when, after a limited cinema release in 1966, it went on to win an Academy Award for Best Documentary Feature. It was not shown on British television until 1985.[10]

In the 1960s the government faced increasing financial pressure and assessed that a need for Civil Defence to preserve the government during nuclear attack was purely speculative, and no longer a priority. Following the Home Defence Review of 1965–66 it was decided by the Wilson government to suspend Civil Defence in 1968. It fell to the Home Secretary of the time, James Callaghan, to announce the decision, largely on financial grounds. Responding to a motion put down by the Conservative Quintin Hogg that, 'this House regrets Her Majesty's Government's decision to disband the Civil Defence Corps and the Auxiliary Fire Service and to abolish the Civil Defence responsibilities of local authorities contrary to the security interests of the

---

111. *Protect and Survive: This booklet tells you how to make your home and your family as safe as possible under nuclear attack.* The foreword explained: 'If the country were ever faced with an immediate threat of nuclear war, a copy of this booklet would be distributed to every household as part of a public information campaign which would include announcements on television and radio and in the press. The booklet has been designed for free and general distribution in that event. It is being placed on sale now for those who wish to know what they would be advised to do at such a time.' *Protect and Survive* was released in May 1980 following an escalation in international tension. Note the new symbol of the protected 'nuclear' family. (BL, PP/258/43)

PROTECT AND SURVIVE

This booklet tells you how to make your home and your family as safe as possible under nuclear attack

Challenge to survival

1

In an area affected by a nuclear explosion, those living beyond the radius of total destruction will be in danger from –

HEAT

BLAST

FALL-OUT

Heat and Blast

The heat and blast are so severe that they can kill, and destroy buildings, for up to five miles from the explosion.

5

---

survival kit

Plan Your Survival Kit
You will need five items to survive
in your Fall-out Room

1. Drinking Water

You will need enough for the family for fourteen days. Each person should drink two pints a day – so you will need three and a half gallons each.

You are unlikely to be able to use the mains water supply after an attack – so provide your drinking water beforehand by filling bottles for use in the fall-out room. Store extra water in the bath, in basins and in other containers.

Seal or cover all you can. Anything that has had fall-out dust on it will be contaminated and dangerous to drink or to eat.

You cannot remove radiation from water by boiling it.

You should try to stock twice as much water as you are likely to need for drinking, so that you will have enough for washing.

12

2. Food

Stock enough food for fourteen days.

Choose foods which can be eaten cold, which keep fresh, and which are tinned or well wrapped. Keep your stocks in a closed cabinet or cupboard.

Provide variety. Stock sugar, jams or other sweet foods, cereals, biscuits, meats, vegetables, fruit and fruit juices. Children will need tinned or powdered milk, and babies their normal food as far as is possible. Eat perishable items first.

Use your supplies sparingly.

3. Portable Radio and Spare Batteries

You radio will be your only link with the outside world.

You will need to listen for instructions about what to do after the attack and while you remain in your shelter.

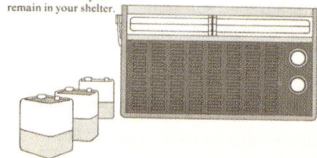

survival kit

13

---

112. *Protect and Survive.* 'Challenge to survival' – for the first time in an official Civil Defence publication, the stark image of the atomic mushroom cloud accompanied the warning that no part of the United Kingdom is safe. *Protect and Survive* details the effects of a nuclear fall-out, outlines how to plan for survival and recognise the warning signs when an attack is imminent. The document asserts that the heat and blast from such an attack are so severe that 'they can kill and destroy buildings for up to five miles from the explosion'. (BL, PP/258/43)

4. Tin Opener, Bottle Opener, Cutlery and Crockery

5. Warm Clothing

14

These further items will be invaluable in the Fall-out Room:

6. Bedding, sleeping bags

7. Portable stove and fuel, saucepans

8. Torches with spare bulbs and batteries, candles, matches

9. Table and chairs

10. Toilet articles, soap, toilet rolls

11. Changes of clothing

15

What to do after the Attack:

Do not smoke.
Check that gas, electricity and other fuel supplies *are* turned off.
Go round the house and put out any small fires.
If anyone's clothing catches fire, lay them on the floor and roll them in a blanket, rug or thick coat.
Use the mains water if you can.

If the mains water is still available also replenish water reserves. Then turn off at mains to avoid contaminating your supplies.

Do not flush lavatories, but store the clean water they contain by taping up the handles or removing the chains.

If the water supply is interrupted extinguish water heaters and boilers (including hearth fires with back boilers). Turn off all taps.

Check that you have got your survival kit at hand for the fall-out room. (See the list of survival items on pages 12-16.)
If there is structural damage from the attack you may have some time before a fall-out warning to do minor jobs to keep out the weather – using curtains or sheets to cover broken windows or holes.

If there is time, help neighbours in need, but listen for the fall-out warning and be ready to return to the fall-out room.

22

What to do on hearing the Fall-out Warning:

(Remember you may hear a fall-out warning without hearing an explosion.)
If you are out of doors, take the nearest and best available cover as quickly as possible, wiping all the dust you can from your skin and clothing at the entrance to the building in which you shelter.
All at home must go to the fall-out room and stay inside the inner refuge, keeping the radio tuned for Government advice and instructions. If you were outside your home when the warning was heard, be sure to wipe or shake off any dust from your skin or clothing before you enter the fall-out room, and change your outer clothing if you can.
The dangers will be so intense that you may all need to stay inside your inner refuge in the fall-out room for at least forty-eight hours. If you need to go to the lavatory, or to replenish food or water supplies, do not stay outside your refuge for a second longer than is necessary.
After forty-eight hours the danger from fall-out will lessen – but you could still be risking your life by exposure to it. The longer you spend in your refuge the better. Listen to your radio. Limit your movements to within

23

113. *Protect and Survive.* The 'five essentials' for surviving in the 'family fortress' (fall-out room). 'Keep your (food) stocks in a closed cabinet or cupboard.' Excellent advice after a thermonuclear war! (BL, PP/258/43

114. *Protect and Survive.* Instructions on what to do after an attack and what to do on hearing the fall-out warning ('Remember you may hear a fall-out warning without hearing an explosion. ... Listen to your radio.') The BBC had a ready prepared text to be broadcast to the nation in the event of a nuclear attack. (BL, PP/258/43

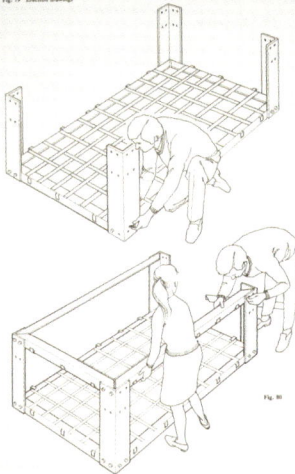
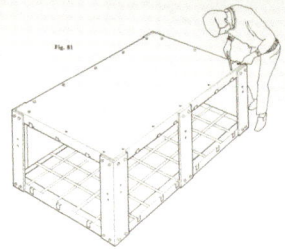
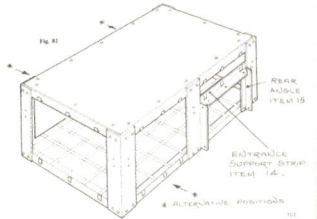

DOMESTIC
NUCLEAR
SHELTERS

TECHNICAL
GUIDANCE

A HOME OFFICE GUIDE

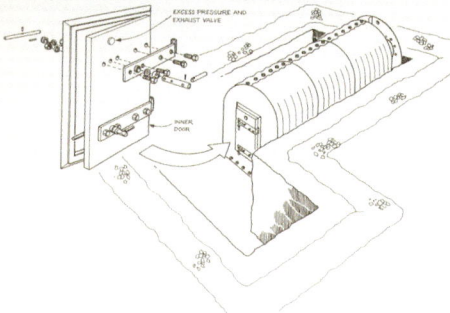

Fig. 88 *End panels and door*

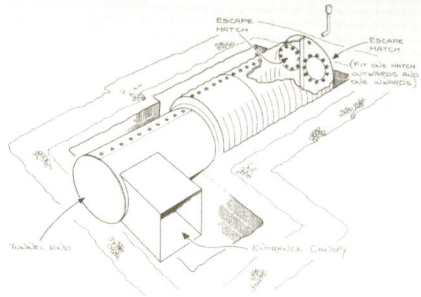

Fig. 90 *Final construction*

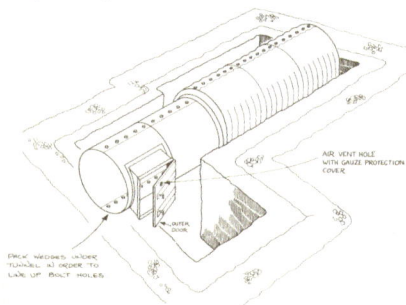

Fig. 89 *Tunnel in position*

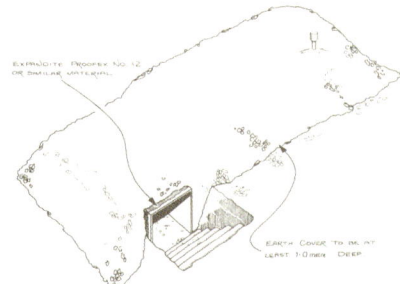

Fig. 91 *Earth cover*

nation', Callaghan replied that he was not 'abandoning' the CDC but rather reducing it to core functions: 'We have not decided that civil defence as a whole is useless. What we have done is to look again at the level at which we can afford to maintain our activities at the present time.'[11]

The final British Civil Defence booklet was prepared for the Home Office by the Central Office of Information in 1976 and was first published by Margaret Thatcher's Conservative government in May 1980. Reflecting recent escalations in international tension, a number of letters had appeared in *The Times* in December 1979 and January 1980 questioning what Civil Defence arrangements were in place in the UK (see later). In fact, in 1975, the animation *Protect and Survive* was adapted for television as part of a series of twenty short public information films designed to prepare people for particular aspects of a nuclear attack. Each film ended with an animated version of the protected family logo as seen on the cover of the booklet, together with a synthesised 'musical logo' composed by Roger Limb. (Limb, a member of the BBC Radiophonic Workshop, would go on to become known for creating electronic music for 1980s' episodes of *Doctor Who*.) The series, produced by Richard Taylor Cartoons (which also produced the *Charley Says* child safety films for the COI), was considered classified material that was intended for transmission on all television channels only if the government determined that nuclear attack was likely within seventy-two hours. However, recordings were leaked to organisations like CND and the BBC, which broadcast it on the *Panorama* programme as a discussion of public affairs, on 10 March 1980, shortly after the Soviet Union's invasion of Afghanistan in December 1979.

'Protect and Survive' was adopted as the new slogan for a new propaganda campaign, which consisted of a mixture of pamphlets, radio broadcasts and public information films that originally had been intended for distribution only in the event of dire national emergency, but they provoked such intense public interest that the pamphlets were authorised for general release. In May 1980 the primary instruction booklet *Protect and Survive* was released (Fig. 111), priced at fifty pence, but was to be widely distributed free to all households *if* the risk of a nuclear attack increased. The pamphlet was published as world tensions were rising. In 1980 nuclear war seemed closer than at any time since the Cuban Missile Crisis of 1962. The Soviet Union was installing SS-20 missiles in Eastern Europe and the Americans were successfully persuading European countries, including the UK, to host its Pershing II ballistic missiles and ground-launched cruise missiles.

In fact, the booklet was only ever intended to play a supporting role; the original campaign plan called for a 'comprehensive radio and television campaign', supplemented by a 'basic handbook' and newspaper advertising. The intention was to 'communicate essential information to the widest possible audience', something

115. *Domestic Nuclear Shelters: Technical Guidance.* Published in 1981, the detailed book was intended for professional engineers, whereas a 'survival made simple' pamphlet version called *Domestic Nuclear Shelters* offered a more basic guide to four different types of shelter. The back cover has a useful food list, including 'canned fruit, fruit juices, fruit squash, drinking chocolate' ... 'if sufficient storage space is available'. (BL, HOME/1/22/81)

made possible by broadcast media. *Protect and Survive* was complemented in 1981 by two booklets that focused on the construction of fall-out shelters: *Domestic Nuclear Shelters*, with basic instructions on how to construct a home shelter, and *Domestic Nuclear Shelters – Technical Guidance*, with detailed designs for long-term permanent shelters, often with elaborate designs (Figs. 115a, b and c). A newspaper campaign, based on the content of the booklet, was also prepared. The content was laid out as a two-page broadsheet and four-page tabloid inserts, and six sets of printers' positives and negatives were created in readiness.

Consisting of over thirty pages, *Protect and Survive* was stylistically more innovative than previous publications in this genre – it is certainly less sanitised, warning on its first page: 'Read this booklet with care. Your life and the lives of your family may depend upon it.' For the first time in an official Civil Defence booklet, the chilling image of an atomic mushroom cloud is shown and juxtaposed against a further warning that no part of the United Kingdom is safe. The booklet then details the effects of a nuclear fall-out, outlines how to plan for survival and recognise the warning signs when an attack is imminent, and advises on what to do immediately following an attack and in the days after (Fig. 114).

Protect and Survive assembled a range of information around four main themes: 'Challenge to survival' (Fig. 112), 'Planning for survival', 'Protect and survive' and 'Your action check list'. Householders are advised on how to make a fall-out room (Fig. 113) and within that an inner refuge, possibly the cupboard under the stairs. Families would be there for at least two weeks, so there are tips on what foods to stock up on and what sanitation arrangements to make. People were urged to store three-and-half gallons (16 litres) of water each, keeping it in the bath and basins, and to remove toilet chains or tape up handles so clean water could be stored in the cistern. If people were not at home during the nuclear strike, they were advised to 'lie flat (in a ditch) and cover the exposed skin of the head and hands'. In the event of someone dying in a fall-out room, 'place the body in another room and cover it as securely as possible. Attach an identification.' A survival kit list includes biscuits, vegetables, meats, fruit, fruit juices, sugar cubes, jams, crockery, notebooks and pencils for messages and dust bags. And a portable radio is needed in order to listen out for advice following the attack. Other items needed in the fall-out room are spare clothes, a table and chairs, toys and magazines, a clock and a calendar.

Although *Protect and Survive* remains a chilling and unnerving government pamphlet, it nevertheless repeats the message of previous campaigns that a nuclear war needs to be prepared for and is eminently survivable. Both the pamphlet and the campaign were subjected to widespread criticism and mockery following its release. Organisations such as the Campaign for Nuclear Disarmament (CND) and the Medical Campaign Against Nuclear Weapons (MCANW) (Fig. 116) passionately

116. *This is the Enemy. Not the Russians. Not the Americans. This is the Enemy.* A typically challenging poster distributed by the Medical Campaign Against Nuclear Weapons (MCANW) in the 1980s. MCANW material emphasised the ineffectuality of being 'prepared' as medical providers for the aftermath of nuclear war and often counter-posed the cost of weapons against the cost of healthcare. (Wellcome Collection, L0075379)

CIVIL DEFENCE

why we need it

contested the government's Civil Defence policy, while it was largely ridiculed in the media and in popular culture.[12] *Protect and Survive* immediately became the subject of detailed and scholarly criticism from anti-nuclear groups and individuals. In 1981, for example, CND and the Bertrand Russell Peace Foundation published a detailed counter-argument entitled *Protest and Survive* – a thirty-three-page document, which also parodied the cover and phrases such as 'keep this handy'. It was written by the historian E. P. Thompson, who reprinted at the front of the document a letter that Michael Howard (Chichele Professor of the History of War, All Soul's College, Oxford) had written to *The Times* on 30 January 1980, which concluded: 'In the absence of a serious civil defence policy, the Government's decision to modernize or replace our "independent deterrent" will be no more than an expensive bluff likely to deceive no one beyond these shores, and not very many people within them.'

To understand the context of *Protect and Survive*, it should be remembered that at the same time as the booklet was being distributed, CND was undergoing a revival and mass anti-nuclear demonstrations were taking place across Western Europe, while the women's peace camp at Greenham Common was set up in 1981. On 14 June 1982, the largest peace demonstration up to that point in history occurred in New York, when a million people gathered in Central Park to protest nuclear proliferation, just as the United Nations was holding a Special Session on Disarmament. In Britain, a short-lived glossy magazine entitled *Protect and Survive Monthly* (*PSM*) encouraged individuals to think about, and prepare for, surviving a nuclear attack. The existence of nuclear weapons at bases such as Greenham Common heightened concerns about nuclear attack. The producers of *PSM* were part of a survivalist movement that advocated Civil Defence. As a result, the magazine contained many advertisements for companies supplying nuclear shelters for the minority that could afford them.

The threat of nuclear war featured widely in popular culture, ranging from Raymond Briggs's 1982 graphic novel *When the Wind Blows*, which obliquely mentions aspects of *Protect and Survive*, to Louise Lawrence's post-apocalyptic children's novel *Children of the Dust*, which refers to the inner refuge designs mentioned in the pamphlets, and the rock band Jethro Tull's song of the same name on their 1980 album *A* that was apocalyptic and critical of the 'Protect and Survive' campaign. The television series *The Young Ones* also ridiculed the campaign. In the episode 'Bomb' the flatmates discovered an atomic bomb that had fallen through their roof and into their kitchen; Neil, ever the pragmatist, set out his personal survival plan: 'I'm going to consult the incredibly helpful *Protect and Survive* manual!'

The BBC play *Threads*, which was shown in 1984, featured three of the animated films in the COI's *Protect and Survive* series and demonstrated that much advice provided to the public would have no impact on survival chances and that those

117. *Civil Defence: Why We Need It.* In response to extensive criticism of *Protect and Survive*, in November 1981 the COI produced for the Home Office this booklet, which attempted to put the case for why civil defence is necessary. (BL, HOME/1/51/81A)

who did not suffer a short and painful death would die in agony of radiation sickness or trauma. In response to extensive criticism of the 'Protect and Survive' campaign, the COI produced, in November 1981, *Civil Defence: Why We Need It*, a new booklet (Fig. 117) that attempted 'to clear up some common misconceptions about civil defence and its value to the United Kingdom'.[13] The foreword contained the following message from the Home Secretary and the Secretary of State for Scotland, which clearly attempted to address some of the criticism levelled by CND and its followers:

> *For over 30 years our country, with our allies, has sought to avoid war by deterring potential aggressors. Some disagree as to the means we should use. But whatever view we take, we should surely all recognise the need – and indeed the duty – to protect our civil population if an attack were to be made upon us; and therefore to prepare accordingly. The Government is determined that United Kingdom civil defence shall go ahead. The function of civil defence is not to encourage war, or to put an acceptable face on it. It is to adapt ourselves to the reality that we at present must live with, and to prepare ourselves so that we could alleviate the suffering which war would cause if it came. Even the strongest supporter of unilateral disarmament can consistently give equal support to civil defence, since its purpose and effect are essentially humane.*

Revealingly, the pamphlet ended with the same slogan used by the COI in the 1960s, namely 'Civil Defence is common sense'. It may have been 'common sense' to the Home Office, but by the 1980s such slogans were clearly contested by much of the public. Nevertheless, the pamphlet did address the specific question 'how would people know what to do if war threatened?'

Full advice to the public about the warning system, and about measures to protect themselves, would be published and broadcast in good time. A wartime broadcast service would be brought into operation to transmit public information virtually non-stop. The advice would be – 'Tune in and listen'. Newspapers, television and radio would carry detailed advice on how to protect yourself and your family within your own home.

'Tune in and listen' referred primarily to the BBC, which would have a pivotal/crucial role in the event of a nuclear attack. The BBC had, in fact, prepared a short statement for broadcast that was essentially a synthesis of the *Protect and Survive* pamphlet:

---

118. *Protect and Survive.* In 1983 the COI prepared for the Home Office a four-page poster/brochure based on the 1980 pamphlet. This document formed part of a briefing pack, but plans to produce a more extensive public education campaign in 1984 never materialised. The poster was intended to be part of the campaign, launched in newspapers as an insert and distributed to government and municipal buildings and homes. Like the original pamphlet the poster also provided a very handy twenty-nine-point 'action' checklist and five things to 'remember' including 'avoid waste'. The poster advised: 'Use the check list systematically, ticking off each item as you deal with it. This will help you to remember all the things you must do.' (BL, HOME/1/34/83)

PROTECT AND SURVIVE

Issued by H.M. Government

How to make your home as safe as possible under nuclear attack.

Read this with care and keep it handy.

Your life and the lives of your family may depend on it.

If Britain is attacked by nuclear bombs or by missiles, we do not know what targets will be chosen or how severe the assault will be.

If nuclear weapons are used on a large scale, those of us living in the country areas might be exposed to as great a risk as those in the towns. The radioactive dust, falling where the wind blows it, will bring the most widespread dangers of all. No part of the United Kingdom can be considered safer than another.

The dangers which you and your family will face in this situation can be reduced if you follow the advice on these pages.

1 Challenge to survival

HEAT AND BLAST

FALL-OUT

Heat and Blast

Fall-out

2 Planning for survival

Stay at Home

Plan a Fall-out room and Inner Refuge

First, the Fall-out room

PROTECT AND SURVIVE

4 Your action check list

Action Before Attack

Warning Sounds

Fall-out Room

Inner Refuge

Survival Kit

Action on Attack Warning

Action After Attack

Sanitation

Fire Precautions

Remember

Remember

Remember

Remember

Flats

Bungalows

Caravans

Now the Inner Refuge

Here are some ideas:

PLAN YOUR SURVIVAL KIT
Five essentials for survival in your Fall-out Room

1 Drinking Water

2 Food

3 Portable Radio and Spare Batteries

4 Tin Opener, Bottle Opener, Cutlery and Crockery

5 Warm Clothing

These further items will also be useful in the Fall-out Room:

Sanitation

Keep these items in the Fall-out Room:

Keep these items just outside the Fall-out Room:

Limit the Fire Hazards

What to do after the Attack:

3 Protect and survive

First – Know the Warning Sounds:

THE ATTACK WARNING

THE FALL-OUT WARNING

THE ALL-CLEAR

What to do on hearing an Attack Warning:

At home

At work or elsewhere

In the open

What to do after the Attack

What to do on hearing the Fall-out Warning:

In the open

At home

Stay in your refuge

Later on

Casualties

On hearing the ALL-CLEAR

BBC TRANSCRIPT TO BE USED IN WAKE OF NUCLEAR ATTACK

This is the Wartime Broadcasting Service. This country has been attacked with nuclear weapons. Communications have been severely disrupted, and the number of casualties and the extent of the damage are not yet known. We shall bring you further information as soon as possible. Meanwhile, stay tuned to this wavelength, stay calm and stay in your own homes.

Remember there is nothing to be gained by trying to get away. By leaving your homes you could be exposing yourselves to greater danger.

If you leave, you may find yourself without food, without water, without accommodation and without protection. Radioactive fall-out, which follows a nuclear explosion, is many times more dangerous if you are directly exposed to it in the open. Roofs and walls offer substantial protection. The safest place is indoors.

Make sure gas and other fuel supplies are turned off and that all fires are extinguished. If mains water is available, this can be used for fire-fighting. You should also refill all your containers for drinking water after the fires have been put out, because the mains water supply may not be available for very long.

Water must not be used for flushing lavatories: until you are told that lavatories may be used again, other toilet arrangements must be made. Use your water only for essential drinking and cooking purposes. Water means life. Don't waste it.

Make your food stocks last: ration your supply, because it may have to last for 14 days or more. If you have fresh food in the house, use this first to avoid wasting it: food in tins will keep.

If you live in an area where a fall-out warning has been given, stay in your fall-out room until you are told it is safe to come out. When the immediate danger has passed the sirens will sound a steady note. The 'all clear' message will also be given on this wavelength. If you leave the fall-out room to go to the lavatory or replenish food or water supplies, do not remain outside the room for a minute longer than is necessary.

Do not, in any circumstances, go outside the house. Radioactive fall-out can kill. You cannot see it or feel it, but it is there. If you go outside, you will bring danger to your family and you may die. Stay in your fall-out room until you are told it is safe to come out or you hear the 'all clear' on the sirens.

Here are the main points again:

Stay in your own homes, and if you live in an area where a fall-out warning has been given stay in your fall-out room, until you are told it is safe to come out. The message that the immediate danger has passed will be given by the sirens and repeated on this wavelength. Make sure that the gas and all fuel supplies are turned off and that all fires are extinguished.

Water must be rationed, and used only for essential drinking and cooking purposes. It must not be used for flushing lavatories. Ration your food supply: it may have to last for 14 days or more.

We shall repeat this broadcast in two hours' time. Stay tuned to this wavelength, but switch your radios off now to save your batteries until we come on the air again. That is the end of this broadcast.

The history of Civil Defence from the end of World War II to the 1980s represents a series of Cold War snapshots that capture intense periods of extreme geopolitical tension when Britain and the world were consumed by the fear of mutual assured destruction (MAD). The age of MAD heralded a new fear, with citizens knowing that they could be annihilated within a matter of minutes at the touch of a button. The fear of impending attack became a part of everyday life and conversation. Devising public information campaigns to inform citizens about the precautions that they should undertake in the event of a nuclear attack posed extraordinary challenges for the COI. By the time of *Protect and Survive* in the 1980s, every conceivable means of communications had been exploited to disseminate its message (Figs. 118a, b and c). The negative publicity this publication received may be why a successor publication was never released despite the increased risk of nuclear attack.[14]

The reasons for the failure of the 'Protect and Survive' campaign to assuage public opinion are twofold. On the one hand, much of the advice given simply did not square with reality and became a source of ridicule. On the other hand, some individuals and organisations drew similar conclusions to that of CND at the time; namely that Civil Defence was a smokescreen to bluff the public into passively accepting the nuclear arms race. The propaganda disseminated by the COI from the 1950s onwards was controversial because it presented facts about how to protect against nuclear weapons' blast, heat and fall-out without giving the nuclear test data that validated those facts. Successive governments saw it as not so much a real attempt to ensure survival as a political necessity to prevent the public from thinking that nuclear war meant certain death. In reality, politicians knew that no preparations, no matter how expensive, would make a substantive difference in the face of an actual attack. For some people, the fear of nuclear destruction was an unbearable source of mental stress. For others, more-personal fears were symbolised by the threat of the nuclear bomb. But preparations for the worst, however unrealistic, could also help social cohesion. Civil Defence activities, including preparations for the aftermath of an attack, paradoxically and somewhat perversely strengthened the bonds of civilian society. Civil Defence encouraged civilian populations to anticipate the terror of nuclear attack. Being prepared – and taking every 'practical' precautions for the aftermath, as advised in the propaganda – allowed for a sense of control over the uncontrollable.

KEEP OUR SECRETS SECRET

One of the curious products of the 'war of nerves' between East and West was a highly concentrated campaign disseminated by the COI aimed at the Civil

Service, the police and the armed forces. It was called 'Keep Our Secrets Secret', and its roots can be traced to the pervasive Cold War paranoia of the 1960s (Fig. 119). For forty years, two superpowers faced each other with fear, distrust and nuclear brinkmanship; a state of paranoia that was exacerbated by a number of spy scandals, show trials and political defections, provoking further alarm in Britain and the United States at the extent to which Soviet infiltration threatened Western democracy.[15]

The Cuban Missile Crisis had confirmed how important espionage was in the Cold War. The Radcliffe Report into security procedures in the public services in Britain, which Macmillan had commissioned following the Portland Spy Ring case, had reported in early 1962 that infiltration of the Civil Service by communists had reached 25 per cent.[16] The last of over 100 recommendations in the Radcliffe Report was that: 'A programme of security education for the public service generally should be drawn up.'[17] In a political climate gripped increasingly by fear, rumour and hysteria, the COI came up with the slogan 'Keep Our Secrets Secret' (Figs. 120a and b) and commissioned an impressive range of posters aimed primarily at the Civil and Security Services, but which also went on display in public spaces. The aim of the campaign was to create a security education campaign to raise awareness of the Soviet espionage threat to state and industrial secrets. In June 1961 an official report blamed lax security at the Admiralty for the Portland Spy Ring. The first posters were produced in the mid-1960s but the campaign continued until the late 1980s. The influential designers Reginald Mount (Fig. 121) and Eileen Evans, who had worked for the Ministry of Information in the war, were both employed on this campaign. The campaign is particularly interesting for the extraordinary range of artistic styles that made up 'security education': ranging from comic format to cartoons styled on propaganda campaigns employed in World War II and modern advertising techniques.[18] ♚

119. *Don't Brag About Your Job.* In the 1950s and 1960s Reginald Mount and Eileen Evans's studio became closely associated with the COI, producing characteristically neat and precise designs for a wide variety of government agencies. Mount also became a consultant designer for the Central Office of Information's Art Services Section. *Don't Brag About Your Job* (1964) is a colour offset lithograph poster by Reginald Mount, intended to encourage secrecy. The illustration is a man wearing a brown and white striped shirt with a blue bow-tie and dark-coloured V-neck jumper. He has his head turned to the side, with his mouth open. The word '*SECRET*' is lettered multiple times in red, flowing from his brain and out of his mouth. All against a white ground. The cartoonish figure is similar to ones drawn by Mount in his anti-smoking and anti-litter campaigns. (BL, PP/277/28A)

DON'T BRAG ABOUT YOUR JOB

KEEP OUR SECRETS SECRET

Printed for Her Majesty's Stationery Office
by The Matfield Press Ltd.
Dd. 8034626 Pro. 13574 10/79

MOUNT/EVANS

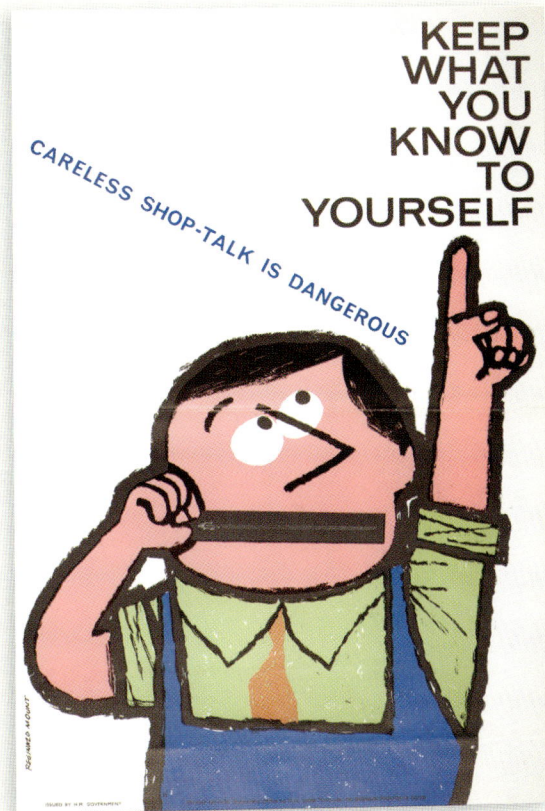

120. *The 'Keep Our Secrets Secret' campaign.* These two examples (opposite and above, left) from the 1980s have their antecedents in the wartime 'Careless Talk Costs Lives' campaign. *You Never Know Who's Listening!* is very much in the tradition of Kenneth Bird (pseudonym Fougasse), the cartoonist whose deflating, humorous, *Careless Talk* posters were among the most popular of the war. One showed two garrulous housewives sitting in a bus, with Hitler and Göring behind them listening to their gossip, with the tag line: 'You never know who's listening!' *How Do You Get a Gas Leak in a Telephone?* is in a modern comic strip format (and its style a form of frenzied humour) to get across its message that careless calls ('gas, gas, gas, trivia...') can lead to 'little leaks' (again a play on words) and to 'big bangs' ('Boom!') ... 'Keep Our Secrets Secret'. (BL, COIN-CIVI/1/1/82 and BL, OMCS/1/7/88A)

121. *Keep What You Know to Yourself.* An interesting variation of the theme was also made for the shop floor. After the Radcliffe Report had revealed communist infiltration of the Civil Service, fears grew of a similar infiltration of trade unions. Reginald Mount produced this poster of a manual worker zipping up his mouth and pointing out that: 'Careless Shop-Talk is Dangerous.' (BL, PP/277/24A)

CHAPTER SIX

THE NERVOUS 1990s

The decade began with violent demonstrations against the 'Poll Tax' (officially known as the Community Charge), followed by the departure of Margaret Thatcher. In 1997 the Labour Party ended eighteen years of Conservative rule as Tony Blair was elected Prime Minister. New Labour was committed to 'efficiency' and the modernisation of public services. As a government agency that had lost its monopoly in the field of communication, the COI came under increasing pressure to demonstrate that it was both effective and represented value for public money. It responded by setting up new specialist services: Sponsorship, Events Management, New Media, and Informability. The New Media Unit launched a website for 10 Downing Street and created the first British Monarchy website, which attracted over one million hits within twenty-four hours of its launch. An ethnic communities information forum acted as a conduit to facilitate more-effective communication with Britain's ethnic minorities and Informability was set up to advise on communication to people with disabilities, following the 1995 Disability Discrimination Act. Informability launched a video magazine for the deaf – *Public Scene* – and an audio magazine for people with sight impairments – *Sound Advice*. The new Sponsorship service secured £1.5 million from the private sector in 1998–99 for public safety campaigns. COI's Merchandising and Licensing Service promoted British Army merchandise via the Internet, raising income and increasing awareness of the British Army as a career for young people.

Although the COI was forced to respond to changing and more-sophisticated communication technologies, its core mission (if indeed it still possessed one) had changed radically from the days of its inception under Clement Attlee's first post-war Labour government. Much of its work consisted of supervising minor public information campaigns of a rather hectoring nature. Gone were the days when it was helping to shape a 'New Jerusalem'. However, it did still have a major campaign to fight, namely the 'Don't Die of Ignorance' campaign of the late 1980s and 1990s.

'DON'T DIE OF IGNORANCE'

In the 1980s a new global threat posed by the AIDS (acquired immunodeficiency syndrome) epidemic persuaded many governments around the world to launch campaigns (mainly television and advertising posters) warning of the dangers of unprotected sexual intercourse. Many of these campaigns broke new ground in terms of their explicit reference to sexual practices and the stark honesty about the scale of the epidemic. Some critics argued that they proved counterproductive because the message was so bleak that it scared people, who 'turned off' or chose not to listen (similar concerns were expressed about the nature of the VD – venereal disease – campaigns in World War II).

In 1987 the British government launched a major public information campaign with the slogan 'AIDS: Don't Die of Ignorance' (Figs. 122a and b). There had been a growing sense of fear bordering on panic about the nature of the AIDS disease, and not just in Britain. Much of this fear was based on ignorance and scaremongering, leading to a growing sense of homophobia with one newspaper even referring to a 'gay plague'.[1] The Conservative Secretary of State for Health and Social Security, Norman Fowler, recognised that there was an urgent need to intervene. The numbers in the UK with the disease were still relatively small, but experience in the United States had suggested that they were likely to increase. By the middle of the decade, scientists were predicting that the cumulative total of UK HIV cases could reach 300,000 by 1992 if nothing were done. An advertising agency, TBWA (who had worked with government on a number of health campaigns, including nurse recruitment, blood donations and rubella epidemics), was commissioned to make adverts intended to shock the nation into action. The spearhead of the initial campaign was a stark, forty-second TV advertisement (*Monolith*) directed by Nicholas Roeg. It was sponsored by the COI for the Department of Health. Under darkened sky, a volcano erupts. Doom-laden images of cascading rocks give way to shots of a tombstone being chiselled. 'There is now a danger that has become a threat to us all,' intones the actor John Hurt ominously in a voiceover. 'It is a deadly disease and there is no known cure. The virus can be passed by sexual intercourse with an infected person. Anyone can get it, man or woman. So far it has been confined to small groups... but it's spreading. So protect yourself...and read this leaflet when it arrives. If you ignore AIDS it could be the death of you. So....[the word etched on to the blackened gravestone is revealed – AIDS].... Don't die of ignorance,' runs the slogan. With its stark, unambiguous warning and bleak message, the advertisement (and an equally stark one featuring an iceberg which, beneath the surface, bore the legend AIDS in giant letters) shocked viewers when they appeared on British screens in 1987. The television commercials were broadcast on both channels for three weeks, and both *Monolith* and the second film *Iceberg* were shown in 1,200 cinemas.[2] A series of advertisements were also run in teenage magazines and the Post Office stamped an AIDS warning slogan on millions of letters.

Immediately, it gave rise to accusations of panic-mongering and complaints that it would terrify any children who happened to be watching. And yet the campaign – the world's first major government-sponsored national AIDS awareness drive – would later be hailed as a success. In addition to the tombstone TV advertisement, a leaflet (which is referred to in the film) was sent to every household in the country, with the advice – 'Anyone can get it, gay or straight, male or female. Already 30,000 people are infected', and a week of educational programming was scheduled at peak time on all four terrestrial channels. The scale of the campaign was unprecedented in the sphere of public health.

While the films *Monolith* (or *Tombstone* as it is often referred to) and *Iceberg* were memorable for their visual quality – suggesting as they do something frightening – they were nevertheless short on information. To compliment the films, Norman Fowler adopted an evidence-based approach, citing the example of successful anti-VD campaigns during the two world wars to show why a combination of shocking facts and condom provision was necessary and effective.[3] He wanted to cut through the prejudice and disseminate the message that AIDS could affect any sexually active person, regardless of sexuality. The then Chief Constable of Greater Manchester Police, James Anderton, infamously referred to victims 'swirling about in a human cesspit of their own making'. Speaking at the launch of the 1987 AIDS awareness campaign, the Secretary of State for Health and Social Security said that 4,000 people in Britain were going to die of AIDS over the next three years. There was no cure, and it would be at least five years before an effective vaccine could be expected.[4]

The leaflet, which was delivered to 23 million households, provided much more detailed information and constitutes the core of Fowler's national awareness campaign – although the information is targeted primarily at what has been referred to as the 'worried well' and less at those who were already infected.

It consisted of ten points, beginning with why the information was being sent, stating that AIDS is not just a homosexual disease – anybody can get it 'depending on their behaviour'. It does, however, warn of the potential scale of the crisis: 'By the time you read this, probably 300 people will have died in this country. It is believed that a further 30,000 carry the virus. This number is rising and will continue to rise unless we take precautions.' Interestingly, the leaflet still refers to AIDS as a virus and there is no mention of HIV.[5]

Point 4 'How Do You become Infected' pulls no punches: 'For most people the only real danger comes through having sexual intercourse with an infected person. This

WHAT CAN'T YOU CATCH THE VIRUS FROM ? 8

The Government's clear medical advice is that you cannot get the AIDS virus from normal social contact with someone who is infected.

You cannot get it from shaking hands. Nor is there any record of anyone becoming infected through kissing.

There is no danger in sharing cups or cutlery. Nor can you catch it from public baths or toilets.

In hospitals, standard disinfection precautions protect patients, visitors and staff.

Giving blood is safe. All the equipment is only used once.

And all the blood used in this country for blood transfusion is rigorously checked.

HOW SAFE IS IT ABROAD ? 9

The AIDS virus exists throughout the world. In certain areas a large number of both men and women have it.

So it is even more important that you follow the advice in this leaflet if you're going abroad.

Otherwise if you do have sex with someone who is not your usual partner, not only might you become infected, but you may also infect your partner when you return home.

Again, in some countries blood transfusions are not checked for the AIDS virus. In those places where the virus is widespread do not, if you can possibly avoid it, have blood from a local donor.

Also, in certain developing countries, medical equipment may not be properly sterilised. If you can, avoid any treatment involving injections and surgical procedures.

If you have any worries about this, discuss them with your family doctor.

DO YOU NEED MORE INFORMATION ? 10

The true picture about AIDS is that, at the moment, relatively few have the virus in this country. Those most at risk now are men who have anal sex with other men. Drug misusers who share equipment. Anyone with many sexual partners. And sexual partners of any of these people.

But the virus *is* spreading. And as it does, so the risk of having sex with someone who is infected increases.

Ultimately, defence against the disease depends on all of us taking responsibility for our own actions.

More detailed information is available from:
Your own doctor.
Clinics for sexually transmitted diseases. (Look in the phone book under Venereal or Sexually Transmitted Diseases or your nearest main hospital.)
Special AIDS line 0800-555777.
Healthline Telephone Service 01-981 2717, 01-980 7222, 0345-581151. (If you're phoning from outside London, use the 0345 number and you'll be charged at local rates.)
Terrence Higgins Trust 01-833 2971.
Welsh AIDS Campaign 0222-464121.
Scottish AIDS Monitor 031-558 1167.
Northern Ireland AIDS line Belfast 226117 (Friday 7.30 pm to 10.00 pm.)
London Lesbian and Gay Switchboard 01-837 7324.
SCODA (Standing Conference on Drug Abuse) 01-430 2341.

For a copy of the more detailed booklet AIDS: What Everybody Needs to Know, write to Dept. A, PO Box 100, Milton Keynes, MK1 1TX. (In Scotland write for The AIDS Problem: What Everybody Needs to Know, to the Scottish Health Education Group, Woodburn House, Canaan Lane, Edinburgh EH10 4SG.)

If you're travelling abroad, read leaflet SA35, Protect Your Health Abroad, available from travel agents.

D O N ' T   A I D   A I D S

Issued by the Department of Health and Social Security.
Printed in the UK for HMSO 1986. Dd 8934669 HSSH J0303 AR

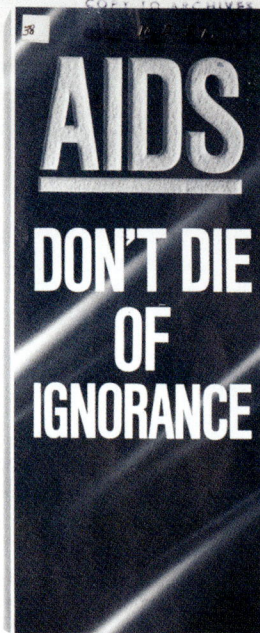

AIDS
DON'T DIE OF IGNORANCE

GOVERNMENT INFORMATION 1987   N.I.

WHY ARE YOU BEING SENT THIS LEAFLET ? 1

This leaflet is being sent to every household in the country. It is about AIDS. And everyone now needs to know the facts. It explains what the disease is. How it is spread. How serious a threat it is. And how it can be avoided.

Because it has to deal with matters of health and sex, you may find some of the information disturbing. But please make sure that everyone who may need this advice reads this leaflet.

The more people know about AIDS, the less likely it is to be spread.

So if you have children, think carefully what they need to know. Whether you approve or not, many teenagers do have sex and some may experiment with drugs.

Even if you think your children don't, they will need advice because they may have friends who encourage them to.

WHY SHOULD YOU BE CONCERNED ABOUT AIDS ? 2

Any man or woman can get the AIDS virus depending on their behaviour. It is not just a homosexual disease.

There is no cure. And it kills.

By the time you read this, probably 300 people will have died in this country. It is believed that a further 30,000 carry the virus. This number is rising and will continue to rise unless we all take precautions.

WHAT IS AIDS ? 3

AIDS is caused by a virus. This can attack the body's defence system which normally helps fight off diseases and infections.

And if this happens people can then develop AIDS – the disease itself. They become ill and die from illnesses they cannot fight off.

HOW DO YOU BECOME INFECTED ? 4

Because the virus can be present in semen and vaginal fluid, this means for most people the only real danger comes through having sexual intercourse with an infected person. This means vaginal or anal sex. (It could also be that oral sex can be risky particularly if semen is taken into the mouth.)

So the virus can be passed from man to man, man to woman and woman to man.

For those who inject drugs, there is the added risk from sharing needles or equipment with someone who is infected.

Finally, babies born to mothers who are infected have a high chance of being born with the virus.

HOW CAN YOU PROTECT YOURSELF FROM AIDS ? 5

Most people who have the virus don't even know it. They may look and feel completely well. So you cannot know who is infected and who isn't. To protect yourself follow these guidelines.

The more sexual partners you have, especially male partners, the more chance you have of having sex with someone who is infected. It is safest to stick to one faithful partner.

FEWER PARTNERS, LESS RISK.

Unless you are sure of your partner, always use a condom (sheath or rubber). This will reduce the risk of catching the virus.

USE CONDOMS FOR SAFER SEX.

It's also best to use a water-based lubricating gel with the condom. Oil-based gels can weaken the rubber. Ask your chemist for advice.

The contraceptive pill is no protection against AIDS.

Anyone who misuses drugs should not inject. If you ever do, never share equipment (needles, syringes, mixing bowls, etc.). You could be injecting the virus straight into your blood stream. It is extremely dangerous.

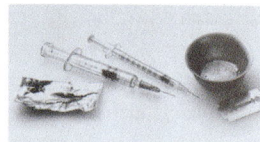

DON'T INJECT. NEVER SHARE.

IF YOU THINK YOU ARE INFECTED ? 6

If you think you may be infected go to your family doctor for advice about having a test. Or go direct to a clinic for sexually transmitted diseases for confidential advice and a test if you wish. If you have the virus, they'll let you know and give you help and support.

WHAT ABOUT THINGS THAT PIERCE THE SKIN ? 7

It is *not* safe to use equipment for ear-piercing, tattooing or acupuncture unless you know it is unused or has been sterilised. Nor is it safe to share a toothbrush or razor of someone who is infected. These things could give you the virus through infected blood.

means vaginal or anal sex. (It could also be that oral sex can be risky particularly if semen is taken into the mouth).' 'How to Protect Yourself' (point 5) consists of three guidelines (in bold): **'Fewer Partners. Less Risk'**, **'Use Condoms for Safer Sex'** and **'Don't Inject, Never Share'**. This section contains the only visual images in the leaflet: a packet of condoms with one removed and ready for use and a picture of a needle, a razor-blade and a drug phial. Interestingly, given the taboos that were circulating about the spread of AIDS, point 8 refers to what you *can't* catch the disease from (shaking hands, kissing, sharing cups and cutlery, public baths or toilets). The final point sets out the present situation ('the virus *is* spreading'), but concludes: 'Ultimately, defence against the disease depends on all of us taking responsibility for our own actions.'

While critics have suggested that the campaign caused a climate of fear around sex (particularly in the gay community) it undeniably helped to raise awareness of the issue of AIDS, and at a time when there were no effective drugs to treat or prevent the spread of HIV. The only answer was to inform people of the risks and attempt to alter their behaviour. In an attempt to consolidate the impact of the AIDS awareness campaign, the COI's new Conference Unit helped to organise the International Conference of Ministers of Health on Aids Prevention, with over 700 delegates from 149 countries and facilities for 600 journalists, which took place in London in 1988 and was jointly sponsored by the World Health Organization and the British government.[6] The summit was in response not only to the elusiveness of a vaccine and a lack of satisfactory drugs, but also to the intense media focus and the apocalyptic predictions of the number of people worldwide who were likely to become infected. The United States also produced its own leaflet in 1988 entitled *Understanding AIDS*, which was similar in fact to *AIDS: Don't Die of Ignorance*. It was sent to 107 million homes, but by the time it had been distributed an estimated 45,000 victims had already died of the disease.

To accompany the *AIDS: Don't Die of Ignorance* leaflet, the COI sponsored a £5 million TV and poster campaign entitled 'Don't Inject Aids' (Fig. 123). Aimed specifically at drug users, it takes up the 'Don't Inject, Never Share' guideline of the leaflet. Once again, the intention was to shock but also to convince drug users that they had to change their habits as they were personally at risk. To accompany the poster the COI sponsored a gritty public information film of the same name that showed a drug user (Michael Reid) who is diagnosed with HIV as a result of injecting illegal drugs. By means of a flashback, Michael is seen injecting the drugs with a voiceover warning: 'The AIDS virus [sic] can live on dirty needles and equipment, so don't share it … because just one fix with an infected needle will really get you out of it.' The film ends with the title 'Don't Inject AIDS', the I in AIDS being a needle pointing upwards.[7]

THE NERVOUS 1990S

122. *AIDS: Don't Die of Ignorance.* The COI leaflet that was delivered to 23 million households in 1987. The leaflet explains the nature of the virus, how it appears to spread and identifies those who seem most at risk. Precautions such as the avoidance of intravenous drug abuse and the merits of the condom as a prophylactic are stressed. (BL, HSSH/1/44/87A).

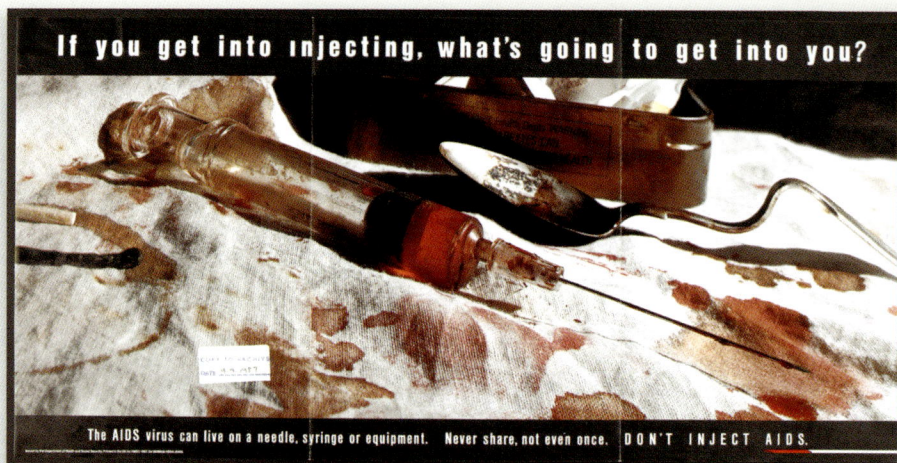

123. *Don't Inject AIDS* (1987). This dramatic, bloodstained poster targets the vulnerable community of intravenous drug users as part of the battle against HIV infection. The emphasis was less on giving up drug use and more on precautionary hygiene, such as the avoidance of dirty needles. (BL, HSSH/1/44/87A)

Launching the government's AIDS awareness campaign in 1978, Norman Fowler claimed that 'public education was the only vaccine we have' and the object of the campaign was to stop the spread of the virus there and then, 'so that the number of deaths did not continue to rise during the 1990s'.[8] In fact, the rates of infection, particularly in the gay community, began to drop in the late 1980s and early 1990s – but that may well have been due to parallel campaigns run by organisations like the Terence Higgins Trust. Nevertheless, the 'Don't Die of Ignorance' campaign played a significant part. In the 1990s, slightly different strategies were being adopted, including the use of humour and greater focus on personal testimony. Institutions such as the Prison Service and the armed forces were targeted by the authorities as posing heightened risks for the spread of the disease. Prisons had been recognised from the outset as posing a special risk and in 1987 a film video and manual had been introduced entitled *AIDS: Inside and Out*. By the time it had been revised in 1995, the manual consisted of fifty-four pages. The aim of both the video (made by John Metcalfe) and the tutors' manual had been to ensure that all inmates had the information they needed to avoid infection with HIV and to help them recognise that 'their own responsible behaviour is the only protection and their own irresponsible behaviour is the only danger'. Evaluative research carried out by the Prison Service since the awareness programme was first introduced showed that 'discussion is very important to the effective delivery of the message'.

Talking About AIDS, which was published in 1995, was a new package with a different approach to *AIDS: Inside and Out* (Figs. 124a and b). In a revealing introduction to the new manual by Len Curran, Director of Health Care and Chair,

AIDS Advisory Committee, HIV/AIDS training is compared to the experience of immunisation against measles: 'When most of the children in a community are immunised, the virus finds it difficult to move around and there are very few cases of measles, and parents begin to wonder if immunisation is really necessary, because the disease doesn't seem to be a problem any more. So, immunisation levels fall progressively. And what happens? After a while, there is another epidemic of measles'. The point being made was that in spite of the successful AIDS awareness programme, both in prisons and in the wider community, 'HIV has not gone away'. Curran wrote: '...more than twenty thousand people in the UK are infected and the numbers continue to grow. This is no time to ease up in our attempt to make sure that *everybody* knows how to protect themselves from HIV. Education is to HIV and AIDS what immunisation is to measles.'

Whereas *AIDS: Inside and Out* focused on the virus, HIV, and the illness it could give rise to, *Talking About AIDS* (both the five films and the manual) was *disease* orientated and designed to impart factual information on all aspects of HIV and AIDS. It's stated aim was focusing on *people*, 'on the thought and feelings and, in the case of those infected with the virus, the ways in which their lives have changed as a result of being HIV positive or living with AIDS'. The package was intended to stimulate discussions to 'help trainees think out what HIV and AIDS mean for *them*'. Three points are stressed in order to develop a greater understanding: that people with HIV do not come from a particular risk group, but are people just like themselves (the most rapid rate of infection at the time of publication had been among the heterosexual population); the experience of living with HIV; and what *they* need to do to avoid catching HIV themselves.

Such concerns chimed with wider changes that were taking place. Rather than simply preaching fear and abstinence, by the mid-1990s a more-sympathetic and nuanced attitude to HIV/AIDS had developed. Teenage magazines, for example, had for some time published sympathetic and informative stories on AIDS and on safer-sex guides. There were other media interventions, such as the *EastEnders*' character Mark Fowler who in 1990 declared he was HIV positive, and *Grange Hill*'s 1995 storyline about Lucy Mitchell's mother, who dies from AIDS-related complications. The *EastEnders* AIDS storyline resulted in a spike in requests for HIV antibody testing, demonstrating the powerful influence public health messages have when embedded within an entertaining, long-running soap opera. Both storylines involved heterosexual characters affected by HIV and sympathetically represented the way this disease affected families and not just individuals.

Talking About AIDS was at great pains to point out that while the predicted epidemic had not materialised, this should not weaken the resources put into HIV/AIDS training. Two points needed to be borne in mind for those that questioned whether such training was really necessary. Firstly, that while the number of inmates infected with HIV remained 'quite small', the number in general was still rising (the most rapid rate of increase was in the heterosexual population). Secondly, the reason that the epidemic had not reached the scale originally feared 'is precisely

124. *AIDS: Inside and Out.* This teaching manual, which included a video, was a revised version of one that was first introduced to the Prison Service in 1987 called *Talking About AIDS.* (BL, HOME/4/121/95A and BL, HOME/4/122/95A)

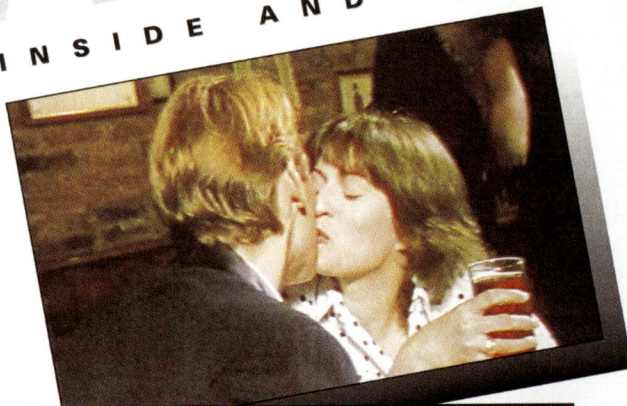

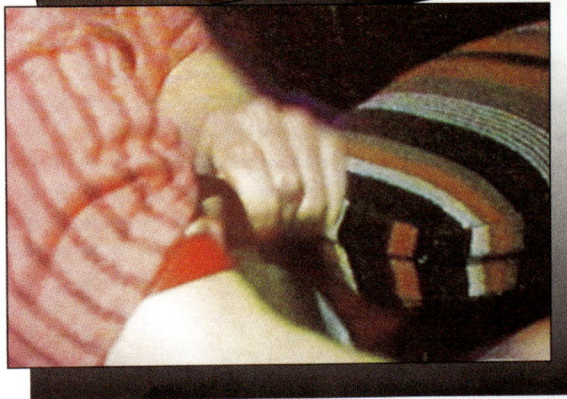

HM PRISON SERVICE

TALKING
ABOUT AIDS

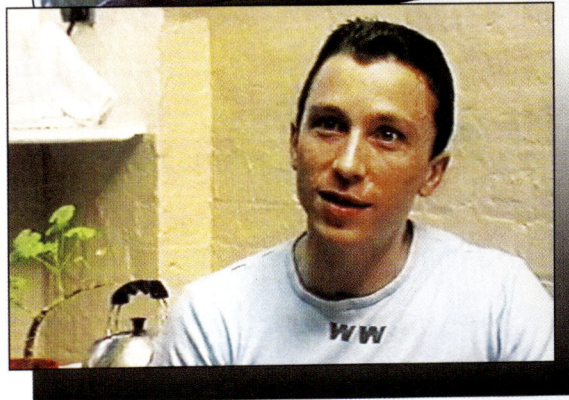

Five short films by John Metcalfe with a manual, 1995

A teaching resource for use with inmates of prisons and young offender
institutions in England, Wales and Scotland

because of the effort that has been put into HIV/AIDS education both within the Prison Service and in the community outside'.

Some people thought that the 'Don't Die of Ignorance' and subsequent campaigns demonised AIDS still further by adding to the already existing levels of fear. However, the general consensus among historians is that the public information campaign (which continued until the mid- to late 1990s) was successful in raising public awareness and in saving lives. New diagnoses of HIV, which reached over 3,000 in 1985, dropped by one-third in three years. The number of new diagnoses stayed relatively stable until 1999. An interesting by-product of the propaganda was that although the campaign targeted HIV, it actually had a profound effect on all sexually transmitted infections. Following the campaign, the number of diagnoses of gonorrhoea in England and Wales dropped from around 50,000 in 1985 to just 18,000 in 1988 – and had dropped to a twentieth-century low by the mid-1990s. Syphilis dropped from around 1,500 annual cases in the mid-1980s to around 150 in the mid-1990s. Between 1985–86 and 1992–93 the government allocated over £73 million to the development of the national AIDS public education campaign. It was a huge amount of money at the time.[9] The 'AIDS' campaign and other active work in the field of HIV prevention in intravenous drug users helped keep rates of infection in the UK in this group relatively low compared to a number of other European countries. Its tactics were imitated around the world.

DON'T PLAY WITH FIRE

AIDS was an unexpected disease that required a (relatively) rapid response. A more mundane, but nevertheless serious, concern was to prevent household fires and to educate children not to play with matches. Fire safety (and safety in the home in general) had been a recurring theme in the COI's portfolio since it had been established in the 1940s. It took two forms: advice for adults (normally the elderly) on how to avoid fire risks in the home (Figs. 126a, b, c and d), and secondly various strategies to keep matches away from children (Fig. 128). Sometimes the two would be conflated (see Fig. 127).

The authorities were invariably encouraging parents to take responsibility for their children in the home (Fig. 125).

While the elderly figured in many of the fire safety campaigns (Fig. 129), the major concern for the Home Office was children and the attraction of matches. In the 1990s a subtler approach was adopted with the creation of *Frances the Firefly*, an animated programme narrated by the actor Richard Briers for three- to six-year-olds. The public information video and film was also accompanied by a lavishly illustrated book (Fig. 130) and a colouring-in poster. The story centred around a young firefly named

125. *Death-Traps in the Home: Safeguard Your Children.* An eye-catching booklet from the late 1950s/early 1960s of the inherent dangers in the home – not just from fires, but also from medicines and drugs for grown-ups and from scalding water. 'More than twice as many young children die from accidents in their homes than on the roads.' (BL, PP/88/1A)

PROTECTING THE PEOPLE

228

WHAT TO DO IF FIRE BREAKS OUT

Delay can be dangerous. If you suspect that there is a fire, take the following precautions before investigating further.

- Close the door of the room where the fire is — this will help to contain the fire and restrict the spread of poisonous fumes.
- Alert the household and get everyone out by the safest route. If you live in a flat, don't use the lift.
- Alert neighbours and call the fire brigade. (don't leave it to somebody else).
- To call the fire brigade, dial 999. You don't need to put money in a public call box. Remember to give the full address of the fire e.g. 12 Smith Street, New Town.
- Try to reduce draughts that may fan the fire. Close all doors and windows (even in rooms away from the fire) if this can be done safely.

TACKLING FIRE

Never attempt to fight a fire yourself unless it is in its earliest stage. Never do so if there is the slightest risk to yourself or others.

- If you suspect there is a fire behind a closed door, don't open it.
- Remember that smoke can be as dangerous as flames.
- If a chip pan catches fire, turn off the heat, smother the flames with a lid or damp cloth, and leave for half an hour.
- If your clothes catch fire, roll on the floor to extinguish the flames.
- If someone else's clothes are on fire — he or she should be laid on the floor and rolled in blankets, rugs or a thick coat.

IF YOU ARE CUT OFF BY FIRE

- Close the door of the room, close any fanlight or other opening, and block up the cracks with bedding etc.
- Go to the window and try to attract attention.
- If the room fills with smoke, lean out of the window. If smoke prevents this, try lying close to the floor where the air is clearer, until you hear the fire brigade.
- If it gets so bad you must escape before the fire brigade arrives, make a rope by knotting together sheets of similar materials. Tie one end to a bed or other heavy piece of furniture.
- If you cannot make a rope, drop cushions or bedding to break your fall. Get through the window feet first, lower yourself to the full extent of your arms and drop.
- If the window will not open, break the glass with a heavy object. Try to clear jagged glass from the lower edge and, if possible, place a blanket over the sill, before escaping.

KITCHEN

- Don't use gloss paint or any oil-based paint on expanded polystyrene tiles. This causes fire to spread rapidly.
- Never block up ventilators. Gas appliances need some fresh air in order to burn correctly. Circulation of air is a vital safety measure in case a gas leak occurs.
- Don't iron — or air — clothes where they could fall on a fire.
- Never store paper near heat.
- Never run an iron (or other appliance) off a lamp holder.
- Don't leave tea-towels to dry over the cooker.
- Make sure that pans are in a safe position on the cooker. Handles should not face into the room or across a lighted burner.
- Keep the flex from the electric kettle well away from the cooker.
- Keep matches out of the reach of children.
- If there is a power failure, always switch off fires, irons, kettles, or similar appliances. They could come on again when you're not at home.
- Chip pans are one of the main causes of fire. Fat and cooking oils heat up until they catch fire by themselves. Never fill a chip pan more than a third to a half full of oil. If you have to leave a chip pan, even for a moment, take it off the heat.

KEEP FIRE SAFELY IN ITS PLACE

Matches are not meant for play keep them safely tucked away

Smoking could mean fire ahead more so if you smoke in bed

these are **the four main causes of fire** in the home

Faulty heaters must be scrapped do not wait until you're trapped

Fire's a danger—don't ignore it always place a guard before it

ISSUED BY H.M. GOVERNMENT

126. *Danger from Fire: How to Protect Your Home.* A booklet produced in the 1980s to provide fire safety advice for every different type of room in the house. In this example the dangers of the kitchen are highlighted. They include: oil-based paints, blocked ventilators, ironing, loose paper, tea towels, pans on cookers, electrical flexes, matches and chip pans. (BL, HOME/1/18/83)

127. *Keep Fire Safely in Its Place.* A simple but concise poster highlighting the four main causes of fire in the home. (BL, PP/166/1A)

Keep matches away from children.

Nicholas: burned at the age of 4; scarred for life.

Prepared by the Home Office and the Central Office of Information, 1974

Printed in England for HMSO by UDO (Litho) Ltd. London. Dd 099342/Pro 3942

128. *Keep Matches Away from Children.* A highly emotive poster from the mid–1970s showing a bandaged and tearful little boy scarred for life at the age of four. The emphasis for this campaign is on parental responsibility to protect children, not on the naughtiness of children. (BL, PP/258/72A)

129. *Fire Kills or Injures 1,700 Elderly People a Year.* This 1980s poster is targeting the elderly but is not necessarily directed at them. An elderly man is shown falling asleep while a cigarette in his hand sets fire to his newspaper. The stark headline is followed by a patronising tag line: 'So make sure *they* [my stress] take special care.' (BL, HOME/1/62/83)

Fire kills or injures 1,700 elderly people a year.

So make sure they take special care

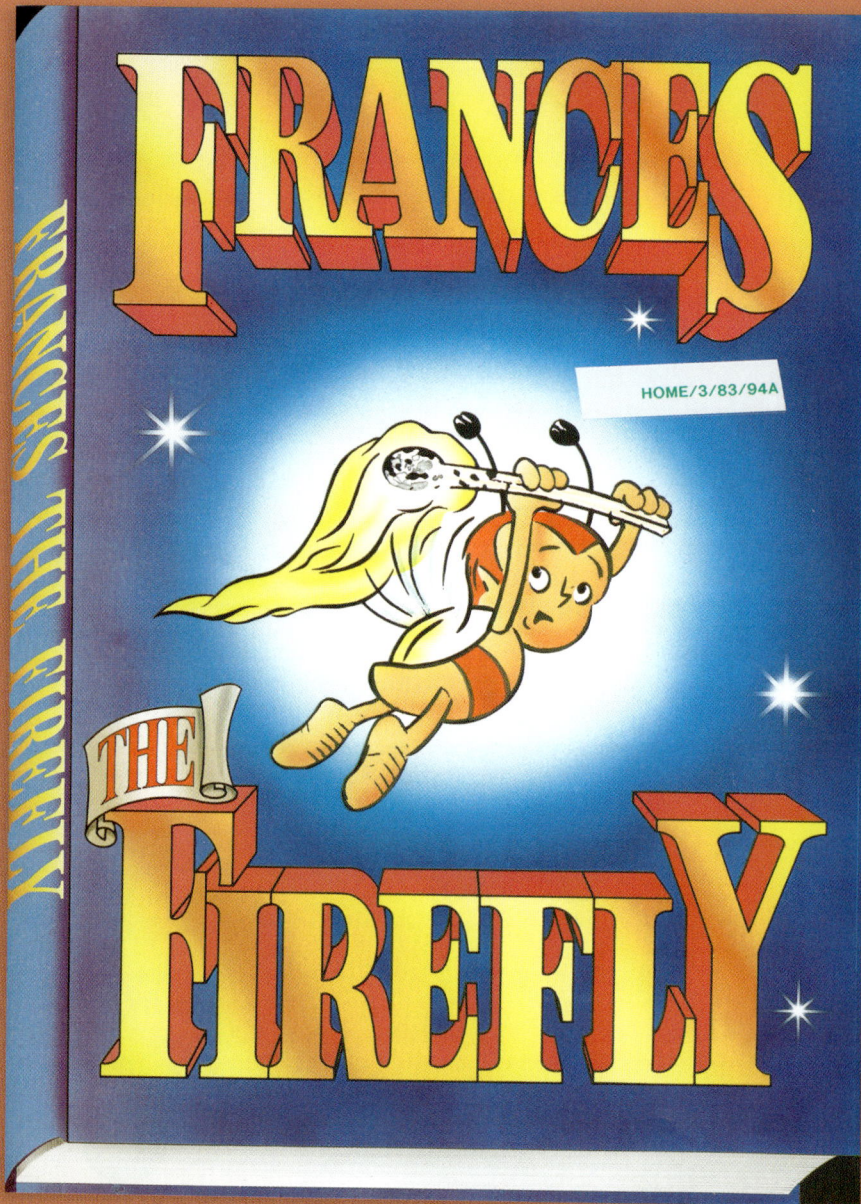

130. *Frances the Firefly*. The cover of the book that accompanied the public information film. Interestingly, on the back there are two messages, one addressed to adults and the other to young children. (BL, HOME/3/83/94)

131. *Frances the Firefly*. Various scenes from both the film and the book. The moral of the story is not to listen to naughty children who try to make you do something you know is wrong and dangerous. Having caused the fire and the damage, Frances has learned her lesson and even tells younger insects her story. Meanwhile, naughty Cocky Roach is banished from King Chrysalis's insect Kingdom. (BL, HOME/3/83/94)

A few nights later, Frances was sitting on a twig in the forest, feeling very sorry for herself. Suddenly, something tapped her sharply on the shoulder.

It was Cocky Roach. Cocky was a naughty young insect who was always getting into trouble. He knew why Frances was upset, and he thought he would play a trick on her.

TAP TAP

Next morning, when the fire had finally been put out, the insects held an emergency meeting. Many of them had been badly burned, including Frances, whose blackened wings were still very painful.

King Chrysalis, a grand butterfly who ruled the Kingdom of the Insects, rose to speak: "We must rebuild our land at once, and make it beautiful again." He looked down at Frances, who was feeling very ashamed of herself.

"I hope you now understand how dangerous fire can be," he said to her in a stern voice.

Frances had indeed learned her lesson. She helped the rest of her friends rebuild the houses and factories, but she was also given a special job to do. Every now and then she gathered together all the younger insects and told them her story.

They would sit and listen to her tale, and understand why they should never play with matches.

And what about Cocky Roach? He was sent away from the Insect Kingdom in disgrace. Even today, you can sometimes see him scuttling amongst the litter in towns and villages, looking for something to eat.

DON'T FORGET – NEVER PLAY WITH MATCHES!

Return to Cir. Sec.
Pubs EH 413
COPY TO ARCHIVES
DATE 11.7.73

NEVER
GO
WITH
STRANGERS

PP/182/14A

194

CHILDREN

Use this bookmarker
and remember the
rules.

- **NEVER** go away
  with a stranger.

- **NEVER** get into a
  stranger's car.

- **NEVER** accept
  sweets or money
  from a stranger.

- **ALWAYS** play with
  friends — never alone.
  And be back home
  before dark.

- **ALWAYS** tell your
  Mum or Dad where
  you are going and
  when you will be back.

- If you are ever
  frightened, ask an
  adult lady for help —
  or go to a police
  officer.

Issued by the Home Office
from a design by the
West Mercia Constabulary

Printed in England for Her Majesty's Stationery Office
by The Soman-Wherry Press Ltd.   Dd223927   3/74

THE NEVER NEVER CLUB

SAY NO, NEVER GO!

Never go with *anyone* — even
someone you know — without
asking Mum or Dad first

Never wander off on the way home
from school or after dark

NN S03

THE NEVER NEVER CLUB

SAY NO, NEVER GO!

THE NEVER NEVER CLUB

THE NEVER NEVER CLUB

Frances. Because she's too young, her tail does not glow and she feels sad. Meanwhile, a naughty cockroach named Cocky Roach, shows her a box of matches that was left by his mum on the kitchen table and gives one to her. She lights the match and flies around with it, until the flame burns her and she drops the match. The match causes a fire in the forest, and Frances's wings are badly burned. The houses are destroyed and the honey factories burnt to cinders. Following an emergency meeting led by King Chrysalis, the insects rebuild the buildings with Frances's help. It ends with Frances being told not to play with matches, and Cocky Roach being banished from King Chrysalis's kingdom (Figs. 131a, b and c). He is found scuttling among the litter bins in towns and villages, never to dare show his face again. The narrator concludes, 'Don't forget – Never play with matches!'

Slogans such as 'Keep Matches Away from Children' and 'Never Play with Matches' are part of wider concerns for children's safety that developed from the 1970s. The 1971 film *Never Go with Strangers* begins with brief animated sequences depicting the classic stories of 'Little Red Riding Hood' and 'Hansel and Gretel', warning children not to be like the title characters and to avoid putting themselves in danger (Figs. 132a and b, and 133a, b and c). Children are encouraged to 'think of a strange car as danger', and as a recurring theme a stranger's car flashes red whenever a child is approached, accompanied by the sound of a dramatic synthesiser chord. In one sequence, a terrified kidnapping victim is shown cowering while the enlarged shadow of an unseen stranger engulfs her.

Charley Says was a series of animations in the 1970s and 1980s that dealt mainly with everyday safety issues which children face, such as not going off with strangers or not playing with matches. They featured a little boy called Tony and his cat named Charley (voiced by Kenny Everett), who served as the boy's conscience and would 'miaow' the warning lesson of the episode, which the boy would then translate and explain.

VE AND VJ DAYS: THE NATION GIVES THANKS

One minor curio associated with the 1990s and the work of the COI was the decision to commemorate the fiftieth anniversaries of VE Day (the unconditional surrender of Nazi Germany) and VJ Day (the victory over Japan, which effectively brought World War II to an end) in May and August 1995 (Fig. 134). This book started with Britain recovering from the trauma of World War II. The COI, having been established in the

---

132. 'Never Go With Strangers'. The 'Never Go With Strangers' campaign in the 1970s used classic tales such as 'Little Red Riding Hood' to warn children not to put themselves in danger. This bookmark, which was distributed to schoolchildren, has on one side a salivating wolf with innocent children at the bottom, and on the other side the rules, set out under the header: 'CHILDREN Use this bookmarker and remember the rules.' (BL, PP/182/14A)

133. The Never Never Club. The 1990s variant of 'Never Go With Strangers' was the Never Never Club, promoted through schools and youth organisations. Children were given a pack consisting of a small wallet containing a bookmark, sticker, badge and card with the Never Never rules about strangers. (BL, HOME/1/1/94).

THE NATION GIVES THANKS

VE VJ

1945
6 7 8 MAY
19 20 AUGUST
1995
DAY

aftermath of war, played an important propaganda role in celebrating victory but more importantly in the creation of a brave new world free from fascist tyranny. To celebrate the fiftieth anniversary of Victory in Europe, the annual May Day holiday in the UK was moved from the first Monday of the month (in 1995 that was 1 May) to the second (8 May) because it was fifty years to the day that the war in Europe had ended. BBC1 ran a special night of programmes to mark the anniversary, including a commemorative episode of *EastEnders*, the Queen lighting the first beacon of peace in a nationwide chain, and a concert featuring some of the stars of the day as the stars of 1945.

Britain celebrated the fiftieth anniversary of Victory over Japan Day (VJ Day) with a gathering of 25,000 war veterans in London on 19 August 1995. Veterans of the Burma campaign gathered outside Buckingham Palace for a memorial ceremony and then marched past the royal residence as the Queen looked on. A World War II Lancaster bomber flew low over the Palace, showering with poppies the thousands who had gathered for the VJ Day ceremony.

The COI was involved in the preparation of commemorative exhibitions and events and, together with the Department of Education, it also prepared a teaching package for schools and educational organisations. The pack contained a personal letter from the Queen, a forty-seven-page booklet with teaching guidance notes and a video. In a nice touch, the material came in a Red Cross food parcel box. In her letter, on Buckingham Palace-letterheaded paper, the Queen refers to the history of World War II as: '...the story of millions of ordinary people fighting, and very many of them dying, to defend the way of life in which they believed and to preserve freedom and democracy. Those like me who lived through that War – I can remember my parents being bombed in Buckingham Palace – know how much following generations owe to those who gave so much.' The teachers' guidance notes end with a section on Great Britain and the wider world – Europe, the Commonwealth, the United Nations and President Roosevelt's 'four freedoms' (freedom of speech and worship, and freedom from fear and from want): 'These aims were shared by many people in Great Britain during the war. The 50th Anniversary of the ending of the Second World War provides an opportunity, not only to commemorate the sacrifices of those that fought for these aims, but also to reflect on how far they have been achieved.' It is ironic that in 1995, by commemorating the national celebrations for victory in the war through 'The Nation Gives Thanks' campaign, the work of the COI had come full circle. It would be the last major national celebration it was involved in. ♛

---

134. *VE VJ Day.* The official poster showing a British soldier being welcomed home from the war by his family. The commemorative celebrations in May and August were held under the banner 'The Nation Gives Thanks'.

CONCLUSION

THE CENTRAL OFFICE OF INFORMATION: BRAVE NEW WORLD?

When Prime Minister Attlee, agreed to the establishment of a central agency to replace the wartime Ministry of Information in 1946 the main arguments for such a transfer of power were that specialisation and concentration could achieve greater economy and higher quality output as well as improved co-ordination at the working level. The policy of the COI was to recruit professionals in the business of public communications.

With more than 1,500 staff, it enjoyed a high degree of autonomy from the beginning. Determined it should not become the Ministry of Propaganda, Attlee ordered that no government minister should be given responsibility for it, although it would answer to the Treasury. On this basis, the COI supplied services for other departments both at home and abroad. It never determined policy and worked invariably (although not always) to a departmental brief, with the sponsoring minister carrying final responsibility. Not having its own minister, though, was a double-edged sword. While it brought COI a high degree of independence, the problem was that it had no political clout to fight its corner when the chips were down – and from its inception it had few political friends. Critics were either suspicious that it was (or could become) a propaganda mouthpiece for the government of the day, or else resented its independence and lack of accountability. Others felt that it undermined departmental responsibility and failed to deliver optimum value for money.

Overseas, it worked for British embassies and high commissions by supplying a wide range of material representing the British way of life and supporting British values in culture, science and industry, and setting up exhibitions. On behalf of the Board of Trade, the COI was responsible for the design and construction of pavilions and stands at overseas trade fairs and for displays at trade promotion events abroad. Inevitably, some of this work overlapped with that of the British Council, which could also lead to political friction.

From the late 1940s the COI experienced a sharp spike in advertising activity, as the post-war Labour government sought to revive the economy and communicate the benefits of the new Welfare State. In 1947–48, the COI spent £1.7 million on press and poster advertisements in a total advertising market worth £20 million. It also spent £1 million on public information films, mostly on themes related to health and hygiene. But much of this activity was curtailed as economic crises forced the government to tighten its belt, and by the mid-1950s the Conservative government had reduced the organisation's overall budget from £4 million to under £2 million. The 1960s witnessed a resurgence of the COI, largely due to two unrelated factors. The first was a rapid expansion in its foreign work as it took responsibility for selling Britain abroad. Books, magazines and films for UK bodies overseas soon accounted for half its budget, and continued to be part of its operations until as late as 1996 when it lost its remaining overseas responsibilities. The second was the emergence of television as *the* mass medium of the twentieth century. Television provided a new platform to communicate with the public and proved an ideal medium for the COI's public information films. Indeed, the 1960s and 1970s proved to be a golden age for public information films. In 1969 COI-sponsored films received more than 34,000 screenings – approximately ninety-five a day – on both the BBC and ITV, all aired for free.

Having established itself as an important conduit for government information, the COI nevertheless remained under constant political pressure to justify itself. Following Margaret Thatcher's General Election victory in 1979, sweeping changes were made to the way the organisation was run, changes that would have long-term ramifications for the COI. By far the biggest change was the structural overhaul that came into effect in April 1984. Prior to this, the COI had been funded directly by the Treasury. Every year it would draw up estimates with the departments according to the communications they required in the months ahead. The Treasury would approve the estimates, then the money was the COI's to spend. Under Thatcher's reforms of the Civil Service, designed to make it more competitive, all this changed. The COI survived as an entity, but became a repayment service. This meant its funding came from individual departments in return for work carried out on their behalf. The result was that the balance of power swung to the departments, as they had the final say on how much would be spent. The balance swung further in 1990, when the COI was given agency status, meaning departments were no longer obliged to use it for their communications. Once again, the COI had continually to justify its existence.[1]

The COI survived the new millennium, but its time was limited. In the past, governments could largely control the flow of information and shape the narrative. But the twenty-first century's new media have brought a host of new questions, not least what is the role of state propaganda and where does it go next? In an age of Facebook and Twitter, is everyone a propagandist? The COI had originally been constructed as a benign force disseminating objective communication – whether it be government policies and their implementation or informing citizens about their rights and entitlements. Its work could also involve changing social behaviour. But in carrying out these objectives, it was always serving its political masters and this could involve contradictory and opposing political objectives from one government to the next. In the twenty-first century, government has to work harder than ever to get its message across and convince its target audiences. Mistrust of authority, social diversity, fragmented audiences and a plethora of communication channels make the task increasingly difficult.

When Tony Blair's Labour government took office in 1997, it placed great emphasis on the need for better news management. Blair's Director of Communication, Alastair Campbell, attempted to manage news and the media as tightly as possible, which frequently resulted in an adversarial reaction from the media. After the disastrous Iraq invasion, a backlash was inevitable – with accusations that 'spin' had taken over from news and information. A review of government communications was launched in 2003, chaired by Bob Phillis. The 2004 Phillis Report had wide-reaching consequences, not least for the COI, whose days were now clearly numbered. Its main recommendation was the appointment of a Permanent Secretary for Government Communication who would be based in the Cabinet Office and would assume strategic leadership for communications across government.[2] The new Permanent Secretary would be tasked, in consultation with departments, to come forward with recommendations 'relating to a redefinition of the overall role of government communications, the structures necessary to deliver this activity and the improved training and development of all communications specialists'. This threatened the very existence of the COI and provided a 'blank cheque' for any government to restructure governmental communications – and by implication close down the COI.[3]

In 2010 the new Conservative/Liberal Democrat coalition government announced a major freeze on marketing and advertising. The coalition government's policy was to support a few campaigns deemed essential, such as those relating to important health issues (Fig. 135) or recruitment to the armed forces. Not surprisingly, the COI's operations were incrementally scaled down. Scrapping the COI was first proposed in March 2011 by Matt Tee, the outgoing Permanent Secretary for Government Communication, following a further review. His report found that the COI's 'trading fund model has skewed its activities and has led to it being too distant from government communication'.[4] As a result, the government announced that the COI would be closed and its remaining functions transferred to the Cabinet Office. After sixty-five years of preparing direct government communication to the public, the Central Office of Information closed on 30 December 2011.

SIXTY-FIVE YEARS OF KEEPING CALM AND CARRYING ON

When the Ministry of Information was dismantled in March 1946 even its former minister Duff Cooper concluded that a centralised propaganda bureau had no

---

135. *Change4Life.* This public health programme was launched in January 2009. It was the first national social marketing campaign to tackle the causes of obesity. *Change4Life* aims to help families lead healthier lives by eating well and moving more. The prevalence of obesity in the UK has trebled since the 1980s. By 2010, 30 per cent of children and 61 per cent of adults were overweight or obese. If the trend is allowed to continue, by 2050 nine out of ten adults could be overweight or obese. The slogan used was: 'Eat well, move more, and live longer... Change4Life.' It was one of the last campaigns the COI worked on before it was closed down.[5] (Crown copyright)

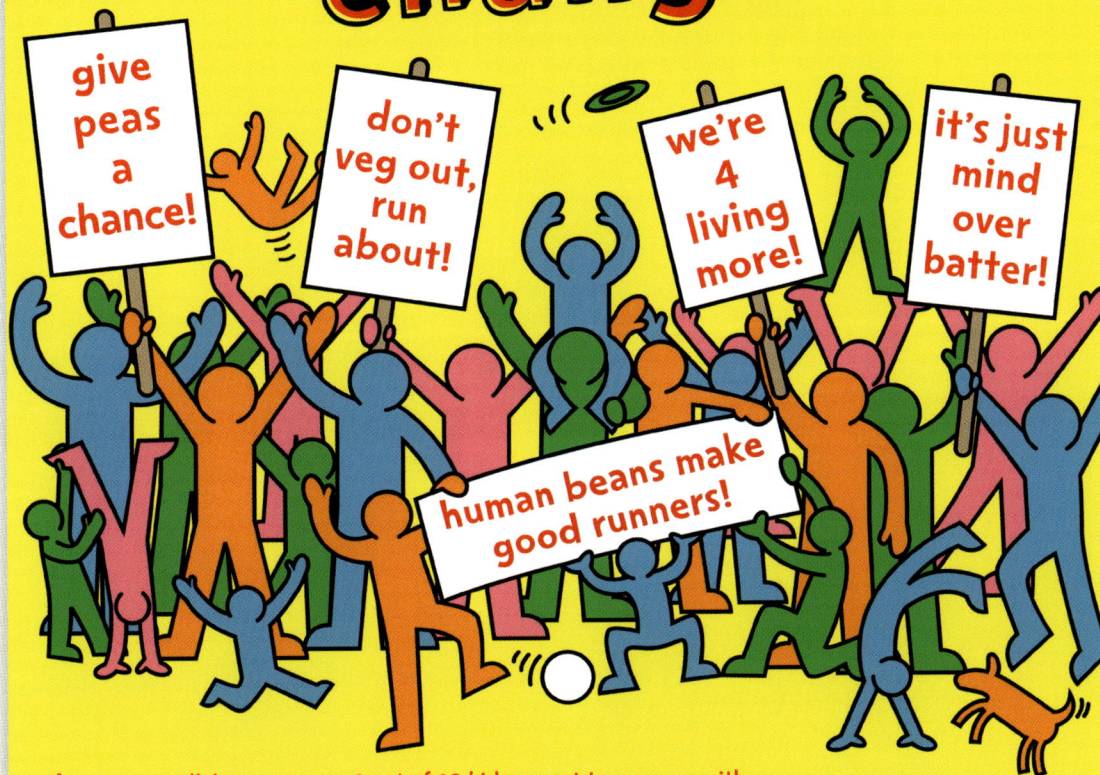

place in a post-war democracy. Writing in his memoirs he noted, 'I believe the truth of the matter to be that there is no place in the British scheme of government for a Ministry of Information'.[6] When the MOI's residual functions passed to the new Central Office of Information it was not without controversy, but few politicians referred to the work of the COI in the pejorative terms reserved for state propaganda. And yet for over six decades the COI continued to intervene in the lives of ordinary people in a manner that would have been unimaginable for the inter-war generation. The term 'nanny state', like other popular political slurs, has contestable historical origins. It is widely attributed to Conservative MP Iain Macleod, who famously used the phrase in his 'Quoodle' column in *The Spectator* in 1965.[7] It has since been widely adopted to convey a critical view of the state's undue interference in individual choice by means of excessive and overprotective policies.

Over half a century later, the censorious 'nanny state' remains a frequent and forceful presence in debates about health and safety policy. Much of the COI's

---

136. *Watch Out! There's a Thief About.* An iconic poster and leaflet from the 1970s. Note that on the back cover of this leaflet, promoting the Good Neighbour Scheme, the thief has stolen the letter o! (BL, PP/258/67L)

output was attacked (largely by Conservatives) for being politically tinged and 'nannying'. It is undoubtedly true that government intrusion has grown beyond anything Macleod had in mind in 1965, after all he was writing before it became illegal not to wear a seatbelt in a car or a crash helmet on a motorbike or to smoke in public spaces. Nevertheless, few (apart from ultra-libertarians) would suggest that such laws should be repealed, since they have almost certainly saved lives.

The COI – like the MOI – never admitted that it was disseminating propaganda, partly because the term 'propaganda' continued to be erroneously associated with lies and falsehood. It preferred the term 'public information' – even when it was patently intent on persuading people to change their behaviour. As such, the output of the COI represents a fascinating insight into the shifting agendas of central government. It tackled a myriad of health, safety and welfare messages; it extolled the virtues of British life and the virility of British business, creativity and enterprise; and it reflected the sea-change in social attitudes. It has been concerned to improve the environment, and during a period in the second half of the twentieth century that witnessed a dramatic rise in the level of recorded crime, it has felt compelled to warn 'Watch out! There's a thief about' (Fig. 136).

The chronological approach that I have adopted, serves, I hope, to illustrate these changing agendas over a considerable period of history. These agendas included concerns about the state of the British economy, the introduction of the National Health Service and the National Insurance schemes, and the constant desire to encourage lifestyles that would make for a healthier and therefore a more prosperous society. To this end, the COI worked tirelessly to educate the public about the dangers of contagion, from 'coughs and sneezes' to the importance of immunisation against diphtheria, polio and measles. There was also the constant promotion of good hygienic practices in daily life ('wash your hands before eating'), which was seen as a key factor in the management of public health. It also broke down taboos by educating people about venereal disease and the nature and threat posed by HIV/AIDS. If this is what constitutes 'nannying', then let us remember that for a certain generation and class the nanny represented a much-loved and benign influence. The 'nanny state' does not have to be a pejorative accusation of undue encroachment on individual liberty, but rather an acknowledgement that in a modern civilised state we recognise the need to be cared for collectively.[8] Or it might be the case that at times people need a nudge to help themselves!

In order to gain the public's attention and interest, the COI produced a body of work that has marked our artistic landscape in the post-war era. An extraordinary group of artists worked at some stage for the COI. These included: Abram Games, F.H.K. Henrion, Hans Unger, Tom Eckersley, Laurence Scarfe, James Fitton, Ronald Searle, Edward Bawden, Andre Amstutz, Charles Tunnicliffe, Reginald Mount, Eileen M. Evans, Norman Thelwell and Royston Cooper. They designed not only some of the most iconic posters, but also pamphlets, leaflets and ephemera. Some of Britain's most distinguished directors, such as Paul Rotha, Humphrey Jennings, Lindsay Anderson, Karel Reisz, John Krish, Don Levy, Peter Greenaway and Nicholas Roeg made films for the COI. These artists, who interpreted changing governmental agendas, invariably adopted state-of-the-art advertising techniques that pushed form and style to new boundaries in order to enforce their messages.

Public information films were an intrinsic part of post-war British culture, revealing changing tastes in fashion (and some very questionable hairdos in the 1970s!), habits, leisure and politics. Rooted in the tradition of the British documentary film movement, they can be viewed as a barometer of changing tastes and are clearly still held in much affection by subsequent generations who experienced a rite of passage viewing these films either in the cinema or on television. In 2006 the COI celebrated its sixtieth anniversary with several events, including a film season at the National Film Theatre and a poll on the BBC website to find Britain's favourite public information film. Nearly 25,000 readers voted in the poll and the clear winner was *Charley Says*, followed by *Tufty* and *Joe and Petunia*. Astonishingly, *Protect and Survive* came seventh!

One of the challenges of writing a history of the COI has been how to capture the rapid technological changes that have led to a shift away from the written word to the visual image on screen, and the speed of delivery associated with the Internet. By the 1990s, the leaflet, pamphlet and poster were largely replaced by moving images either on television, the Internet or social media. It is much more difficult attempting to analyse, for example, a television advertisement on AIDS that you are unable to show than it is to discuss a poster or pamphlet that can be shown and interrogated on the page.

In terms of content and effectiveness, it is quite clear that some of the most powerful campaigns, such as 'Don't Drink and Drive', the anti-smoking campaigns, and the health and nutritional drives, etc. have helped to change attitudes and behaviour. It is easy to forget how deeply embedded smoking and drinking were in everyday lives. Driving after drinking alcohol was hardly debated and was taken as the norm, just as using a seatbelt was at first viewed as an irritant and resisted. Remember also that COI propaganda was not viewed in isolation. Such propaganda did not exist in a political and media vacuum. It would often be part of a much-wider debate whereby politicians from departments sponsoring a campaign would appear on radio and television to defend a specific cause. The debate might then widen out to include medical, scientific and educational experts who would add support or criticism, such as on the benefits of giving up smoking or regularly visiting a dentist. The cigarette companies, on the other hand, would try (initially at least) to undermine the medical arguments by focusing on the 'pleasure' and 'sexiness' historically associated with tobacco advertising. Once a campaign had started, there might also be other media interventions. In the case of the 'AIDS' campaign in the United States, the commercial success of the film *Philadelphia* in 1993 starring Tom Hanks and Denzel Washington is credited with changing attitudes by creating a more-sympathetic awareness to the disease and those that suffered from it. In the UK, Mark Fowler's extraordinary moving story line in *EastEnders* had a similar effect on public perception. As indeed did photographs in 1987 of Princess Diana shaking the hand of a man with AIDS without wearing gloves while she attended the opening of the Middlesex Hospital AIDS ward in London, the first ward in the United Kingdom dedicated to the treatment of HIV/AIDS. Such media coverage undoubtedly played a pivotal role in dispelling the fear and stigma surrounding HIV/AIDS.

On the other hand, it is fair to say that campaigns to persuade citizens to become more socially aware, such as the 'Keep Britain Tidy' campaign, were largely preaching to the converted. They may have persuaded the 'casual recalcitrant' to pick up a piece of litter in the countryside, but were hardly going to have much impact on serial rubbish dumpers!

As it was being closed down, the COI's chief executives issued a final statement:

COI was born out of the wartime Ministry of Information and came into being on 1 April 1946. It closed on 30 December 2011. For 66 years it has performed a key function as an efficient and effective centre for government communications, supporting and delivering results on behalf of a diverse range of clients in Whitehall and right across the wider public sector. Ever since it was formed, COI has driven best practice, value for money and has championed accountability standards and robust evaluation. These principles must now lie at the heart of all government marketing and communications activity. On behalf of the taxpayer, COI has worked tirelessly to play its part in saving lives, saving money, and enabling the government of the day to engage the public more effectively with its policies. Supported by a wealth of evidence, COI's impressive legacy is one of which its clients, its suppliers and, most importantly, its staff can look back on with immense pride.[9]

Did it achieve these objectives and if so, what sort of legacy has it left? From the outset, the COI promoted an idealised notion of Britain and its people; from encouraging immigration to redefining the diversity of the nation. British citizens were invariably portrayed as members of an ordered and civil society. The propaganda it disseminated was by turn affectionate, humorous, informative, stirring and, at times, disturbing. It could also be hectoring, and occasionally it was irritatingly patronising. But much of its work was peppered with the COI's mix of humour and gentle persuasion. Above all it sought to stimulate a sense of civic responsibility underpinned by the belief that this could be achieved by involving the nation in a fuller discussion of public affairs. Straddling many decades and taken as a whole, the work of the COI constitutes a revealing social history – a fascinating portrait of a people struggling to come to terms with ravages and deprivations in the aftermath of World War II, while at the same time searching for a new post-colonial identity. By and large it excelled at getting its message across and its work provides compelling testimony that the Central Office of Information was an overwhelming force for good. ♛

NOTES

PREFACE

1. For a detailed analysis of the role of the Ministry of Information, see D. Welch, *Persuading the People: British Propaganda in World War II* (British Library, 2016). This work on the Central Office of Information is conceived as a companion volume.
2. For a more-detailed exposition of my thinking on propaganda, see D. Welch, *Propaganda: Power and Persuasion* (British Library, 2013). See in particular the introductory chapter, 'A Brief History of Propaganda', 1–40.
3. E. Bernays, *Propaganda* (Ig Publishing, 2005 edition).

CHAPTER ONE

1. For a detailed analysis of the role of the Ministry of Information, see *Persuading the People: British Propaganda in World War II* (British Library, 2016). This work on the Central Office of Information is conceived as a companion volume.
2. The National Archives (hereafter TNA), CAB 66 (War Cabinet)/42, WP (43) 476, 23 August 1943.
3. TNA, INF 1 (Ministry of Information committee minutes and memoranda, etc.)/941, Bracken to Bernard Sendall, November 1943.
4. *Evening Standard*, 28 June 1944. Churchill demurred and asked Bracken to retain the MOI until the defeat of Japan. Shortly after the end of the war in Europe, in May 1945, Bracken left the MOI to become First Lord of the Admiralty in the caretaker government. TNA, INF 1/942, Prime Minister to Minister of Information, 5 March 1945.

5. TNA, INF 1/941, Sir Alan Barlow to Radcliffe, 28 March 1944. (In British research policy, the Haldane principle is the idea that decisions about what to spend research funds on should be made by researchers rather than politicians. It is named after Richard Burdon Haldane, who in 1904 and from 1909 to 1918 chaired committees and commissions which recommended this policy.)
6. TNA, PRO CAB 87/74, WP (44) 482, MGO 47.
7. Ibid.
8. TNA, PRO CAB 128/, CM (45). See Morrison's report to the Cabinet in November prior to this meeting in which he supported the idea of a central information agency 'with ideas and a positive contribution of its own to make'. TNA, PRO CAB 129/5, CP (45) 316, Report dated 23 November 1945.
9. *Hansard*, House of Commons, vol. 417, col. 916. The announcement of the establishment of the COI can be found in *Hansard*, House of Commons, 7 March 1946, vol. 420, cols. 520–21.
10. A temporary exception was made for certain departments arising from war conditions such as the Ministry of Food.
11. The announcement of the establishment of the COI can be found in *Hansard*, House of Commons, 7 March 1946, vol. 420, cols. 520–21. Fraser had turned down the post of economic publicity adviser to Hugh Dalton at the Exchequer in favour of the Director-Generalship of the COI.
12. Quoted in Sir Fife Clark, *The Central Office of Information*, (London, 1970), 35–6. After the war, Fife Clark had been Chief Information Officer of the Ministry of Health and was Director-General of the COI from 1954 to 1971.
13. The Crombie Committee, under the

Chairmanship of Sir James Crombie, was to establish terms of reference and to advise on the creation of a professional group of Civil Servants to provide the necessary links between government and the media. The committee included the Director-General of the COI (Sir Robert Fraser) and the Prime Minister's Press Adviser, Mr (later Lord) Francis Williams.

14. Figures taken from Sir Fife Clark, *The Central Office of Information*, 126. In 1966 staffing had risen to just over 1,660, the highest in its history.

15. HC Debate, 23 May 1949 vol. 465 cc963–1017. https://api.parliament.uk/historic-hansard/commons/1949/may/23/central-office-of-information-1 (retrieved on 30 December 2018).

16. Summary of the Report of the Independent Committee of Enquiry into the Overseas Information Services, April 1954. Cmnd. 9138. Cited in P. Taylor, *British Propaganda in the 20th Century: Selling Democracy* (Edinburgh University Press, 1999), 233.

17. It was not until the 1960s that funding for the COI increased significantly. In 1969–70 its gross Vote had increased to almost £16 million. For the COI's full annual budgets from 1946 to 1970, see Fife Clark, *The Central Office of Information*, Appendix VI, 172.

18. https://api.parliament.uk/historic-hansard/commons/1949/feb/15/propaganda-film-cost. *What is Life* was directed by Michael Low and featured Richard Massingham and Russel Waters. (Retrieved on 20 December 2018.)

19. J. Cole-Morgan, 'Public Relations in Central Government', in S. Black (ed.), *The Practice of Public Relations* (Routledge, 2011), 63.

20. These changes can be gleaned from the COI's annual handbooks, for examples of the 1950s and 1960s see British Library (hereafter BL), PP (Central Office of Information)/34/7A and 8A and BL, PP/34/18A.

21. J. Cole-Morgan, 'Public Relations in Central Government', 66.

22. William Haley served as Director-General of the BBC from 1944 to 1952, and from 1952 to 1966 he was editor of *The Times*. For an informative discussion of the early history of the COI, see T. Wildy, 'From the MOI to the COI – Publicity and Propaganda in Britain, 1945–1951: the National Health and insurance campaigns of 1948', *Historical Journal of Film, Radio and Television*, vol. 6, no. 1, (1986), 3–18.

23. For a detailed analysis of the COI's relations with the media during this early period, see M. Moore, *The Development of Communication Between the Government, the Media and the People in Britain, 1945–51*, Unpublished Ph.D. Thesis: Department of International History, London School of Economics and Political Science, October 2004.

24. Fife Clark, *The Central Office of Information*, 71–78.

25. Peter Hennessy, *Never Again: Britain 1945–51* (Jonathan Cape, 1992), 118.

CHAPTER TWO

1. Labour Party manifesto, *Let Us Face the Future*, 1945.

2. Bevan made this claim in a ministerial meeting on publicity for the 'Appointed Day' for the introduction of the two schemes, 5 July 1948. Bevan argued that the schemes came into operation on different timetables, which inevitably affected the publicity. NA, CAB124/1015, 12 February 1948. I am greatly indebted for much of this discussion to Tom Wildy's excellent article, 'From MOI to the COI – Publicity and Propaganda in Britain, 1945–1951: the National Health and insurance campaigns of 1948', in *Historical Journal of Film, Radio and Television*, vol. 6, no. 1 (1986), 3–17.

3. Quoted in D. Kynaston, *Austerity Britain 1945–51* (Bloomsbury, 2008), 280.

4. This had been borne out by a public opinion survey conducted during the war after the recommendations of the Beveridge Report had been published: 'There was overwhelming agreement that the Beveridge plan *should* be put into effect. There was, however, a much smaller proportion believing that in fact it *would* be put into effect.' The survey discovered that the greatest interest was 'most marked amongst the poorer people' ... 'and greatest

amount of opposition existed amongst the wealthier people....' 'The proposal that doctors' and hospital services should be extended, free of charge, to every person... was heartily endorsed with 88 per cent of the public welcoming the idea.' NA, PREM, (1942/3), 4/89/2. See also economic survey for 1948, NA, CAB, 124/1050.

5   General Practitioner surgeries remained private businesses that could be bought and sold, and the NHS effectively gave these practices contracts to provide healthcare. Similar compromises were worked out with dentists. The Catholic Church was also opposed to the new welfare provision and managed to negotiate the opting-out of Catholic hospitals from the new NHS.

6   NA, CAB, 124/1015, memorandum by Morrison, 'Social Services; Publicity for 5 July 1948: Home Publicity as on 26 February 1948', 5 March 1948.

7   Wildy, 'From MOI to COI', 9.

8   Attlee's speech entitled 'The New Social Services and the Citizen' took place on 4 July at 9.20 pm, a slot established during World War II for announcements of national importance. In typically understated fashion, Attlee warned not to expect too much to start off with, and linked the schemes to productivity while emphasising their comprehensiveness and universality. The full broadcast can be found at: https://www.youtube.com/watch?v=9rqyzWzDONQ

9   In the period leading to the launch, the BBC devoted eleven programmes to the NHS (about two hours of airtime) and thirty-five programmes to Insurance (over seven hours of airtime). This suggests that the BBC thought that the Insurance scheme required more explanation than the NHS. Wildy, 'From MOI to COI', 12.

10   In this debate the public was represented by Honor Croome, a BBC Economist. BBC Talks Scripts, Film No. 170, 'The National Health Service', *Friday Forum*, BBC Home Service, 21.15 BST, 20 February 1948.

11   *Daily Mail*, 3 July 1948.

12   *Manchester Guardian*, 5 July 1948. *Daily Mirror*, 5 July 1948.

13   *The Times*, 5 July 1948. Interestingly enough, most of the national newspapers relegated the launch of the NHS to their inside pages.

14   Kynaston, *Austerity Britain*, 282.

15   NA, Ministry of Health (MH) 55/963, Fife Clark to Rowland, Read, 2 October 1947. The written archival minutes always refer to the document as a 'pamphlet' whereas in the publicity campaigns it was invariably referred to as a 'leaflet'.

16   NA, CAB 124/1015, memorandum by COI, 'Social Security Publicity', 24 December 1947.

17   The MNI pamphlet *Social Security in Britain 1948* was published in a plain blue cover with no diagrams and covered the whole range of insurance provision that it claimed had largely been agreed by the coalition government following the Beveridge Report (what it termed 'what sort of Britain was to emerged once victory had been won'). BL, PP/68/23A.

18   The film can be viewed at: https://www.youtube.com/watch?v=ebRbHDzG3pg.

19   The film can be viewed at: https://www.britishpathe.com/video/choose-your-doctor-trailer/query/national+health+service.

20   Text taken from the production file. Catalogue reference, NA, INF 6/1969. The films can be viewed at: https://www.youtube.com/watch?v=nOlSyKhy474.

21   *The National Health Service* (1948, BL, PP/40/34A), 4.

22   *The National Health Service*, 2.

23   Quoted in Kynaston, *Austerity Britain*, 328.

24   N. Timmins, *The Five Giants: A Biography of the Welfare State* (HarperCollins, 2001), 192.

25   *The National Health Service* (1948, BL, PP/40/34A), 36.

26   *Manchester Guardian*, 9 August 1949.

27   Quoted in *Sixty Years of the National Health Service: A Proud Past and a Healthy Future* (COI/DH Publication, 2008), 9. The document is also online at: http://www.sor.org/sites/default/files/images/old-news-import/Sixty_Years_NHS.pdf. For a view that challenges many of our assumptions on the roots and antecedents of the Welfare State see, C. Renwick, *Bread for All: The Origins of the Welfare State* (Allen Lane, 2017).

28   M. Panter-Downes, *The New Yorker*, 8 January 1949.

29   See Roberta Bivins; https://peopleshistorynhs.org/the-appointed-day-celebrated-or-silent/.

30   *Life Blood* (BL, PP/78/16A).

31 *The National Health Service*, 3.

32 With health costs rising far more than initial forecasts had suggested, the 1951 Budget precipitated Bevan's resignation (he was, by this time, Minister of Labour). The Chancellor Hugh Gaitskill's budget breached the principle that the NHS was free at the point of delivery by introducing charges for part of the cost of dental treatment, spectacles and prescriptions [National Health Service Amendment Act of 1951]. Harold Wilson, President of the Board of Trade, and John Freeman, a junior minister at Supply, joined Bevan in resigning in April 1951.

33 For a more-detailed analysis, see D. Welch, *Persuading the People: British Propaganda in World War II* (British Library, 2016), 22–45. In 1945, the Ministry of Food and the COI published the first *Manual of Nutrition* (still going to this day). Originally the work of Dr Magnus Pyke (later to become a television celebrity), it has become a standard work and grew out of Pyke's wartime research at the Ministry of Food. It contains detailed but simple advice on a range of topics ranging from carbohydrates, fats, proteins, food consumption and physical work to recommended nutritional allowances. Multiple copies of these manuals can be found in the British Library (PP/Box 114).

34 Gallup polls discovered that over half the population disapproved of bread rationing and Mollie Panter-Downes in her regular column in *The New Yorker* observed that the British people had a strong 'aversion to the darker, more nutritious, but obstinately disliked loaf' that the government was promoting. *The New Yorker*, 9 March 1946.

35 The National Food Survey was established in 1940, and looked at the household eating habits of the urban working class. In 1950 the survey was extended to be a national sample of Great Britain.

36 The austerity and bureaucracy of British post-war life was ruthlessly satirised in George Orwell's 1949 novel, *Nineteen Eighty-Four*.

37 After rationing ceased in July 1954, these services were provided through the Family Allowances Scheme as 'benefits in kind', and the Milk in Schools Scheme, which was introduced in 1934 and administered by the Board of Education. This scheme eventually became the responsibility of the Ministry of Health and later the Ministry of Education. In April 1955 the Ministry of Food and the Ministry of Agriculture and Fisheries were amalgamated to form the Ministry of Agriculture, Fisheries and Food. As from 1 October 1955, the Minister of Health assumed responsibility for welfare foods, but the Ministry of Agriculture, Fisheries and Foods acted as procurement agent.

38 On studying the Medical Research Council's (MRC) report, Professor Michael Wadsworth, Director of the Medical Research Council National Survey of Health and Development, said that it was an indication of the complete change in children's lifestyle over the years: 'In 1950, the average diet was still influenced by post-war austerity but this study shows that the food and nutrient intake of young children at the time was better than today.' As for the higher calorie intake in 1950 as a result of eating more animal fat, this, according to the MRC report, was almost certainly counteracted by a much more physically energetic lifestyle. BBC News 30 November 1999. Accessed 31 July 2018: http://news.bbc.co.uk/1/hi/health/542205.stm. See also *The Guardian*, 30 November 1999: https://www.theguardian.com/uk/1999/nov/30/jamesmeikle.

39 Together with the *Food Calendars* the Ministry of Food also published press guides known as *Food Facts*. Every week an estimated seven million housewives read tips on the best use of rationed and unrationed food and dietary information, and according to one government source they 'helped to reconcile the housewife to an austerity diet'. NA, CAB 134/369. 4 March 1949.

40 D. Macunovich, *Birth Quake: The Baby Boom and its Aftershocks* (Chicago University Press, 2002). After the immediate-post-war rise, the rate dropped dramatically by the early 1950s. Then the UK rate rose from about 1956 to a peak at about 1965, before slowly dropping away.

41 However, some groups continued to be sceptical or outright hostile. The Anti-Vaccination League and British Union for the Abolition of Vivisection opposed BCG (which had been introduced in 1953 to combat TB) and diphtheria immunisations in the 1940s and 1950s, arguing that they relied

on animal cruelty, false science and vested commercial interests.

42   For an interesting collection of essays on visual culture, illness and public health, see D. Serlin (ed.), *Imagining Illness: Public Health and Visual Culture* (Minnesota University Press, Minneapolis, 2010).

43   Cited in Kynaston, *Family Britain 1951–57* (Bloomsbury, 2009), 626.

44   Cf. Roland Quinault's excellent synoptic piece, 'Britain 1950' in *History Today*, vol. 51, Issue 4, (April, 2001).

45   G.T. Hankin, *The United Nations at Work* (HMSO, 1952). The illustrated booklet cost three shillings and sixpence or ten copies for thirty shillings. PP/113/28A.

46   Fife Clark, *The Central Office of Information*, 16.

47   Cf P. Taylor, 'Power, Public Opinion and the Propaganda of Decline: The British Information Services and the Cold War, 1945–57' in P. Taylor, *British Propaganda in the 20th Century: Selling Democracy* (Edinburgh University Press, 1999), 227–242.

48   CAB 129/7 CP (46) 54, Report of the Committee on Government Information Services, 9 February 1946.

49   Third annual report of the Central Office of Information for the year 1949–50 (HMSO, 1950).

50   T. Dykes, 'Portrait of a People', a short introduction to the accompanying BFI booklet of the DVD collection of COI films from 1940 to the 1970s of the same name. 1–2.

51   To assist the first wave of immigrants, the COI produced a series of promotional films intended to help them acquaint themselves with Britain and its customs. Compare, for example, *A Journey by a London Bus* made in 1950 (with the Colonial Film Unit) about two African students https://www.youtube.com/watch?v=yBOcLnyMX-M. For example, after 1948, Caribbean arrivals numbered between 500 and 700 a year, and by 1956 there were just over 40,000 such immigrants in Britain.

52   For an analysis (including historical documents) of the origins of the Cold War, see D. Welch, *Modern European History 1871–2000: A Documentary Reader* (Routledge, 1999), 206–226.

53   NA, FO 953/1051, 'Information, Propaganda and the Cold War', (unsigned) memorandum, 10 December 1951.

54   For a detailed analysis of the IRD, see P. Lashmar and J. Oliver, *Britain's Secret Propaganda War 1948–1977* (Sutton, 1998).

55   Following the end of the Korean War, the monthly literary magazine *Encounter* was founded by the poet Stephen Spender and the journalist Irving Kristol. It was secretly funded by the CIA (after discussions with MI6) and was explicitly anti-communist and intended to counter Cold War neutralism.

56   Cited in Kynaston, *Family Britain*, 322.

57   In 1962 the Central Office of Information for the Foreign Office produced a very interesting and moving film *The Shadow Of The Wall* that told the tale of two Berlins. This propaganda film was produced to help Britons understand why the East German communist authorities constructed the Berlin Wall in 1961.

58   Third annual report of the Central Office of Information for the year 1949–50 (HMSO, 1950).

59   Taken from the Summary of the Report of the Independent Committee of Enquiry into the Overseas Information Services, April 1954 (London HMSO), based on Committee of Enquiry into the Overseas Information Services, 18 July 1952, Cmnd. 9138. The 1954 report was known as the Drogheda Enquiry and was highly critical of consistent investment in information services. It concluded presciently: '...this is essentially a struggle for men's minds – a war of propaganda which is likely to continue for some time to come.'

60   A third series was entitled 'How the Other Half Lives' and dealt with topics such as *The Life of a West African Cocoa Farmer* (BL, PP/111/15A) and *The Daily Life of an African Peasant Farmer in Kenya* (BL, PP/111/21A). These were in a larger format, consisting of five pages of text with no illustrations. They were mainly targeted at schoolchildren in Britain and the Commonwealth and were intended to provide an insight in the 'first person' into the daily lives of citizens of the Commonwealth. For example, the peasant farmer in Kenya begins: 'My name is Leonard Githui. I am one of the Kikuya people, and I live on a smallholding near Nyreri in Kenya. I am going

to write about my smallholding and how my family and I live on it...'

61 In a tart exchange in the House of Lords with Viscount Hinchingbrooke, who questioned the competence of the COI to plan such an undertaking, Morrison replied: 'The noble Lord is ill-informed, if I may say so. It is not so much a question of planning as that the Central Office of Information is an expert exhibition authority. It is very competent in that field, and it is primarily in that respect that its services are being utilised. I presume that the noble Lord would not like us to set up another Department. That would hardly be economical.' *Hansard* report, 2 March 1949. https://api.parliament.uk/historic-hansard/commons/1949/mar/02/festival-of-britain.

62 Quoted in Eric Nahm, *Britain Since 1945: The People's Peace* (Oxford UP, 1992), 1.1.

63 Barry Turner, *Beacon for Change: How the 1951 Festival of Britain Shaped the Modern Age* (Aurum Press, 2011).

64 Cf *Gaumont-British News*, 17 May 1951. https://www.britishpathe.com/video/VLVA85D98D2ZZBN3THKD41T49SBY7-FESTIVAL-OF-BRITAIN-AT-NIGHT/query/festival+of+britain. The Crown Film Unit also produced an historical record of the event *Festival of Britain in Colour* (1951) https://www.youtube.com/watch?v=m9uGlfvyH0M. In 1951 the Central Office of Information produced two fascinating documentary films, *Brief City* and *Festival in London*. The latter was directed by Philip Leacock and targeted at the Commonwealth. The film begins by referring to the festival as: 'As a milestone between past and future. To enrich and enliven the present. A diverse place, of serious fun, and light-hearted solemnity. Reclaimed from the bomb-wrack, and the decay of years. Here, in the heart of London...That's us. Or some of us. For we're more than that... We are the Lion and the Unicorn. The Lion is our strength; the Unicorn our imagination. We smile at our follies and our most profound beliefs. Such as tradition. Such as peace. Such as justice....'

65 *Manchester Guardian*, 29 September 1951. The Festival of Britain was not universally popular and not just with Conservative politicians opposed to what they perceived was a socialist propaganda exercise.

Telephone operators at the box office, for example, were reported to answer with a brisk: 'Festering Britain, here.'

CHAPTER THREE

1 Figures taken from BARB (Broadcaster's Audience Research Board Limited): https://www.closer.ac.uk/data/television-ownership-in-domestic-households/.

2 The COI pamphlet providing detailed information on how best to use slicing machines can be found in the British Library COI collection at BL, PP/151/54A, 1970.

3 *Pedestrian Crossing* (1948) can be viewed at https://www.youtube.com/watch?v=ApPA80XU464. Full text of the films at http://www.nationalarchives.gov.uk/films/1945to1951/filmpage_pc.htm.

4 Information taken from the RoSPA's website, https://www.rospa.com/about/history/.

5 The poster can be found in D. Welch, *Propaganda: Power and Persuasion* (British Library, 2013), 139.

6 *Kerb Drill with Batman* (1967) can be viewed at: https://www.youtube.com/watch?v=ValVCxonmX8

7 By 1970 the COI was spending £957,000 on road safety campaigns, the highest expenditure for any of its campaigns. British Army recruitment was second, accounting for £920,000. Fife Clark, *The Central Office of Information*, 96–7.

8 The pamphlet ('This year I am Going to Reduce Casualties Even More') can be found in the British Library's archives, BL, PP/245/56A).

9 Government estimates suggested that seatbelts prevented an estimated 60,000 deaths and 670,000 serious injuries in the twenty-six years since 1983 when seatbelts were made mandatory for drivers and front seat passengers. Research published by the Department for Transport indicated that annually about 565 people who died in traffic accidents were not wearing a seatbelt and, in 2007, over 300 of these might have survived had they been belted in. https://www.dailymail.co.uk/motoring/article-1206112/Clunk-click-trip-The-modest-seatbelt-celebrates-50-years-lifesaving-today.html.

10 In 2014 the National Archives, in a remarkable act of self-censorship, quietly removed all of Jimmy Savile's *Clunk, Click every trip* public information films from its website after the extent of Savile's child abuse became clear.

11 Fife Clark, *The Central Office of Information*, 99.

12 Fife Clark, *The Central Office of Information*, 100–101.

13 Letter from the COI announcing the 'anti-litter campaign for 1964' including the new Abram Games poster. It also announced the 'litho circle, arrow and basket design', which would become ubiquitous wherever a litter basket was in (or outside) a building. Letter dated 3 April 1964. (BL, BS/81/19)

14 These leaflets can be found at BL, PP, Boxes 153 and 159.

15 Macleod quote cited in P. Hennessy, *Having it So Good: Britain in the Fifties* (Penguin, 2007), 221.

16 The film can be viewed at https://www.youtube.com/watch?v=s_6Tz6EqKSk.

17 Mount designed a similar lithograph poster with the same format and message for men. The caption read: '... So this guy gives up smoking and he reckons he saves enough in a year to get himself two jackets and a transistor radio and a gold watch and a new suit. On top of which he reckons he feels a lot better for it. Me, I still smoke thirty a day and I haven't got two jackets or a transistor radio or a gold watch or a new suit. But man have I got a shockin' cough!'

18 Figures for 2017 from the Office for National Statistics (ONS) suggest that in the UK, 17.0 per cent of men smoked compared with 13.3 per cent of women, which equates to around 7.4 million people in the population. https://www.ons.gov.uk/peoplepopulationandcommunity/healthandsocialcare/healthandlifeexpectancies/bulletins/adultsmokinghabitsingreatbritain/2017.

19 I have relied heavily in this section on the peerless and pioneering works of Professor Virginia Berridge. The quote is from Berridge, 'Smoking and the sea change in public health, 1945–2007', *History & Policy*, 4 June 2007. Online at: http://www.historyandpolicy.org/policy-papers/papers/smoking-and-the-sea-change-in-public-health-1945-2007. See also Berridge, *Marketing Health: Smoking and the Discourse of Public Health in Britain, 1945–2000* (Oxford University Press, 2007).

CHAPTER FOUR

1 John Boyd-Carpenter, 'Why the pound is weak' (letter), *The Times*, 20 October 1967, 11.

2 The origins of the Buy British campaign can be traced back to the Empire Marketing Board (EMB), which was established in 1926 in order to encourage the British public to buy Empire products and thereby foster closer imperial economic relations. The EMB's innovative role in the development of government public relations techniques and information services can also be seen as a forerunner of the COI. See, S. Constantine, *Buy and Build: The Advertising Posters of the Empire Marketing Board* (HMSO, 1986).

3 Fife Clark, *The Central Office of Information*, 103. Much of my information on decimalisation is from this 'official' source.

4 A £1 coin was introduced in 1983, and a £2 coin in 1997.

5 *Hansard*, 2 August 1961 vol. 645 cc1480-606 https://api.parliament.uk/historic-hansard/commons/1961/aug/02/european-economic-community.

6 In the 23 June 2016 Referendum, the government once again produced an 'advisory' pamphlet entitled: *Why the Government believes that voting to remain in the European Union is the best decision for the UK*. The fourteen-page document is much glossier than its 1975 predecessor and, revealingly, it does not contain a personal statement from the Prime Minister, David Cameron, who had called the referendum. Instead, it focused on three main arguments: protecting jobs, a stronger economy and providing security.

7 The information pack *A Project on Race Relations* can be found in the COI archive at BL, PP/162/63A, 1973.

CHAPTER FIVE

1 G. Orwell, 'You and the Atomic Bomb', *Tribune*, 19 October 1945.

2   Quoted in M. Gowing, *Independence and Deterrence: Britain and Atomic Energy, 1945–1952, Volume 1: Policy Making* (Macmillan, 1974), 184. For a wide-ranging analysis of these issue see, M. Grant, 'The imaginative landscape of nuclear war in Britain, 1945–65' in M. Grant and B. Ziemann (eds.), *Understanding the Imaginary War: Culture, Thought and Nuclear Conflict, 1945–90* (Manchester University Press, 2016), 92–115.

3   *The House in the Middle* (1954) shows the impact of atomic tests at the Nevada Proving Grounds (later the Nevada Test Site) on specially constructed homes – some well-kept and some filled with trash and combustibles, and also homes painted with reflective white paint. It claims bizarrely that cleanliness is an essential part of civil defence preparedness and that it increased survivability!

4   These figures are quoted in the COI 1958 and 1960 Civil Defence campaign guides, which are discussed below.

5   The first manual of Civil Defence was published in 1956. These manuals, which contained technical and medical (essentially first aid) information for CDC personnel, would subsequently be revised in 1959 and 1963. *Manual of Civil Defence: Vol I Pamphlet No. 1. Nuclear Weapons* (HMSO, 1956). The document can be downloaded online as a PDF: https://archive. org/details/ManualOfCivilDefenceVol1- Pamphlet1NuclearWeapons.

6   These programmes are on YouTube.

7   M. Grant, *After the Bomb: Civil Defence and Nuclear War in Britain, 1945–68* (Palgrave Macmillan, 2010). Grant draws a similar conclusion to that of CND at the time; namely that Civil Defence was a smokescreen to encourage an acquiescent acceptance on the part of the public that the arms race was an inevitable fact of life.

8   *Hansard*, 2 December 1963 vol. 685 cc940- 50. The full debate can be followed on-line at: http://hansard.millbanksystems.com/ commons/1963/dec/02/civil-defence- handbook-no-10.

9   James Chapman, 'The BBC and the Censorship of *The War Game*', *Journal of Contemporary History*, (2006), vol. 4, (1), 84.

10   *The War Game* finally was televised in the United Kingdom on BBC2 on 31 July 1985, as part of a special season of programming entitled 'After the Bomb' (which was also Watkins's original working title for *The War Game*). 'After the Bomb' commemorated the fortieth anniversary of the bombing of Hiroshima and Nagasaki. The broadcast was preceded by an introduction from British journalist and broadcaster, Ludovic Kennedy.

11   Callaghan announced that spending on Civil Defence would be reduced from £25–27 million in 1968 to £7–8 million in 1969–70. *Hansard*, 29 February 1968 vol. 759 cc1784- 896. Online: https://api.parliament.uk/ historic-hansard/commons/1968/feb/29/ civil-defence.

12   In the UK, the Medical Campaign Against Nuclear Weapons (MCANW) was formed in 1980 and grew to a membership of around 3,000 from the professional community. MCANW campaigned across the country, often counter-posing the cost of weapons against the cost of healthcare. Their campaigning material emphasised the ineffectuality of being 'prepared' as medical providers for the aftermath of nuclear war, and the moral imperative to ensure that it never happened.

13   NA, *HO322/980*. 'Review of Home Defence Planning', briefing paper prepared for ministers, November 1981.

14   In 2004 'Preparing for Emergencies' was a public information campaign advising citizens on what to do in the event of a natural disaster, accident or terrorism. It contained some residual elements of the 'Protect and Survive' campaign ('Go home, stay in, tune in'). In 1986 the COI was removed from the process of producing new Civil Defence publicity and in future the Home Office would work directly with the advertising industry.

15   In 1962 the COI produced (for the Foreign Office and with the Information Research Department responsible for content and editorial policy,) a new, quarterly counter- propaganda magazine, *Anglia*, which continued to disseminate British national values and interests to the Soviet Union until 1992. See, S. Davies, 'The Soft Power of *Anglia*: British Cold War Cultural Diplomacy in the USSR', *Contemporary British History*,

vol. 27, (2013), Issue 3, 297–323. In 1989, as the Berlin Wall collapsed and *glasnost* spread, Russian demand doubled for the COI's *Anglia* magazine. *UK Today*, a similar COI TV news programme, was so successful that ninety countries requested it.

16 The Portland Spy Ring was a Soviet spy ring that operated in England from the late 1950s until 1961. The discovery of the ring, operating out of a house in Ruislip, northwest London, sent shockwaves around the intelligence services of the world because it was one of the first examples of 'deep-cover' agents – those who blended into society under false names rather than posing with 'official' covers in diplomatic roles. The incident involved Harry Houghton and Ethel Gee, who were arrested in January 1961 and accused of stealing top secret information from the Royal Navy›s Underwater Defence Establishment in Portland, Dorset. The following year, John Vassall was sentenced to eighteen years' imprisonment for spying for the Soviet Union. The Vassall scandal together with the Portland Spy Ring greatly embarrassed the Macmillan government, but was soon eclipsed by the more-dramatic Profumo Affair. For a discussion of the Radcliffe Report, see HL Deb 08 May 1963 vol. 249 cc705-806705.

17 TNA, *T 216/964*, Report of the Committee on Security Procedures in the Public Service 1961 (Radcliffe Committee).

18 In 1962, following the Portland Spy Ring and the Vassall affair, the COI commissioned several instructional films using fictional scenarios to dramatise the Cold War threat to security personnel. The aim was to provide security training for military and civilian personnel handling classified material. Films included, *It Can't Happen to Me* (1962); *Persona Non Grata* (1964), a feature-length dramatised security training film in which a Russian diplomat tries to recruit a lonely British Civil Servant as a spy; *The Lecture* (1968); and *Any One of Us* (1970). See S. O'Sullivan, 'This Film is Restricted: Training Films of The British Security Service', *Historical Journal of Film, Radio and Television*, vol. 38, no. 2, (August, 2018), 274–95.

CHAPTER SIX

1 A number of newspapers during this period displayed a shocking blend of ignorance, prejudice, bigotry and intolerance. Cf. *The Mail on Sunday*, 6 January 1985. The headline that accompanied the article by Barbara Jones, the *Mail*'s Medical Correspondent, claimed: 'Britain Threatened by Gay Virus Plague... 20,000 infected....and it's getting worse.'

2 *Monolith* can be viewed at: https://www.youtube.com/watch?v=iroty5zwOVw. *Iceberg* can be viewed at: https://www.youtube.com/watch?v=yVggWZuFApI.

3 Fowler, for example, had to circumvent Margaret Thatcher's attempts to water down the explicitness of the campaign. Thatcher's concerns focused on the language used to explain the sexual practices, specifically unprotected anal sex, which could lead to HIV infection. When Fowler circulated a memorandum giving details of his planned publicity text, Thatcher wrote: 'Do we have to have the section on risky sex? I should have thought it could do immense harm if young teenagers were to read it.' Nigel Wicks (Principal Private Secretary) wrote that she 'thinks that the anxiety on the part of parents and many teenagers, who would never be in danger from AIDS, would exceed the good which the advertisement would do'. TNA. PREM 19/1863, 28 August 1985–31 December 1986. See also, N. Fowler, *AIDS: Don't Die of Prejudice* (Biteback, 2014).

4 *The Guardian*, 9 January 1987.

5 According to the NHS website the distinction between HIV and AIDS is as follows: HIV (human immunodeficiency virus) is a virus that damages the cells in your immune system and weakens your ability to fight everyday infections and disease. AIDS (acquired immune deficiency syndrome) is the name used to describe a number of potentially life-threatening infections and illnesses that happen when your immune system has been severely damaged by the HIV virus. While AIDS can't be transmitted from one person to another, the HIV virus can. https://www.nhs.uk/conditions/hiv-and-aids/.

6   Following the International Conference of Ministers of Health on Aids Prevention, AIDS: World Health Summit held in London, on 3 February 1988 the House of Lords debated the response to the predicted AIDS epidemic. The debate was initiated by Lord Kilmarnock, who provided figures to show that compared to other countries the figure in the UK was still relatively small: 'Canada, with less than half our population, had 1,334 cases at the end of September 1987 and expects this to rise to 7,000 by 1991. France, with a population almost equal to ours, had 3,073 recorded cases by the end of last year, a number which will inevitably double this year. Our numbers are lower. At the end of last year, there was a cumulative total in the United Kingdom of 1,227 cases, of whom 697 had died. But this was a 2.4-fold increase on the previous year's end.' *Hansard*, HL Debate 03 February 1988 vol. 492 cc1077–114 https://api.parliament.uk/historic-hansard/lords/1988/feb/03/aids-world-health-summit (retrieved on 26 February 2019).

7   *Don't Inject AIDS* can be viewed at: https://www.youtube.com/watch?v=nCouCttEllw (retrieved on 26 February 2019).

8   *The Guardian*, 9 January 1987.

9   The 1980s AIDS campaign', *BBC News*. 16 October 2005. http://news.bbc.co.uk/1/hi/programmes/panorama/4348096.stm (retrieved on 26 February 2019).

CONCLUSION

1   For an excellent overview, see D. Tiltman, 'COI: Sixty years in the public eye', *Campaign*, 29 March 2006. https://www.campaignlive.co.uk/article/coi-sixty-years-public-eye/550197 (retrieved on 6 March 2019).

2   The Phillis Report was keen to separate the role of a Director of Communication, which is an overtly political appointment, working in the Prime Minister's office, at the centre of government, from that of a Permanent Secretary for Government Communications who is part of the Civil Service and who must remain impartial.

3   Ironically, the Phillis Report actually praised the work of the COI: 'We examined the work of the Central Office of Information (COI), which undertakes paid-for communications activity on behalf of government departments and agencies. In the main it was praised by its customers and those outside government for its expertise in marketing and bulk media buying for government advertising campaigns' (p.12). The full reports can be accessed at: http://readinglists.ucl.ac.uk/items/92E98ABE-470C-9EC9-99E9-169D2546DD13.html (retrieved on 5 March 2019).

4   The report concluded: '...the COI appears to enjoy a stronger reputation outside of government than within'. 'Government to cut 1,000 jobs and axe COI', *The Guardian*, 18 March 2011 (retrieved on 4 March 2019: https://www.theguardian.com/media/2011/mar/18/government-communications-budget-cuts?INTCMP=SRCHa). The announcement was made by Francis Maude, the Minister for the Cabinet Office.

5   For an example of the video campaign launched in 2009, see 'Change4life Childhood Obesity': https://www.youtube.com/watch?v=SYhbBidlcMI (retrieved on 5 March 2019).

6   D. Cooper, *Old Men Forget* (London, 1957), 287–88.

7   *Spectator*, 3 September 1965.

8   Cf. P. Johnstone, 'Britain's Gone from Nanny State to the Naggy State', *Daily Telegraph*, 15 July 2015.

9   The statement was issued by the COI's chief executives Emma Lochhead and Graham Hooper, dated 29 March 2012, in their foreward to the *Central Office of Information Annual Report and Accounts for the Period 30 December 2011* (HMSO, 2012). https://assets.publishing.service.gov.uk/government/uploads/system/uploads/attachment_data/file/60817/22659_HC_462_COI_2_8_12.pdf

SELECTED READING

Berridge, Virginia. *Marketing Health: Smoking and the Discourse of Public Health in Britain, 1945–2000*. Oxford University Press, Oxford, 2007.

Chapman, James. 'The BBC and the Censorship of *The War Game*', *Journal of Contemporary History*, vol. 4, (1), (2006), 84.

Clark, Sir Fife. *The Central Office of Information*. London, George Allen & Unwin, 1970.

Crofts, William. *Coercion or Persuasion? Propaganda in Britain after 1945*. Routledge, Chapman & Hall, New York, 1989.

Fowler, Norman. *AIDS: Don't Die of Prejudice*. Biteback Publishing, London, 2014.

Grant, Matthew. *After the Bomb: Civil Defence and Nuclear War in Britain, 1945–68*. Palgrave Macmillan, London, 2010.

Grant, Matthew. and Ziemann, Benjamin. (eds.) *Understanding the Imaginary War: Culture, Thought and Nuclear Conflict, 1945–90*. Manchester University Press, Manchester, 2016.

Hennessy, Peter. *Never Again: Britain 1945–51*. Jonathan Cape, London, 1992.

Hennessy, Peter. *Having it so Good: Britain in the Fifties*. Penguin, London, 2007.

Kynaston, David. *Austerity Britain 1945–51*. Bloomsbury, London, 2008.

Kynaston, David. *Family Britain 1951–57*. Bloomsbury, London, 2009.

Rennie, Paul. *Modern British Posters: Art, Design & Communication*. Black Dog Publishing, London, 2010.

Renwick, Chris. *Bread for All: The Origins of the Welfare State*. Penguin, London, 2017.

Serlin, David. (ed.) *Imagining Illness: Public Health and Visual Culture*. Minnesota University Press, Minneapolis, 2010.

Taylor, Philip M. 'Power, Public Opinion and the Propaganda of Decline: The British Information Services and the Cold War, 1945–57' in Taylor, Philip M. *British Propaganda in the 20th Century: Selling Democracy*. Edinburgh University Press, Edinburgh, 1999.

Turner, Barry. *Beacon for Change: How the 1951 Festival of Britain Shaped the Modern Age*. Aurum Press, London, 2011.

Vaizey, Hester. *Keep Britain Tidy and Other Posters from the Nanny State*. Thames & Hudson, London, 2014.

Welch, David. *Propaganda: Power and Persuasion*. The British Library, London, 2013.

Welch, David. *Persuading the People: British Propaganda in World War II*. The British Library, London, 2016.

Wildy, Tom. 'From the MOI to the COI – Publicity and Propaganda in Britain, 1945–1951: the National Health and insurance campaigns of 1948', *Historical Journal of Film, Radio and Television*, vol. 6, no. 1, (1986), 3–18.

INDEX

(Page numbers in *italic* refer to illustrations; c signifies caption text)

PICTURE CREDITS

All the images are from the Central Office of Information Archives held at the British Library, except those listed below. All are © Crown copyright.

Pages 28, 69, 70 and 207: Wellcome Collection.

Pages 36–37: Crown copyright, reproduced with the permission of The British Film Institute under delegated authority from The Keeper of Public Records.

Pages 72, 148 and 193: The National Archives.

Page 147: Welch Collection.

Page 149: The Advertising Archives.

Page 172: British Cartoon Archive, University of Kent, Canterbury.

ACKNOWLEDGEMENTS

I would like to thank the publishing team at the British Library, notably my editor John Lee, copy editor Christopher Westhorp and Sally Nicholls who did such a splendid job compiling the visual content. The archive that I worked from proved especially challenging and it was impossible to include all the material which I had chosen. Nevertheless, we managed as a team to overcome these difficulties, especially thanks to Ian Cooke who went out of his way to help me find material in an archive that proved, at times, counter-intuitive! Thanks also to my wife Anne for reading (and improving) the manuscript. Finally, I would like to dedicate this volume to our grandchildren, Lucas, Olivia and Lilah. The Central Office of Information closed before they were born and so they never experienced its dissemination of largely benign public information that was intended to encourage a well-informed public to discharge good citizenship. In an age of social media, fake news and an increasingly victimhood culture, there is arguably greater need today for such a public information agency. In its absence, I can only hope that my grandchildren live informed and responsible lives – with the proviso that they are not overprotected.